DISASTER RITUAL

Explorations of an emerging ritual repertoire

P. Post, R.L. Grimes, A. Nugteren,
P. Pettersson & H. Zondag

PEETERS

LEUVEN - PARIS - DUDLEY, MA

Library of Congress Cataloging-in-Publication Data

Disaster ritual: explorations of an emerging ritual repertoire / P. Post ... [et al.].
  p. cm. -- (Liturgia condenda ; 15)
  Based on: Rituelen na rampen / Paul Post, Albertina Nugteren, Hessel Zondag.
  Includes bibliographical references (p.) and index.
  ISBN 90-429-1291-X
  1. Memorial rites and ceremonies. 2. Disasters--Religious aspects. 3. Memorial rites
and ceremonies--Netherlands. 4. Netherlands--Religious life and customs. I. Post, Paulus
Gijsbertus Johannes, 1953- II. Post, Paulus Gijsbertus Johannes, 1953- Rituelen na rampen III. Series.

BL619.M45D57 2003
393--dc21   2003043389

© 2003, Peeters, Bondgenotenlaan 153, B-3000 Leuven

D. 2003/0602/49
ISBN 90-429-1291-X

DISASTER RITUAL

CONTENTS

LIST OF ILLUSTRATIONS

1. Amsterdam (The Netherlands, Bijlmer): front of memorial wall (Bijlmer disaster, 1992), showing a part of the tile mosaic, with the tree visible behind the wall (photograph: A. Nugteren, 2001)
2. Laren: ceramic butterfly vase in the Roman Catholic basilica at Laren (The Netherlands, North Holland), with the names of the dead in the aeroplane accident at Faro, Portugal (1992) (photograph: A. Nugteren, 2001)
3. Bovenkarspel: granite book in Bovenkarspel (The Netherlands, North Holland) as a memorial to the victims of the Flora disaster (1999), with a memorial text and poem by Ida Gerhardt (photograph: A. Nugteren, 2001)
4. Eindhoven: temporary monument near the site of the aeroplane crash, Hercules disaster, The Netherlands, Eindhoven, 1996 (photograph: Hercules Disaster Foundation, 1996)
5. Eindhoven: memorial monument, Hercules aeroplane diaster, The Netherlands, Eindhoven, 1996 (photograph: Hercules Disaster Foundation, 1996)
6. Eindhoven: memorial monument, Hercules aeroplane diaster, The Netherlands, Eindhoven, 1996, after the commemoration of July 15, 2001 (photograph: A. Nugteren)
7. Enschede: floral tribute after the fireworks disaster, Hengelosestraat fire station, The Netherlands, Enschede, May, 2000 (photograph: I. Albers)
8. Enschede: floral tribute after the fireworks disaster, The Netherlands, Enschede, May, 2000 (photograph: I. Albers)
9. Enschede: floral tribute after the fireworks disaster, The Netherlands, Enschede, May, 2000 (photograph: I. Albers)
10. Enschede: 'Draag een steentje bij' (Do your bit) action after the firework disaster, The Netherlands, Enschede, June, 2000 (photograph: I. Albers)
11. Enschede: fencing around disaster area, fireworks disaster, The Netherlands, Enschede, May, 2000 (photograph: I. Albers)
12. Enschede: hoarding around disaster area, fireworks disaster, The Netherlands, Enschede, May, 2000 (photograph: I. Albers)

PREFACE

This book is the result of a research project into rituals following disasters. Funding from the Van der Gaag Foundation, administered by the Royal Dutch Academy of Arts and Sciences, enabled a project group of three researchers to explore the subject in 2000 and 2001. As a ritual study, the project was taken on as part of the research programme at the Liturgical Institute, at Tilburg. The Tilburg Faculty of Theology lent generous cooperation to the project.

The general aim of the project was to explore the ritual repertoire after disasters. This would have to be a multidisciplinary undertaking, situated in the domain of ritual studies.

The group carrying out the project consisted of Dr. Tineke Nugteren, Dr. Hessel Zondag and Prof. Dr. Paul Post, who approached the project from the disciplines of comparative religion, psychology of religion and ritual and liturgical studies, respectively. Post also served as project leader. The contact person with the Van der Gaag Foundation was Prof. Dr. L. Laeyendecker. There were two supervisory committees. For the Royal Academy of Arts and Sciences Prof. A. Felling, Dr. J. Platvoet and Prof. Dr. L. Laeyendecker offered critical oversight. The project group itself found Prof. Dr. R. Kleber and Prof. Dr. R. Van Uden prepared to provide their expertise and function as a sounding board.

The project fit well into ongoing and planned research in the framework of the national research programme of the inter-university Liturgical Institute. In fact, the ritual-liturgical dynamic is central in that research programme. One important contribution from the Tilburg Faculty of Theology to this programme is the surveying and testing of the contemporary ritual milieu. The project is thus a specimen of Tilburg's approach to the study of liturgy. The dynamics of cultus and culture, multidisciplinarity and operating within the stage of ritual studies are important perspectives within the general basic programme of liturgical inculturation and the *liturgia condenda*. In this sense, this book also fits with the forthcoming English version of Gerard Lukken's book *Rituelen in overvloed (Rituals in abundance)*, also planned for this Liturgia Condenda series.[1]

---

[1] See LUKKEN: *Rituelen in overvloed* (1999) = *Rituals in abundance* (to appear as *Liturgia Condenda* 16, 2003). As this book was completed the English edition of Lukken's book was not yet available, so all references here are to the Dutch edition.

The first report of this investigation appeared in the Dutch book *Rituelen na rampen* in 2002.[2] It was presented in Tilburg in May, 2002, at a symposium devoted to the same subject. During the preparation of the Dutch book the decision was soon made to also bring the project onto the international stage, and to strive for an English edition of the research report. Ultimately it was decided to publish not an integral English version of the Dutch text, but a fundamental revision of it. This revision would first of all involve a more ritual-liturgical orientation. All emphasis would be placed on the ritual repertoires in context, and much less than in the Dutch version on the coping dimension. Although Dutch disasters in the 1990s would continue to form the principal focus, the research would also take on a more international perspective and context. The Dutch book however remains the basis for this English version.

The first, introductory chapter (in particular section 1.1.) lays out the subject and approach used, and the limitations placed on the research field. It is proper to already mention here the exploratory nature of the project. To a great extent this is pioneering work. The book thus closes with a series of perspectives and recommendations for further research. The subject was strictly delimited, chiefly in terms of time and place. Although The Netherlands forms the principle context for the cases analysed and the whole exploration, there is always an international perspective. With the cooperation of Per Pettersson from Uppsala/Karlstad and Ronald Grimes from Ontario, two relevant international case studies could be introduced: the great disaster with the ferryboat Estonia in Scandinavian waters in 1994 and the attacks of September 11, 2001. An important line in the research is the constant worldwide interference among rituals after disasters.

During the project the investigators were constantly reminded of how vital their theme was, and how closely involved it is in current affairs. None of the cases chosen are closed files. This constantly and directly confronted the team with the question of distance and involvement, which is discussed at a number of points, and in a number of contexts, in this study. The terrorist attacks on Tuesday, September 11, 2001, in New York and Washington, D.C., which have generally been spoken of as a disaster, took place while the final editorial work was being done on the last chapter of the Dutch book.

---

[2] POST, NUGTEREN & ZONDAG: *Rituelen na rampen* (2002).

Parts of this project were presented in classes, lectures, workshops and seminars, articles and interviews.[3]

Although this is emphatically a cooperative, multidisciplinary project, all the main issues were discussed together, and the book is presented as a coherent whole, there was a certain division of labour. Nugteren wrote Chapter 2, and sections 3.1, 3.4 and the first draft of Chapter 6. Zondag wrote 3.3. Post wrote 1.1, 1.2.2, 1.2.2, 3.2, 3.5 and Chapter 5. Pettersson wrote 4.1 and Grimes provided 4.2. For 1.2.2, on the concept of ritual, and Chapter 5, on contemporary ritual dynamics, use was made of other completed and ongoing research.

We owe a debt of thanks to all the individuals and institutions who provided their cooperation. The sections of the book originally written in Dutch were translated by D.H. Mader.

Paul Post, Tilburg/Naarden, May, 2002

---

[3] See for instance the paper on ritual-liturgical perspectives on the phenomenon of silent processions delivered at the international Societas Liturgica Congress devoted to Life Cycle Rituals, in Santa Clara, CA, USA, August, 2001: Post: 'La marche silencieuse' (2001); IDEM: 'Silent procession' (2002).

1. INTRODUCTION

1.1. APPROACH, STRATEGY AND STRUCTURE

General

Increasingly, after a disaster, people turn to rituals. In the Dutch situation it appears that presently an, as it were, 'off the shelf' repertoire has been developed, whose outlines are ready to be filled in as needed. Silent processions and memorial services are organized with care and punctuality; one encounters preparations for a lasting monument in remembrance of the event, or to maintain a tradition of annual commemorations. Some of the contours of the background of this growing interest in ritual after disasters are easy to identify. In general, our culture is experiencing a great dynamism in ritual. Gerard Lukken has observed that the earlier crisis in ritual has been replaced by rituals in abundance.[1] This general interest in rites and symbols seems to be focused around rituals at transitional points in life – *rites de passage* – and crisis rituals. Obvious examples are rites accompanying death, in particular in cases felt to be undeserved, sudden death.

The interest in ritual repertoires after disasters is very diffuse. Often it is chiefly the effect, the 'purpose' of the ritual which is directly or indirectly of concern. The question constantly arises of how ritual can be of use: does prayer help?[2] Although ritual is still spontaneously connected with religion – after a disaster priests and clergymen are often called in as 'ritual experts' – rituals after disasters clearly involve a wider category of acts, both individual and collective. In a general therapeutic context rituals are recommended as an element in the process of handling grief and other emotions following a disaster. For example, there is a continuing discussion in Germany and The Netherlands about small roadside memorials marking sites of fatal traffic accidents. Some civil authorities advocate a policy of tolerance for a specific period because of the role that these 'second gravestones' play in the grieving process; others prefer a centralised policy with officially prescribed memorial markers; still others

---

[1] LUKKEN: *Rituelen in overvloed* (1999).
[2] GIJSWIJT-HOFSTRA & EGMOND: *Of bidden helpt?* (2000).

want to forbid them altogether lest our roadsides come to look like one large cemetery.[3]

As well as the recognition of the value of rituals for their function in the processing of traumas, there is also criticism. Especially the repertoire of memorial rituals following the death of Princess Diana, and the silent processions after attacks that are popularly characterised as 'senseless' violence (assaults in public space) in the late 1990s in The Netherlands, provoked critical articles and essays.[4] In only a few cases has this ritual/critical perspective been worked out further in a somewhat more well-founded manner. Two authors who have done so are Jacques Janssen and Toine van den Hoogen.[5] Janssen, a sociologist and cultural psychologist, evaluated Dutch silent processions, the often massive marches in silence after fatal cases of street violence, from the perspective of Durkheim's religious and symbolic theory. He ultimately sees them as a search for 'positive mass' and coherence in a context of the decline of participation in churches and confrontation with contingency. A 'homeless majority' is seeking suitable forms of social communication about the meaning or meaninglessness of an undeserved death or disaster, about grief and disrupted order. What remains are forms of minimal ritual, such as the silent procession; shared grief is a sort of mental and spiritual first aid. In his critique, the cultural-theologian Van den Hoogen takes his cue from the perspective of remembrance (*anamnesis*) as a fundamental Jewish-Christian category. Rituals of remembrance bring us back to the places where things went wrong, and prevent us from reducing adversity and accidents to a question of mismanagement.

In these reflections, be they journalistic or academic, rituals after disaster often stand in a negative light. The tone is often one of 'unmasking' them. Ritual offends the authors because it is hollow and empty, is manipulated by the mass media, and particularly because it is useless and ineffective from the perspective of consequences for better policy and disaster prevention: "The Dutchman celebrates his disasters at a level that begins to take on the form of narcissism".[6] Religion, theology and ritual are all marginalised:

---

[3] Some provincial authorities have now forbidden permanent memorial markers along public roads. See POST: 'Paysage rituel' (1996) 251-255.

[4] We will return to the phenomenon of the silent procession in this book in Chapt. 2, and specifically Chapt. 3.5.

[5] JANSSEN: 'Stille omgang' (2000); VAN DEN HOOGEN: 'Is de zonde nog te redden?' (2000).

[6] *Ibid.*, 4.

The only hope is to be more robust and practical in our organising the world, and with stricter enforcement of the law and longer sentences for offenders. The rest is religion, theology, ritually praying that this cup pass by our door![7]

This diffuse interest in ritual after disasters is the stimulus for this project. We hope chiefly to gain further oversight of the matter. This study is intended as a first exploration of the complex ritual repertoire of rites after a disaster. In this, we have opted for a specific context, The Netherlands, but without neglecting the international perspective. After all, we want to see how each disaster ritual is on the one hand a localised ritual, and on the other hand exists by the grace of all sorts of international references. For us disaster ritual is the preeminent locus for catching the complex contemporary ritual dynamic. From that perspective, this project is part of a longer-running Dutch liturgical studies focus, namely surveying and assaying the dynamics in the ritual marketplace, with an eye to liturgy and liturgical inculturation. Therefore in this book we will also examine the repertoire of rituals associated with disasters from the vantage of contemporary ritual dynamics (Chapter 5). In a general sense one could say that the project focuses on the functions, qualities and context of collective, public rituality as associated with disasters.

This investigation can be counted as part of the multidisciplinary field of ritual studies; here especially the previously tried and tested collaboration among the social sciences, humanities and liturgical studies takes shape.[8] Implicitly – and in the final chapter, explicitly – there will be attention given to liturgical and liturgical studies perspectives. Thus this book has a ritual/liturgical character.[9] As well as contemporary ritual dynamics, other themes relevant to current liturgy and liturgical studies, such as active participation, the relationship of the community and individual, ecclesiastical liturgical ritual in relation to forms of civil ritual, liturgy in the public domain and the functionality and instrumentality of ritual, will come under scrutiny.

Although every disaster (both the terms *disaster* and *ritual* will shortly be subject to further definition and delimitation, and will be given a working definition; see 1.2) has both a collective, social dimension and

---

[7] *De Volkskrant*, May 17, 2000.
[8] For a further elaboration of the platform of *ritual studies*, see 1.2.2.
[9] For this 'ritual/liturgical' perspective, see: POST: 'Life cycle rituals' (2002); IDEM: 'Rituell-liturgische Bewegungen' (2002).

a more personal, individual dimension, the project will focus particularly on the collective, public or semi-public rituals associated with disasters. Depending on the research perspective (see below), within the scope of that repertoire a greater or lesser stress can placed on the individual or group, on those directly involved or on outsiders.

Vacuum

A preliminary survey of the literature from scholarly research indicates how empty the field is when it comes to rituals associated with disasters. While there are studies available on the role of the media in respect to disasters, on governmental policy, information and crisis management, medical services, psycho-social and psychotraumatology and sociological aspects of disasters, and while disasters are also discussed from the perspective of women and children, ritual has received almost no attention.[10] At the very most there is an historical collection with some notice of rituals,[11] memorial rituals associated with undeserved sudden death in traffic in Germany and The Netherlands receives some attention,[12] and there is a study of rites associated with the Hillsborough Stadium disaster.[13]

---

[10] As a somewhat random selection of the literature available, listed alphabetically, see: VAN AVESAATH & DE BRUIN: *De psychosociale gevolgen van rampen* (1994); BAEYENS: *Herald of Free Enterprise* (1992); BARTON: *Communities in disaster* (1969); BLAIKIE et al.: *At risk* (1994); BOURRIAU: *Understanding catastrophe* (1992); DAVIS: *Manmade catastrophes* (1992); VAN DUIN, ROSENTHAL & VAN BEELEN-BERGSMA: *De Herculesramp* (1996); DYNES: *Organized behavior in disaster* (1969); DYNES, DE MARCHI & PELANDA: *Sociology of disasters* (1987); ELLEMERS: *De februari-ramp* (1956); IDEM: 'Rampen in Nederland' (2001); ENARSON & HEARN MORROW: *The gendered terrain of disaster* (1998); FRERKS: *Omgaan met rampen* (1998); GIJSWIJT-HOFSTRA & EGMOND: *Of bidden helpt?* (1997); QUARANTELLI: *Disasters* (1978); ROSENTHAL: *Rampen, rellen, gijzelingen* (1984); VAN DER VELDEN, ELAND & KLEBER: *Handboek voor opvang* (1997); WALLACE, ROWLES & COLTON: *Management of disasters* (1994); WOUTERS: *Er valt een gat* (1993); ZINNER & WILLIAMS: *When a community weeps* (1999); cf. also: FOOTE: *Shadowed ground* (1997). For more literature see elsewhere in this book, particularly the section on disaster, 1.2.1, below. In this perspective it is particularly telling that the fine chapter 'Disasters' by Fritz disappeared when the much-used collection *Contemporary social problems* was reprinted, cf. FRITZ: 'Disasters' (1961).

[11] GIJSWIJT-HOFSTRA & EGMOND: *Of bidden helpt?* (1997).

[12] POST: *Ritueel landschap* (1995) 42-46 in 4.4, with literature in notes 92 and 97, supplemented by: FRANKE, FRIEDRICHS & MEHL: 'Unfallskreuze' (1994).

[13] GRAY: 'Bridging the gap' (1989); DAVIE: 'You'll never walk alone' (1993); POST: *Ritueel landschap* (1995) 42-46, note 92.

The rest of the discussion is dominated by fleeting journalistic notice of the regular explosions of public rituality accompanying disasters (i.e. silent processions) and high-profile deaths and murders (for example, Princess Diana, the murdered Belgian girls ('the Dutroux affair'), aeroplane crashes and instances of street violence).[14] What the disaster of September 11, 2001, in New York will lead to can not yet be said as this book is ready to go to press, but here too it appears that a further analysis of ritual is not high on the agenda, although after September 11 there were sessions devoted to disaster ritual at several international conferences in the field of ritual and religious studies. That even within the domains of ethnography and ritual studies disaster ritual hardly receives any attention can be termed remarkable. In this connection – an important indirect connection, as we shall soon see in this study – one can point only to the repeated references to the ritual explosion after the death of Diana, Princess of Wales. In this, however, it is striking that attention was focused on the hybrid funeral service or the role of the media.[15]

This picture, gained from a first survey of the literature regarding ritual and disaster, also applies to disaster ritual and the coping perspective. There too there appears to be a remarkable vacuum. Rituals as yet play only a slight role in the study of adequate coping strategies. At the most the coping qualities of ritual are mentioned in studies of coping and religion, or coping among the elderly.[16] In the realm of ritual studies reference can however be made to a line of research that increasingly is discussing the coping qualities of ritual, often religious in nature (see research into therapeutic rituals, rituals and grief processing, 'adequate' funeral and cremation rituals, 'effective' rites in individual pastoral care; for this see also studies into the functionality of ritual in general).[17]

---

[14] In the course of this book we will repeatedly refer to this; for examples see: POST: *Het wonder van Dokkum* (2000) 109, note 39 and BAL: *De stille tocht* (2000); for a survery of newspaper and magazine articles, see: POST, NUGTEREN & ZONDAG: *Rituelen na rampen* (2002) Chapt. 1, note 13.

[15] Cf. GRIMES: *Deeply into the bone* (2000) 275-280; SPEELMAN: 'The 'feast' of Diana's death' (2001).

[16] KOENIG: *Religion, health and aging* (1988); IDEM: *Research on religion* (1995).

[17] For examples of what are termed therapeutic rituals: VAN DER HART: *Overgang en bestendiging* (1978); IDEM: *Afscheidsrituelen* (1981); IDEM: *Rituelen* (1984); cf. further: MULDER: *Geloven in crematieliturgie* (2000) and particularly MENKEN-BEKIUS: *Rituelen in het individuele pastoraat* (1998); see further in this book case 3.3.

Perspectives

A number of perspectives will be employed in this study. We will briefly develop the most important here in their various relationships, in order to further clarify the concept and approaches of this work.

Ritual

The first perspective can be indicated briefly. It involves ritual input, the ritual perspective. By now it is rather generally acknowledged in the social sciences, humanities and comparative religion that it is precisely through rituals that certain subjects can be approached most productively. In a general sense, a researcher can penetrate a culture deeply through its rituals. Therefore ritual repertoires have become a favourite research field, which long ago ceased to be the sole terrain of cultural anthropologists, ritualists or liturgists.[18]

Interference

A further important perspective is what is termed ritual interference. This term is used to designate the multiplicity of interactions among ritual repertoires.[19] It is not specific functions or qualities of rituals that are involved here, but the manifestation and nature of the ritual repertoire and the complexity or composition of the ritual source. Rituals are always arrangements or montages assembled of various materials, often derived from diverse primary and secondary contexts. Many newly arisen rituals, termed 'emerging rituals'[20] – a realm to which a large proportion of rituals after disasters belong – consist of a combination of ecclesiastical/ religious, general/religious, profane/secular or perhaps interreligious ritual. There is also the interesting phenomenon that in the case of disasters, there is often what might be termed multiple, double or complementary

---

[18] For ritual input in general see: POST: 'Het rituele perspectief' (1998); IDEM: *Het wonder van Dokkum* (2000) 11ff.; IDEM: 'Interference and intuition' (2000) 56 under 3.3. and DEKKER, ROODENBURG & ROOIJAKKERS: *Volkscultuur* (2000) Chapt. 4 and 5.

[19] For interference, and an extensive bibliography, see particularly POST: 'Van Paasvuur tot stille tocht' (1999); from this perspective what is termed contiguous or adjoining ritual is already included in the descriptive survey in Chapt. 2.

[20] For emerging rituals, see: GRIMES: *Reading* (1993) Chapt. 2, 23-38; MITCHELL: 'Emerging ritual' (1995). See further Chapt. 5.

ritual. In addition to traditional prescribed ritual focused on the more private or individual context (rites of mourning, viewing, the wake, burial or cremation) after a disaster there are also – before, after or along with these – collective, public or semi-public rituals (condolence registers, memorial services, silent processions, etc.). The same applies to material memorials. In addition to the individual grave there is a general memorial monument, each with its own form of ritual activity (annual memorial observances, etc.).

Although the accent in this study is on collective, public ritual, it is of great importance to focus on this interference among ritual repertoires in the project, particularly from the perspective of victims, the grieving, and those left behind.

Finally, in addition to the question of what factors play a role here, there arises the question of the nature, identity and 'quality' of the ritual. Is disaster ritual a typical example of postmodern emerging ritual? Is it ultimately to be seen as a general memorial ritual? Do ecclesiastical/Christian references dominate it, or is it a liturgical repertoire escaped from the church building? Is it an exponent of instrumental ritually averting evil? Or is it perhaps a modern variant of popular religious ritual?[21] From whence comes the need to seek out the public realm? And finally, what role does the media play in this?

Appropriation

Further, the ritual source has a complexity that both nuances and complicates every ritual. In fact, with increasing frequency ritual repertoires are being viewed in the context of designation and appropriation processes.[22] This important research approach relativises the perspective of 'designation' which often dominated research, i.e., how culture and cultural elements are imposed from above or outside. It also focuses on appropriation, the specific manner of dealing with culture that is rooted within the group or community itself. This essentially shifts the accent in the investigation from top-down to bottom-up, viewing the community as the central locus where culture takes form. Rather than a unilateral

---

[21] For a summary of this: POST: 'Van paasvuur tot stille tocht' (1999) and IDEM: *Het wonder van Dokkum* (2000).

[22] Cf. FRIJHOFF: 'Toe-eigening' (1997); POST: *Het wonder van Dokkum* (2000); IDEM: 'Interference and intuition' (2000) 59 under 3.5, with extensive bibliography in note 22.

accent on the designation by, for instance, academics or authorities (for instance, in the case of disasters, by 'experts', and the culture of scenarios), the focus moves to the wider process of production, distribution and consumption of culture, from the prescribed to the experienced practice as it is celebrated. This shift of attention in research is different from, and encompasses more than interest in the receiving parties. It means, for example, that a ritual is not seen only as ritual supply, or is understood in terms of regulations and instructions, but is seen primarily as bearing meaning in a process of interpretation and assigning significance, by which groups and individuals experience and fill in a received ritual repertoire.

Just as in a general sense it is true of the first perspective of the ritual approach (we are primarily concerned with the search for rituals, and describing, characterising and analysing them), the perspective of appropriation also places certain demands on source material and research techniques. This will be discussed separately. However, we will here indicate that ritual narratives, the accounts of personal experience in which those involved report their ritual experiences and appropriation of the repertoire, can be a valuable source.

Ritual criticism

Subsequent to the phases of research that will be dominant in this study (characterisation, inventorisation, analysis), there is also a more evaluatory phase. We here connect with the research perspective that, with Ronald Grimes, can be termed ritual criticism.[23] Because of the context of our explorations, in part involving case studies, this ritual critical attitude can be less intuitive than is generally the case in journalistic or expository contributions. In our explorations, through a series of interrelated contextual analyses of ritual, we will attempt to introduce a modest, clear and solidly based critical perspective. In this, both specific parts of the repertoire (such as the silent processions mentioned above) and disaster ritual in a general sense will also be placed in the broader context of shifts in the ritual market.

---

[23] This term was coined by Ronald Grimes in 1990 (GRIMES: *Ritual criticism* (1990)) and has since played a key role in his work; cf. most recently: GRIMES: *Deeply into the bone* (2000).

Ritual inculturation

With respect to rituality there is increasing realisation of the importance of the aspect of inculturation, which depends on the degree to which specific forms of symbolic action are connected with general rituality in a dominant culture. Briefly, this involves the connection between the defining qualities of (in this case) certain forms of marking and commemorative rituals and the context of the tendencies and qualities of the dominant rituality. In our postmodern culture the connection between cultus and culture, bound up with 'honest', 'adequate', 'legitimate' or 'relevant' ritual (these being the sort of terms with which people readily denote the ideal of ritual inculturation[24]), is especially linked with or dependent upon dynamics in the field of rituality and the falling away of prescribed forms of and spaces for ritual coupled with it. The traditional connections between ritual and culture have disappeared; new connections are being sought. We constantly see people in search of suitable ritual repertoires, for adaptations or new creations, for language, forms and space for ritual ("Sir, have you gotten any good rituals in today?"). This is the background of the repertoire of emerging rituals mentioned above, and for the disappearance of the boundaries between ecclesiastical/religious, general/religious, profane/secular and interreligious ritual. One can think here of the way military authorities in Europe are wrestling to come up with fitting 'modern' ceremonies and rituals, or on the search everywhere in the world for suitable national (and sometimes also international) rituals of reconciliation (i.e., South Africa, Rwanda, the former Yugoslavia, Afghanistan), but also, on a smaller scale, of experiments and searching particularly in the field of life cycle and transition rituals.[25]

Rituals after disasters are a preeminent locus for discovering and observing this inculturation process. Here we therefore locate more generally the fundamental perspective of the project: how can we bind our rituals of commemoration to the culture? Where can signals of vital potential for inculturation be picked up? And what are the inculturating, vitalising qualities there, or the qualities which militate against vitality

---

[24] LUKKEN: *Rituelen in overvloed* (1999); MULDER: *Geloven in crematieliturgie* (2000).

[25] Cf. BARNARD: 'De Nationale Herdenking' (2001) 187-193. We also return to this in the discussion of the phenomenon of the silent procession, under 3.5.

and inculturation?[26] We will have to seek out the connections with general rituality in postmodern culture. This can only happen after a careful examination, a survey of the surrounding ritual culture.

In general, every ritual case study (if it is a good one) is also a wider study of ritual tendencies in our culture. Our exploration is thus at the same time a sample and testing of the contemporary ritual/symbolic milieu that possess a wider reach than the disaster ritual alone that is being investigated. After all, every ritual study is ultimately a cultural study, for, as has been said, it is precisely through ritual repertories that one can penetrate deeply into a culture.

Liturgical inculturation: ritual-liturgical perspectives

Although, as we said before, this study must be considered primarily as a ritual study, a liturgical studies and liturgical perspective is also present. The project is part of a long-running and general series devoting attention to Dutch liturgical studies research (and in particular, to the programme conducted by the Liturgical Institute at Tilburg), which can be characterised as investigation of contemporary ritual dynamics. All of the subsidiary perspectives discussed above can be found in a liturgical studies research design which has previously been presented frequently, and which is employed in this connection.[27] A phase of surveying and analysing the contemporary ritual milieu is one important component in it. Supplementing the perspective of ritual inculturation just discussed, the continual search for an adequate connection between ritual and its anthropological and cultural setting, there will also be that of liturgical inculturation – or honouring the inextricable link between the two, that of ritual/liturgical inculturation. In addition to the general ritual perspective of constant reflection on the dynamic of cultus and culture, there is now also a focus on liturgy. This deals with the place and identity of Christian rituality and the *liturgia condenda*. Each liturgical study, supported by the perspective and the task of liturgical inculturation, is in essence also a ritual study. Because this study, as we have said, primarily

---

[26] Cf. for the perspective of inculturation: LUKKEN: *Rituelen in overvloed* (1999) 122-143; POST: 'Interference and intuition' (2000) 54, note 15; IDEM: *Het wonder van Dokkum* (2000) 126-128.

[27] POST: 'Interference and intuition' (2000); IDEM: 'Programm und Profil der Liturgiewissenschaft' (2002).

involves an investigation of a widely present ritual repertoire in context, we will resist the temptation to devote a separate excursus to research design in liturgical studies. We will devote only a few sentences to this 'ritual-liturgical' inculturation perspective.

In the context of the Liturgical Movement (perhaps it is by now much better to speak of this without the capital letters and in plural ('liturgical movements'), because what we customarily term the Liturgical Movement is in fact a complex and multi-layered process), the realisation grew that the general/human givens with regard to ritual must be taken seriously. Accordingly, reflection was devoted to ritual and symbol, language and act, to the sensory and physical, and to other non-verbal elements. Each of these anthropological/ritual dimensions necessarily brought with it its own expertise, with a series of new alliances, methods and techniques.

In the course of this integral approach to liturgy, people became aware of the multiple contexts of liturgical expression. In the wider framework of liturgical renewal, the fundamental realisation grew that liturgical studies had to take seriously not only the general basic/human givens regarding ritual (that is to say, the 'anthropological' context in the stricter sense), but also the multi-layered, complex cultural context. It was acknowledged that each liturgical study was both an anthropological study and a cultural study.

Against this background the somewhat tautological term 'ritual-liturgical' was introduced. In this construction, not only is liturgy placed consistently and systematically in the wider context of ritual and thus liturgical studies declared a ritual study, but, to our minds, one also hears echoes of the double human and cultural condition or context mentioned above.

For the ritual-liturgical analysis advocated here as integral, and in the final research phase involved with theological evaluation, liturgical studies finds here a natural alliance or partner. For the argument which follows, we will take this alliance as a guide for a further exploration and discussion, in the conviction that with the exploration of the ritual-liturgical milieu and the ritual-liturgical competency we ultimately will provide an important contribution to liturgical studies as a theological project.

Closely linked with that same ritual-liturgical perspective is the perspective of the margin. Liturgical studies show that researchers are increasingly interested in the margins surrounding the traditional areas of liturgical Christian sacramental repertoire. They are aware of the fact that the traditional parish structure is still our parameter, but perhaps in the margins, in areas outside and around the traditional parish structure, we will find forms of inspiring rituals. By analysing the margins further we may find inculturating qualities. In short, that is the perspective of ritual-liturgical marginality. The paradox we now face is that people feel alienated from the rites of the Christian centre, the parish, and that participation in marginal rituals prevents them from feeling alienated, because there they can find solidarity with the all-embracing culture and can break through their isolation. This openness resulting from the borderline position may increase the possibility of integrating the traditional culture of one's own ecclesiastical domain. If we look at all the movements surrounding the parish, we can distinguish between different loci of innovation and marginality which strikingly concern especially the domains of ritual and liturgy. We would link this perspective with the threshold areas – at the moment an important perspective in practical theology and catechetics – between Christian faith and the world, of 'transitional spaces' and 'border communities.'[28] Disaster ritual is perhaps the terrain par excellence for providing us with more insight into this spacious transitional area of core liturgy and surrounding culture. It is this perspective that justifies including this ritual study in a liturgical studies series bearing the series title '*Liturgia condenda.*' Important themes such as liturgy and media, the tension between the individual and the communal and the public and private domains can be surveyed immediately through this connection. These are therefore all subjects which will return as we draw up our final balance and perspective in the last chapter.

Sources, methods and research strategies

The ritual source is central to this study. It is an exploratory study that can be counted as part of the platform or podium of ritual studies. In the course of the discussion of the concept of 'ritual' we will shortly have more to say regarding this platform (see 1.2.2). Here the methodological note will be sufficient, that one mark of ritual studies is their pronounced multidisciplinary character. In this case, various religious studies, particularly liturgical studies, comparative religion, psychology and ethnography/ethnology which are involved.

The multidisciplinary method of working is conceived as being essentially characterised by an effort to learn to understand the methods of

---

[28] ROEBBEN: 'Spiritual and moral education' (1999), here 88f.

other disciplines and appropriate them, in order to then be able to treat the results independently and integrate these into a new entity.[29]

Our exploration is an exercise in qualitative research. The qualitative research method is here seen as a way of investigating the qualities, nature and character of a phenomenon. Rituals are therefore, as previously remarked, employed as an indispensable primary source, and further the perspective of those involved, the appropriation of the ritual by the participants, is taken into consideration to as great an extent as possible. As is customary in qualitative research, the collection and examination of the data is not wholly separated from analysis and evaluation. Data is provisionally analysed so that this analysis can in turn direct subsequent collection and examination. Thus one can denote the process as dialectic. Here too we join with the profile of the platform of ritual studies as a critical study of rites, as that was and is being developed particularly by Grimes. There inductive and deductive approaches to the material interact constantly. This interplay will recur in this study as well. There are ritual explorations, the case studies with phases of inventorisation, characterisation, context analysis and evaluation, and there are more conceptual, theoretical explorations, particularly of disaster and ritual, and there is a more broadly conceived contextual and comparative exploration of contemporary ritual dynamics.

More focused on the research strategies is first of all and generally the ethnological tradition of 'opening up' the ritual source through participatory observation and description. Here it is the ritual performance which is central. If one seeks to do justice to the complexity of ritual as performance, the interaction within which various elements such as space and appointments, implements, music, words, acts, and roles of the various participants all play a part, one must employ various methods and techniques which supplement one another in order to 'open up' this source. Because it is not possible (or at best only possible to a slight degree) to engage in actual, direct and timely participatory observation (cf. immediate memorial service, or annually recurring commemorative rituals after a disaster), various convergent source materials will be used. In this study these will include sound and video recordings, descriptions and reports, text materials, reconstructions, conversations with participants and interviews.

---

[29] We are conscious that others might use the term interdisciplinary for this perspective. Of the trio of multi-, inter- and intra-disciplinary, we nevertheless deliberately opt for employing the least ambitious and pretentious, 'multidisciplinary'.

In this connection we want to briefly and specifically mention ritual narratives, accounts of personal ritual experience, as a part of the more comprehensive genre of the personal narrative. A file of narratives of this sort were collected for this project, and used only here and there in its compilation. As we will further indicate in the closing chapter, these constitute a privileged source for further study.

Structure

The exploratory nature of the project is reflected in the structure of this book, especially in Chapters 2 and 3. The structure is defined by the fact that this is first and foremost a report on an exploratory investigation which was carried out by three researchers who each had their own accent in the research and represented different research traditions (psychology of religion (Zondag), comparative religion (Nugteren), ethnology, ritual and liturgical studies (Post)). In this study they encounter each other on the platform or podium of ritual studies, already mentioned and discussed further in 1.2.2.

In general, there were four successive phases in the research project, which in part define the structure of this book as a research report. First there was the orientational, introductory phase (Chapter 1). Here clear working definitions are provided for the central concepts of disaster (1.2.1) and ritual (1.2.2). Next there is the exploratory, descriptive, empirical phase, central to which are a series of exemplary and thematically focused surveys (Chapters 2 and 3). These provide a general overview of disasters and the ritual repertoire, keeping in mind the parameters set forth previously in Chapter 1 (a primarily Dutch perspective, period 1990-2001; Chapter 2). This survey is also widened out internationally in the case of both disasters and the ritual repertoires. It flows into an attempt at a typology of the ritual repertoire, with particular attention for what is termed contiguous ritual.

After this general survey the study zooms in on several selected disasters and on components or aspects of the repertoire of rites after disasters (Chapter 3). Here a choice is first made for both a definite period, to wit the 1990s, and for a definite context, to wit The Netherlands. Just as each ritual study is essentially a local study, so, if it is well chosen, characterised, analysed and placed into a wider research perspective, each local case transcends that limited local context. Although, as we will see repeatedly, disaster ritual is uniquely defined by local factors, there is at the same time always an international dimension. This has everything to do with the impact these major disasters have; the September 11 disaster was commemorated around the world, and the silent procession after the New Year's fire in Volendam, in The Netherlands in 2001, was broadcast in more than 20 countries. The international dimension is also often injected because disasters are frequently connected with international traffic. One example is the 1992 crash of an El Al freight liner into an Amsterdam residential neighbourhood in which many immigrants lived; people of more than 36 nationalities were involved in the memorial services. In addition, the often complex ritual interferences, which we have listed as an important perspective, are more focused on the ritual repertoire.

A particular general theme in disaster ritual is illuminated in each of five Dutch cases. In section 3.1 the focus is on the multicultural dimension in the Bijlmer disaster, the aeroplane crash in Amsterdam in 1992 just mentioned; in 3.2 on the search for fitting ritual from the Christian-liturgical and general-religious forms, through the memorial service for the Hercules disaster, the crash of a military personnel transport plane in Eindhoven in 1996; and on the aspect of dealing with trauma through the procession and memorial service following the Volendam cafe fire, 2001 (3.3), and the memorial monument and annual commemorative service (3.4). The final case study, devoted to the phenomenon of the silent procession, begins with the procession in Enschede following the explosion of a fireworks factory in a residential neighbourhood, 2000, but is developed in a wider context (3.5) and as such serves as a prelude to the fifth chapter, on ritual dynamics.

The international perspective is explicitly introduced in a second exploratory round (Chapter 4) through two non-Dutch cases: the sinking of the ferryboat 'Estonia' (Scandinavia, 1994) and September 11, 2001.

These case studies are followed by more broadly conceived contextual and analytic chapters in which first the current general framework of rituality is explored (Chapter 5). Although a contextual and analytic perspective is expressly present with the discussion of the ritual repertoire in the concrete case studies (that is particularly the case in the development of the intercultural and multicultural dimension in 3.1 and the silent procession in 3.5), rites after disasters are now placed in a broader context. With regard to ritual, there is the question of the contemporary dynamics of the ritual market, and the trends and qualities that can be identified there.

The final phase of the project involves synthesis and evaluation. The final portion of the book corresponds to this, and has the character of the familiar 'balance and perspective' (Chapter 6). Here, on the basis of the ritual-critical perspective discussed above, several of the important dimensions will be taken up again, and perspectives for future research set out. Finally, the ritual-liturgical perspective mentioned above again comes up for discussion.

1.2. CENTRAL CONCEPTS

1.2.1. Disaster: definition and characteristics

Introduction

Along with rituals, disasters are the central object of this study. As with ritual, on further examination it is not easy to give a precise definition of a disaster, particularly because in the case of disasters context and perspective will play an especially important role. It is thus more useful to speak in terms of working definitions, or, better still, characteristics. If one fully enters into the perspective of trauma, of suffering experienced, then each individual case of illness or death can mean a disaster. What for outsiders is a marginal loss can be a disaster for someone directly involved. Definitions also appear to be strongly influenced by specific contexts that determine the perspective in which disasters are discussed. Those assembling news reports or annual retrospectives employ different parameters, it would appear, than psychologists specialising in trauma processing and policy-makers whose focus is on public safety and social work.[30]

For our project it was necessary to formulate a clear definition of a disaster, upon which critical distinctions could be made. After an exploration of definitions and characteristics presently in circulation, we opted for the method of using several relevant qualifiers, a method that we will also follow in the definition of ritual, below. Thus we arrive at a working definition that will be further focused for the project by the addition of two more practical distinctions or choices geared to the performance of this study. A detailed typology of disasters is not offered here, but only later in connection with a broad inventory.

---

[30] Cf. for instance ANNUAL BOOK OF THE YEAR, *Encyclopaedia Britannica*; KLEBER, BROM & DEFARES: *Traumatische ervaringen* (1986); IDEM: *Coping with trauma* (1992); VAN DER VELDEN, ELAND & KLEBER: *Handboek* (1997) 15-22; FRITZ: 'Disasters' (1961).

Exploration of definitions and characteristics

In a very general sense there are – apart from very general and popular figurative language use: "That man is really a disaster for our firm!" – three major directions to be distinguished in the use of the concept of 'disaster'. There is the focused, specific delineation of disaster. This can flow out of the search for an adequate definition or characterisation, or from a series of characteristics or qualities (qualifiers). It is nevertheless striking how often studies in the humanities, but also in the social sciences, forego any further clarification of the concept.[31] A second line is oriented exclusively to the aspect of the experience of suffering, as mentioned above. In principle then a large number of events, if not everything, can be a disaster for someone. 'Disaster' refers to the dimensions, the extent of the suffering experienced in the life of an individual. A third direction is more ascriptive and recycles this dimension of suffering metaphorically. Unemployment, sexual abuse, senseless violence, global warming and such can then be termed 'disasters'. All three directions have in common that by 'disaster' they understand a considerable calamity, misfortune and suffering, a line that is rather generally to be found in the primary definition in the entry for 'disaster' in dictionaries.[32]

We now turn our attention to the first direction, of more specific characterisations. Although the definition of disaster has decidedly not been a separate and dominant theme within the social sciences, as has been the case for ritual, one can find further definition of disaster in the literature dealing with processing of trauma, and that on policy dealing with social work and public safety. In most cases this involves the enumeration of a series of qualities or characteristics. We will give several examples from both fields.

The Dutch law dealing with disasters chooses a very specific perspective of public safety and assistance:

> A disaster is an event leading to the creation of a serious disruption of general safety, through which the lives and health of many persons, and/or large material interests are threatened to a serious degree, and which demands the coordinated deployment of services and organisations of various disciplines.[33]

---

[31] Cf. for instance GIJSWIJT-HOFSTRA & EGMOND: *Of bidden helpt?* (1997) and KLEBER: *Het trauma voorbij* (1999).

[32] Cf. *disaster, catastrophe.*

[33] VAN DER VELDEN, ELAND & KLEBER: *Handboek voor opvang na rampen* (1997).

The definition of C.E. Fritz is more generally socially oriented: a disaster is:

> ...an event, concentrated in time and space, in which a society, or a relatively self-sufficient subdivision of a society, undergoes severe danger and incurs such losses to its members and physical appurtenances that the social structure is disrupted and the fulfillment of all or some of the essential functions of society is prevented.[34]

For the most part psychology that specialises in the treatment and handling of traumatic experiences seeks a suitable set of qualifiers.[35] We focus here particularly on the characteristics as they were developed by R. Kleber, D. Brom and P.B. Defares since 1986. In 1986 they began with a set of four:[36]

(a) an acute situation that is or could be life-threatening for animals or humans, and can cause great damage;
(b) a relatively large group of people are or could be involved;
(c) disruption of the normal pattern of a society, or a part thereof;
(d) a more than unusual effort from rescue workers or governmental authorities is demanded.

Several general dimensions which will help in our process of defining and distinguishing clearly already emerge here, but at the same time there is a question of to what extent all four aspects together make a dramatic occurrence into a disaster. Emphasis on aspect (c) would mean that the uproar caused by the series of disappearances of girls, later found abused or murdered, in the mid-1990s in Belgium (the 'Dutroux affair') would qualify as a 'disaster' without further ado. The fourth qualifier is also very much linked to context and perspective.

In 1992 we find the same authors presenting an altered set of qualifiers, which we would want to accept as a guide.[37] A disaster is then characterised by:

(a) powerlessness of the individual;
(b) loss of structure in everyday life;

---

[34] FRITZ: 'Disasters' (1961) 655.
[35] VAN DER VELDEN, ELAND & KLEBER: *Handboek* (1997) 15-22 provides a summary.
[36] KLEBER, BROM & DEFARES: *Traumatische ervaringen* (1986); cf. VAN DER VELDEN, ELAND & KLEBER: *Handboek* (1997) 15-22.
[37] KLEBER, BROM & DEFARES: *Coping with trauma* (1992).

(c)   the extent of the destruction and human suffering;
(d)   its collective nature;
(e)   unexpectedness.

The first three characteristics correspond with those of a traumatic event (loss of control, loss of certainty, and suffering). This set has a number of important implications. A disaster is a collective occurrence; it overcomes a group, and not an individual. This means that people cannot approach the consequences of a disaster on the individual level alone. The social, cultural context must always be involved. Next, human suffering is central, although again that can be closely connected with loss of or harm to animals, nature or material goods.

This set of five qualifiers has been elaborated in a number of ways in social science literature. For example, attempts are made to further designate or rank the seriousness of loss or destruction.[38] The proposed criteria or parameters include:

(a)   objects: goods, houses, personal possessions, means of transport and communication;
(b)   conditions: social structures and other circumstances at the individual, group or social level, health or other support institutions;
(c)   internal resources: individual characteristics such as self-esteem, ability to cope, imparting meaning, trust in the future, pride, competition, sense of control;
(d)   power: finances, food, fuel, knowledge that can be employed to tap or protect other resources.

There is no generally accepted classification for disasters. Several attempts have indeed been made to arrive at a taxonomy, but these remain rather abstract, and insufficiently developed.[39] Rather generally, however, there is a distinction made between natural disasters and disasters caused by man.[40] This distinction is employed to afford further insight into certain aspects of a disaster. One can think of:

(a)   duration of danger: this would tend to be longer for disasters caused by man (i.e., Chernobyl);

---

[38] Cf. VAN DER VELDEN, ELAND & KLEBER: *Handboek* (1997) 17.
[39] The authors are here particularly referring to BERREN, BEIGEL & GHERTNER: 'A typology' (1980).
[40] Cf. VAN DER VELDEN, ELAND & KLEBER: *Handboek* (1997) 18.

(b) predictability; this is generally greater for natural disasters;
(c) magnitude; natural disasters are generally considered greater;
(d) the question of guilt; this distinguishes disasters caused by man,
     while a natural disaster simply happens.

By now it is generally acknowledged that this distinction, when examined further, is not terribly sharp. The realisation has become rather widespread that people cause natural disasters, and that in their form and
impact (collectivity and the extent of human suffering) disasters caused
by man do not necessarily differ from natural disasters. It is therefore
appropriate that we do not introduce this distinction at the conceptual
level. Certainly, however, a general, purely phenomenological descriptive
typology is appropriate, such as is employed by the annual survey in the
Encyclopaedia Britannica.[41] Ranked in order of the average length of the
sections involved, the eight groupings are natural disasters, aeroplane
disasters, traffic disasters, maritime disasters, fires and explosions, mine
disasters, rail disasters, and a miscellaneous section which includes,
among other things, large-scale cases of food poisoning. One of the striking points is how four of the sections together arise from the category of
travel and commerce (disasters with aeroplanes, trains, automobiles and
busses, and ships).

Working definition

Against the background of the preceding exploration, we can propose a
working definition for this study into rituals accompanying disasters. For
us, there are three basic qualifiers which together to a greater or lesser
extent will distinguish a disaster:

(a) There is major, extensive destruction and human suffering. In addi-
     tion to damage and human suffering, generally in the form of the loss
     of human life, large scale, magnitude, impact and infamy are central
     here. These factors lie behind the almost stereotypical adjective
     'national'. We easily speak of 'national' disasters; in the media or other
     literature one almost never encounters local or regional disasters.
(b) Closely connected with (a), the calamity, the great misfortune, is
     collective in nature. It does not involve the individual, but always the
     larger group.

---

[41] ANNUAL BOOK OF THE YEAR, supplement to the *Encyclopaedia Britannica*.

(c) Third, it involves a sudden, unexpected occurrence. A disaster is
     instantaneous in nature, and not chronic.

In our opinion, these qualifiers are sufficient to make adequate distinctions in a general sense. We will employ these characteristics in this project, and particularly in the general exploration of the disasters and the
selection of specific case studies. In this we are fully aware that this is a
working definition which serves to identify specific cases. In an examination more oriented to case studies of the phenomenon of disaster, there
will always be borderline cases that can be discovered and proposed for
inclusion. For instance, there can always be questions about the precise
scale of magnitude of the impact, and the precise extent of the collectivity,
as well as the ratios with regard to harm to people, nature and goods.
The instantaneousness is also relative. A recent example of this latter was
the infection of a large number of visitors at the West-Friesian Flora, an
agricultural and garden exhibition at Bovenkarspel, The Netherlands, in
February, 1999, with the dangerous legionella bacteria. Because it was
only after some time that the source of the infection was localised, and
people continued to die from the infection over a long period, one could
identify this as a disaster of a peculiar nature. The media spoke of
'a silent disaster'. Nevertheless, in most cases, through our qualifiers it can
be quickly determined whether or not we are dealing with a disaster.
Natural disasters, major train, aeroplane, ship, bus and auto accidents,
avalanches, explosions and such are disasters. Individual automobile accidents, outbreaks of swine fever, cases of sexual abuse, or assaults on the
street in the genre of 'senseless violence' do not fall into the category.
Nor was the sudden death of Princess Diana a disaster.
    Although we will follow this distinction as strictly as possible, nonethe-
less because of ritual interferences misfortunes and calamities that can not
be qualified as disasters will still enter fully into our discussion via the
ritual repertoires (more will be said on this later). With this we introduce
an important perspective in our project. In the delineation of objects for
study we rather strictly choose for disaster rituals, and in inventorying,
exploring, characterising and analysing them we leave victims of various
sorts of violence (assaults, accidents and such: cf. Olof Palme, Yitzhak
Rabin, Princess Diana, the 'Dutroux affair', cases of 'senseless street
violence', etc.) out of the picture. These do however come into consideration in the contextual analysis of the ritual repertoire, in which their
silent processions, memorial services and similar elements in the repertoire seem to join in one current, without distinctions, from the Heizel

stadium drama (Belgium, 1985), through the sinking of the ferry Herald of Free Enterprise (Belgium, 1987), Palme's assassination (Sweden, 1986), the Hillsborough stadium disaster (England, 1989), the sinking of the ferry Estonia (Scandinavia, 1994), the Bijlmer disaster (air crash, Amsterdam, 1992), the 'Hercules disaster' (air crash, Eindhoven, 1996), the 'Dutroux affair' (disappearance, abuse and murder of girls, cf. the 'White March', Brussels, 1996), numerous victims of 'senseless violence' in The Netherlands in the 1990s (particularly Leeuwarden, Amsterdam and Gorinchem), the fireworks disaster in Enschede (2000), the sinking of the Russian submarine Kursk (August, 2000), the New Year's cafe fire in Volendam (2001) and the attack on the Twin Towers, New York, September 11, 2001.

Before adding two delineations to the qualifiers, we would briefly note that the questions of guilt or cause play no role. We do not make a distinction between natural disasters, as not being caused by man, and other disasters that are indeed caused by man.[42] Nevertheless, there are three remarks necessary here.

It is noteworthy that in surveys of disasters, terrorist attacks, even through their impact may be great, almost never appear in the category of disasters. The suspicion must be that unconsciously the element of human responsibility still plays a role here. For example, it is our impression that the international media labelled the sinkings of the Estonia and the Kursk disasters more quickly and easily than the attacks in Oklahoma City (1995) and New York (September 11, 2001). For the rest, this provokes the question of what other factors – for instance, the location of the attacks – may play a role here too. There would appear to also be a striking difference here in perspective between Western Europe and North America on the one hand, and attacks which have also claimed many victims in Eastern Europe, Asia, the Middle East, South America and Africa.

Also – and this is our second remark – the element of 'undeserved' plays a more or less indirect role. Through its sudden and unforeseen character, the suffering caused by a disaster is by nature 'undeserved'. But it must immediately be said that this still involves a somewhat

---

[42] It is striking how certain researches continue to employ this distinction. One example is Bäckström, the sociologist from Uppsala, who in his analysis of the sinking of the Estonia (1994, more than 900 dead) made a strict distinction between disasters to be blamed on technical or human failures and natural disasters (unpublished lecture, Soesterberg, The Netherlands, June 7, 2002), See further Chapt. 4.1.

associative category which definitely cannot be the antithesis of 'deserved', and therefore perhaps is just as unfortunate as the expression 'senseless violence' which has come into general circulation. 'Undeserved' does not so much touch on the question of causality and guilt. Rather, it says something about the nature of the misfortune that has struck. Just as people in the Middle Ages spoke of an 'unforeseen death', thereby indicating that this involved a sudden death in which the deceased did not have the opportunity to receive the Last Rites,[43] people today speak of a sudden undeserved death from the assumption that persons of advanced age normally die at home or in a hospital or nursing home.

A third and last note involves the general, rather vague fact that in the modern Western context many (if not all) disasters are experienced as a sore assault on an order susceptible to control by management and technology. A disaster provokes an immediate double reaction: an assiduous search for responsibility or cause, with as its background the suspicion of failure, human or otherwise, and efforts at future prevention. 'Investigation' is the watchword for both reactions – or better, 'investigations', in the plural. As the Estonia disaster shocked Scandinavian self-confidence in their social and technological order and autonomy, in general in the rest of the Western world we proceed from the often unconscious idea that most categories of disasters, including natural disasters, are the property of countries and regions where (as everyone knows or assumes) people have their affairs much less in order. Until recently the example par excellence of a Dutch disaster was the great flood of April 1953, with which the term 'disaster investigation' was connected right up through a recent survey of Dutch culture in the 1950s.[44] That almost exemplary position would seem to have applied internationally for a long time too; for instance, Fritz cites the great flood in the chapter on disasters in his familiar 1961 standard work *Contemporary Social Problems*.[45] A telling indication of the persistence of this hidden assumption was the way that the media termed the fireworks disaster in Enschede an 'un-Dutch disaster'.[46]

[43] This is the background for the great popularity of St. Christopher, down to this very day: the presence of this patron saint would prevent an unforeseen death.

[44] SCHUYT & TAVERNE: *Welvaart in zwart-wit* (2000) section 'Rampenonderzoek' 142-146.

[45] FRITZ: 'Disasters' (1961) 651.

[46] Cf. among others DE HOOG: 'De ramp, de rituelen', in *de Groene Amsterdammer* May 27, 2000.

Further delineation of time and place

Finally, to the three characteristics that make a misfortune or calamity into a disaster, we will add two very practical delineatory criteria, specifically related to our project. First, we will focus exclusively on disasters which have had a predominately Dutch dimension. That may be because the disaster took place in The Netherlands, or because there were many Dutch victims, or because for some other reason there was wide Dutch interest. As we have said before, this in no way precludes an international perspective. For instance, in the general description of the repertoire in Chapter 2, and also in the various surveys, the international perspective will be expressly present. Particularly in the discussion of the phenomenon of the silent procession the relation between the local and international dimensions will be raised. At the same time, the silent procession would seem an unique and typically Dutch ritual after a disaster, although linked with and determined by a series of international references. Here too one can point to the disaster of September 11, 2001. One the one hand the disaster in New York found a global, worldwide response in scores of rituals; on the other hand it was, and is, strongly nationally and locally defined. European memorials were obviously stripped of American/nationalistic dimensions, and for instance no silent procession was held in The Netherlands because there was a 'ritual niche' or *topos*.

As a second delineation we have selected a certain period: in our exploration we will focus on rituals associated with disasters in the period from 1990 to 2001. That is a purely pragmatic choice, behind which there is no substantive or programmatic reason at all. We had to limit our field, chiefly because in the general exploration and inventorying we wanted to place 'Dutch' disasters in an international perspective.[47]

1.2.2. Ritual: definition and indications

Introduction

As well as disaster, ritual is a central concept in this exploration. Even more than by the disaster concept, an adequate characterisation or definition of 'ritual' is not easily achieved. Not only is there a long and complex tradition on this point, but especially the conceptualisation of

---

[47] See Chapt. 2. Cf. further the literature listed in 1.1., note 10.

ritual is connected with diverse theories with regard to ritual and symbols. For many the use of the terminology ('ritual', 'rite', 'ritualising' or
'rituality' and such) requires precision, and betrays certain theoretical
accents.[48]

In the context of this project we have opted for pluralistic further indi-
cators for identifying ritual. On the one hand, our working definition will
be stated briefly; on the other hand some insight will be offered into
contemporary lines of force in the ritual studies situation. We will thus
go further than just a clearly stated working definition, and, more than
in the case of the concept of disaster, on the basis of a brief historical
exploration will also sketch the background of the working definition.
Accordingly we will also present and develop several research perspectives more generally. These involve qualities and functions of ritual, as
well as the important perspective of the dynamic of cultus and culture
and inculturation. Before this proposed characterisation and development of ritual we will turn to the important platform of ritual studies,
the field in which we intend to situate our exploration of rituals accompanying disasters.[49] Finally, it is thus our intention to provide more than
merely a sound characterisation of qualities and dimensions of rituality
relevant to this study. In the discussion we will especially focus on theoretical reflection on ritual. Later, in the handling of the context, the
stratum of ritual developments and trends, as well as the diverse analyses
in that field – likewise an important component in the modern study of
rites – will be explicitly discussed.[50]

---

[48] For a survey see: BOUDEWIJNSE: 'The conceptualisation of ritual' (1995); GRIMES:
Beginnings (1982); IDEM: *Ritual criticism* (1990); IDEM: *Reading* (1993); IDEM: *Marrying
and burying* (1995); IDEM: 'Ritual' (2000); IDEM: *Deeply into the bone* (2000); BELL:
Ritual theory (1992); IDEM: *Ritual* (1997); RAPPAPORT: *Ritual and religion* (1999);
LUKKEN: *Rituelen in overvloed* (1999); POST: 'Ritualiteit' (2001). This section on ritual
draws on POST: 'Ritualiteit' (2001). See further: all of part A: 'Symbolische orde'
in BARNARD & POST: *Ritueel bestek* (2001). Cf. AUNE & DEMARINIS: *Religious and social
ritual* (1996); RITUELEN EN RELIGIE (special issue) (1997); HUMPHREY & LAIDLAW:
The archetypal actions (1994); MENKEN-BEKIUS: *Rituelen in het individuele pastoraat*
(1998) Chapt. 2 and 3: 17-70.

[49] See the elaboration of the statement of our research question/problem and our
method and manner of working, in 1.1 above.

[50] See Chapt. 5.

Rituals: abundant interest

Rituals are 'in'. Much is being said and written about them in academia and the media. The title of a recently published critical study on the place of Christian ritual in our culture by Gerard Lukken is telling in this regard: *Rituals in abundance*.[51] The media is regularly full of expressions of surprise about explosions of ritual, for instance accompanying the death of Princess Diana, but also following cases of what is being termed 'senseless violence'. Funeral rituals, traditional and postmodern, also get plenty of attention from journalists – but also from artists, policy-makers and planners (in government and the funeral industry), and those studying rituals.

Rituals have been discovered by scholars from various fields in the humanities as an effective entry into the extremely complex system that a culture is, past and present.[52] The interest in rites on the part of psychologists, traumatologists and therapists is striking.[53] Rituals are often used instrumentally in diverse situations for healing or caring for the mind or body, particularly in the more alternative segment of therapy and counselling, whether this involves the until recently popular healings of alternative priests and gurus, New Age ritual quests or the spatial/ritual control of energy currents in the art of optimal placement (*Feng Shui*): everywhere there is that dominant, complex jumble of an abundance of rites and symbols.

In addition to old ritual traditions (real, or, more often, invented), there are entirely new rituals. Older, particularly ecclesiastical, religious rituals appear to be losing their influence, and a whole new repertoire is rising around them. AIDS Memorial Day is one such modern tradition, but other groups, such as the relatives of cancer victims or traffic deaths, by now also have their own annual commemorations, often with newly created rituals.

---

[51] LUKKEN: *Rituelen in overvloed* (1999); for the announcement and review see: POST: 'Acht woorden' (2000) and ROUWHORST: 'Rituelen in overvloed' (2001). An English edition of this book (*Rituals in abundance*) is planned in the series *Liturgia condenda*.

[52] A recent example is the introduction to Dutch ethnology, DEKKER, ROODENBURG & ROOIJAKKERS: *Volkscultuur* (2000) especially Chapt. 4, 'Vieren en markeren. Feest en ritueel' (ROOIJAKKERS 173-230) and 5: 'Percepties van sacraliteit. Over religieuze volkscultuur' (NISSEN 231-281).

[53] In addition to the very vague and broad domain of healing (see GRIMES: *Deeply into the bone* (2000) 307ff), for The Netherlands reference can be made to the ongoing research of Menken-Bekius: cf. MENKEN-BEKIUS: *Rituelen in het individuele pastoraat* (1998).

On further examination one discovers that in this remarkable popularity and interest the term 'ritual' – like for that matter the closely related term 'symbol' (of which more below) – is often employed intuitively or associatively. The precise meaning of the concepts is often not taken into account. 'Ritual' is rather casually connected with traditional ecclesiastical/ religious acts, for example, or with 'ceremony' (national celebrations, for instance), or the conspicuous rites that mark cycles in time or transitions in life (Christmas, baptism, burial). It is striking that in our everyday use of language 'ritual' and 'symbol' have taken on a certain, often pejorative connotation. Ritual and symbol stand for behaviour that recurs with regularity, without influence or impact. How this 'debased' use of terms surrounding ritual and symbol constantly plays itself out against the background of the classical tension between symbol and reality will not be developed further here.

In the following we focus on the further indication of what ritual is. From the long tradition of reflection on the concept of ritual and the symbolic order in various academic disciplines and subdisciplines (within the social sciences, primarily sociology, psychology and anthropology and ethnography/ethnology; within the humanities primarily philosophy, comparative religion and theology) we will only note some of the lines of force. Finally we will turn our attention to what is termed ritual studies, together with semiotics one of the two academic disciplines that are especially devoted to the conceptual analysis of ritual.

A first coherent identification of the concept: sign, symbol, rite and myth

Rituals – or more generally formulated and including the whole of the ritual repertoire, rituality – exists by the grace of what is termed symbolic order. In a very general sense it can be said that rituality is supported by the interplay of signs, symbols, myths and rites. Some brief indication of these concepts will not be out of place here.[54]

A sign is any form, linguistic or physical, a word or thing, that calls a particular content up in our mind. A symbol is a sign with added value. Every symbol is a sign, but not every sign is a symbol. Three dimensions determine this symbolic added value. A symbol supposes engagement or participation. Symbolism, the play with symbols in ritual acts, demands

---

[54] For our sketch see POST: 'Het liturgische spel' (1986); IDEM: 'Ritualiteit' (2001); cf. LUKKEN: *Rituelen in overvloed* (1999).

a particular attitude or disposition. Encounter, the coming or bringing together of diverse things or persons, plays a role; there must be an openness. The root word, the Greek *symballein*, to bring together, to cast together, already hints at this. In the background looms the image of the two potsherds or two halves of a piece of wood used when children were abandoned: the one half was left with the child, the other kept by the father or mother. Later, when in the caprices of life the child and parents might encounter one another again (Greek mythology develops this idea nicely) the meeting could be sealed by the bringing together (*symballein*) of the two halves.

The second characteristic that makes a sign a symbol is its iconicity. A symbol exists (works, but be careful not to understand this metaphor mechanically!) because there is a correspondence reaching into the symbolic dimension between that which is evoked or becomes present in the reference, and that through which this happens. Water plays an important role in many initiation or cleansing rites. Water of course already bears within itself dimensions of cleansing or refreshment, and in specific religious contexts also of passage through or over water, and the water of death and water of life. In the sign that is a symbol, that which is symbolised is already present; there is a certain correspondence between the two.

Third, to an important degree symbols are defined by conventions and codes. We are dealing here with what are termed cultural codes, the conscious – or generally unconscious – context that determines 'leverage', the referential function of symbols.

After sign and symbol, we can now globally define rite and myth. A rite (for ease we will use rite and ritual interchangeably, although it is possible to make a formal distinction between the two) is an action in which symbols play a role. Ritual is thus symbolic action in word and gesture. One could say that myth is an exegesis of that symbolic act. It offers an elucidatory context, the story accompanying the ritual-symbolic material. Rites are the language of symbols, and symbols are the building blocks of myth. We will not here enter into the question of the precise relationship between rite and myth, and in particular the question of which has primacy.[55]

---

[55] For an introduction to this, with references, see LUKKEN: *Rituelen in overvloed* (1999) 55-58.

From the general scheme of sign, symbol, rite and myth we have sketched, we can now choose a number of directions for further theoretical development and reflection on symbolic acts. For instance, one obvious path is the phenomenological approach. Ritual is approached formally as a phenomenon in which first the fundamental dimensions of time, space, action and actors (performers, participants) are examined. One can also focus on the interaction of the character of the sign/symbol, its content and its user in the play of ritual. This particularly expresses the concept that ritual is a form of communication: symbolic action is communication, among people themselves and between people and a higher reality. This line of communication, which distinguishes a sender and receiver, and where mediation and media play a crucial role, is therefore an unusually effective manner of approaching and studying the complex world of rites and symbols. It is also important, before the definitions and characterisation of ritual, to indicate how this perspective of communication is present in many conceptual definitions of ritual.[56]

We will however stop with this first and provisional indication, and in the following section turn our attention to current lines of conceptualising ritual in ritual studies.

The platform of ritual studies

After a phase dominated by symbolic philosophy and cultural anthropology there arose an academic field that can be situated on the interface of various disciplines (chiefly comparative religion and the social sciences) which concentrated its full attention on rituality: ritual studies. It would be well to rehearse some points with regard to this. For them one can refer to a recent survey article on ritual and ritual studies by one of its pioneers, Ronald Grimes.[57] Ritual studies blossomed as an interdisciplinary enterprise in the United States, and precisely in the early 1970s when ritual began to obtain a new image, no longer being connected with the conservative, traditional, religious-ecclesiastical and

---

[56] For a long time Gerard Lukken employed this perspective in his definition of rites; it has recently been taken up again by MARGRY: *Teedere quaesties* (2000) 20ff, when he characterises ritual as "the whole complex of symbolic acts, objects and language which is repeated in a more or less fixed pattern with a specific purpose involving communication".

[57] GRIMES: 'Ritual' (2000) Chapt. 18.

boring. Diverse persons and interest groups encountered one another on that podium. These involved – and still involve – chiefly four groups: scholars in comparative religion, anthropologists, liturgists, and people from the colourful world of ritual performance such as dramaturgists.[58] The establishment of the *Journal of Ritual Studies* in 1987 was important for further profiling the platform. Initially the platform for ritual studies was characterised by three strong fields of interest: a primary theoretical, conceptual interest, an interreligious and intercultural interest, and an emphatically comparative slant. It is chiefly through the influence of people like Grimes that the profile of ritual studies has by now clearly broadened.

To our mind it is important to see how ritual studies now has become a platform where diverse researchers can encounter one another. In a general sense, what they have in common is the study of rites. This broad platform has many corners where the interplay of disciplines takes shape, often in very diverse ways.

Looking further now at the aspect of developing conceptual theories with regard to ritual, there are two general lines that can be distinguished. First, the 'ritologists' are still important – a group of researchers very strongly orientated to theory and method, mostly coming from anthropological or religious studies disciplines. For years their central themes have been characterising and defining ritual/ritualising/rituality, the question of the origins and development of ritual, the relation between rite and myth, ritual and religion, ritual and sacrality, the ritual expert, etc. Figures representing this sector or pattern are Catharine Bell, Roy Rappaport, Frits Staal, and to a certain degree Ronald Grimes. In recent years the 'harder' scientific approaches to ritual, such as neurobiology and biogenetics are clearly increasingly influential here.[59]

A second sector increasingly distances itself from this very formal, abstract approach and prefers to investigate rituality on the basis of concrete case studies. Ritual practice goes hand in hand with theoretical

---

[58] This initial orientation is reflected by the interest in the platform for ritual studies shown by three bodies in the U.S.A., to wit the American Academy of Religion, the American Anthropology Association, and the North American Academy of Liturgy.

[59] For a reflection of this, see: SCHILLEBEECKX: 'Naar een herontdekking' (2000) = 'Hin zu einer Wiederentdeckung' (2001). Cf. D'AQUILI & LAUGHLIN: 'The neurobiology of myth and ritual' (1979); D'AQUILI & NEWBERG: *The mystical mind* (1999).

development. In addition to Grimes, who has already been mentioned, reference can be made here to recent work by Martin Stringer.[60] Particularly with regard to this second sector it is important to note that ritual studies is no longer only, or even primarily, an American or Anglo-Saxon platform. For example, I would count figures such as Arno Schilson, from Mainz, and the Belgian sociologist of religion Liliane Voyé as belonging to this sector.[61] But Dutch research could also be named here.[62]

With regard to this case-study oriented approach to ritual, it is noteworthy how especially rituals accompanying life phases have come to occupy central stage recently.[63] Within ritual studies there are now all sorts of accents which can be found when it comes to the characterisation of what defines and distinguishes ritual.[64] Three groups can roughly be distinguished here:

(a) There is one group who principally see ritual as unchanging, independent of its human agents. Here ritual is chiefly seen as 'highly symbolic acting', as that is found in the classic and traditional repertoire of rites in the annual cycle and at transitional points in life. Names representing this school are Victor Turner, Mary Douglas and Rappaport.

(b) A second group nuance that 'changeless' and 'high rituality' and demand attention for everyday rites, and particularly for new, 'emerging' rituals, often on the margins of society.[65] Grimes can be named as exponent of this school.

---

[60] Cf. GRIMES: *Marrying & burying* (1995); IDEM: 'Ritual' (2000); STRINGER: *On the perception of worship* (1999); see also the collection of case studies: AUNE & DEMARINIS: *Religious and social ritual* (1996).

[61] Cf. SCHILSON: 'Fest und Feier' (1994); IDEM: 'Das neue Religiöse' (1996); IDEM: 'Den Gottesdienst fernsehgerecht inszenieren?' (1996); IDEM: 'Musicals' (1998); VOYÉ: 'Effacement' (1998).

[62] Cf. for instance POST: *Het wonder van Dokkum* (2000) and POST, PIEPER & VAN UDEN: *The modern pilgrim* (1998).

[63] Cf. GRIMES: *Marrying and burying* (1995); IDEM: *Deeply into the bone* (2000); DE VISSCHER: *Een te voltooien leven* (1996).

[64] For this see among others WOOLFENDEN: 'How ritual forms holiness' (2000). See further the literature mentioned in note 48.

[65] For the genre of emerging rituals, see MITCHELL: 'Emerging ritual' (1995) and GRIMES (1993) 23-38.

(c) A third group place all their emphasis on the ritual process. Ritual
     and content coincide, and the ritual performance is definitive. Here
     Bell can be named.[66]

It is important to note how the latter two groups break through and
relativise the classic concept of ritual as fixed symbolic acting.

It is within this framework of the distinctions within ritual studies
that the numerous and often very divergent definitions of ritual are
situated. For the rest, we will leave out of consideration here a fourth
school, related to the third line that places emphasis on the ritual process,
which appears to want to cut away all the ground under the sense of ritual studies by suggesting that ritual is an academic, Western invention
and construction, which bears no relation whatsoever with actual ritual
practice (cf. Staal).[67]

In the survey article regarding ritual and ritual study by Grimes mentioned above, he accurately calculates the balance with regard to the category of ritual. He demonstrates how there is still no consensus about the
delimitation of the category.[68] This is all the more a sticky point when
we connect ritual with other adjoining concepts such as ceremony, magic,
liturgy or religion. There is, for example, the continual and complicating question of whether ritual is religious.

Grimes sees Victor Turner (1920-1983) as the twentieth century's most
influential and high-profile theoretician in the field of ritual. In the footsteps of Arnold van Gennep – and in contrast to Émile Durkheim, who
saw ritual as consolidating and preserving social reality – Turner emphasized the transformation that takes place in a ritual. Turner made ritual
into an extremely dynamic concept. All ritual is defined by a 'before' and
an 'after', with between them an interval of liminality. Through this
ritual acquired dynamism, and a distinction could be made between, on
the one hand, ceremony which validates the status quo and, on the other,
the transformational ritual.[69]

---

[66] For Bell see especially her two most recent books: BELL (1992) and (1997). Cf.
here also in their entirely own manner: HUMPHREY & LAIDLAW: *The archetypal actions*
(1994).

[67] Particularly Staal annoyed 'ritologists' by his astute manner of emphasising and
substantiating 'meaninglessness': STAAL: 'The meaninglessness' (1979).

[68] GRIMES: 'Ritual' (2000); IDEM: *Deeply into the bone* (2000).

[69] For Turner's oeuvre we refer only to: TURNER: 'Betwixt and between' (1967); IDEM:
The ritual process (1969); IDEM: *Dramas* (1974).

Against this general background, with Grimes we can distinguish three ways of defining or characterising ritual:[70]

(a) First and foremost there are the very global, loose and inclusive – and thus vague – definitions. Edmund Leach speaks of ritual as 'culturally defined sets of behavior'.[71] One can think in this respect of the general characterisations of ritual as 'symbolic acting' and 'communication' introduced above. A good specific example is the definition by Davis-Floyd, still to be found in circulation: "A ritual is a patterned, repetitive and symbolic enactment of a cultural belief or value; its primary purpose is transformation".[72] The problem with definitions of this sort is always their breadth: they can easily include brushing one's teeth daily.

(b) Next there are the focused characterisations from divergent theoretical explorations. The ethnologist Honko writes of 'traditional, prescribed communication with the sacred'.[73] In his work Rappaport remained very consistent in his characterisations, right through his final great synthesis which appeared posthumously, *Ritual and Religion in the Making of Humanity*.[74] For him, ritual is "the performance of more or less invariant sequences of formal acts and utterances not entirely encoded by the performers".[75] Ritual is here designated as belonging to the previously distinguished unchanging category. For Rappaport ritual is passed down by tradition and others; it is seldom 'new': "new rituals are likely to be largely composed of elements taken from older rituals".[76] This question of 'new' rituals, their derivation and interference, will recur repeatedly as a key element in our exploration of rituals associated with disasters.

Another attempt at focus is the introduction of multiple terms. For instance, as we have said, distinctions are made between rite and ritual, between ritualising and ritualisation, whereby for instance dimensions such as conscious dealing with ritual, and the individual, collective and traditional can be distinguished.

(c) A third direction attempts to circumvent the dilemmas involving the broad and focused by not so much looking for a comprehensive

---

[70] In addition to GRIMES: 'Ritual' (2000), I here rely on IDEM: *Deeply into the bone* (2000), where indirectly an image is likewise given of the conceptualisation of ritual.

[71] Cf. GRIMES: 'Ritual' (2000) 260.

[72] GRIMES: *Deeply into the bone* (2000) 24.

[73] Cf. GRIMES: 'Ritual' (2000) 261.

[74] RAPPAPORT: *Ritual and religion* (1999).

[75] *Ibid.* 24.

[76] *Ibid.* 32.

definition as seeking characteristics or lists of qualifiers. These efforts proceed in various ways. These can be extensive lists of qualities (cf. Grimes in his pioneering work *Ritual Criticism*, below[77]). They can be a series of dimensions or functions of ritual (Lukken; likewise see below[78]). But they can also be a limited number of very fundamental characteristics, which once again calls up the suggestion of a focused characterisation, as in (b). As an example of this one can cite the characteristics from neurobiology. For instance, according to D'Aquili and Newberg[79] ritual conduct is defined by four fundamental characteristics:

(a) it is structured, or constructed according to a certain pattern;
(b) it is rhythmic and repetitive in nature; that is to say, it will occur in the same way, or nearly the same way, with a certain regularity;
(c) it attempts to synchronise affective, perceptual-cognitive and motor processes within the central nervous system of the individual participants;
(d) it synchronises these processes among the various individual participants.

This more biological manner, which has again attracted abundant interest in ritual, and also liturgical and theological studies (see Schillebeeckx as a recent example[80]), will not be further developed here, because these characteristics appear to arise chiefly from theoretical discussions in regard to how rituals work.

For our purpose, it is instead important to see that there are often two tracks: a focused working definition is presented, which subsequently is worked out in terms of qualities and characteristics. In the development, recourse is readily made to distinct 'functions' of ritual that can be traced back into the social sciences.

Grimes himself provides a good example of this. On the one hand he distances himself from ritologists who search for an adequate characterisation and argues for the more open approach of qualities that aid in identifying rituals. On the other hand, among the personal narratives in his most recent book on rites of passage,[81] in addition to series of ritual

---

[77] GRIMES: *Ritual criticism* (1990).
[78] LUKKEN: *Rituelen in overvloed* (1999).
[79] D'AQUILI & NEWBERG: *The mystical mind* (1999) 89ff., esp. 99.
[80] Cf. SCHILLEBEECKX: 'Naar een herontdekking' (2000) = 'Hin zu einer Wiederentdeckung' (2001).
[81] GRIMES: *Deeply into the bone* (2000).

qualities he in fact does present a definition of a rite. He does this by setting out three mutually related domains:[82]

Ritual: "sequences of ordinary action rendered special by virtue of their condensation, elevation or stylization".

Spirituality: "practiced attentiveness aimed at nurturing a sense of the interdependence of all beings sacred and all things ordinary".

Religion: "spirituality sustained as a tradition or organized into an institution".

The refinement of presenting these characterisations in their interrelationship is that an attempt is thereby made to avoid playing the social against the individual, to avoid separating the sacred from the profane, and the spiritual from the religious. Because the question of religion and ritual is not a primary perspective in our exploration, we will not further deal with Grimes's triple characterisation. It is enough to note that he points the way toward a general characterisation of ritual as repertoires of actions in which condensation, stylisation and elevation – or put more generally, 'particularisation' – can be detected, a characterisation that subsequently can be 'dressed out' with qualities or characteristics.

It is our intention to introduce here such a double track, having the nature of a indicative, qualitative characterisation of ritual. We will subsequently develop our working definition through a series of qualities and characteristics.

We propose the following as our working definition:

Ritual is symbolic action, whether religious in nature or not, with a more or less fixed, recognisable and repeatable pattern or course. In short, it is ordered symbolic action or action with a special design (to borrow a characterisation from the ethnologist Bernet Kempers[83]).

This definition can be fleshed out with a series of qualities, characteristics, functions and dimensions. It will always involve certain elements which will function as investigative themes in our exploration of rituals after disasters.

Qualities and dimensions of rituality

Qualities of ritual

In order to provide a picture of the development of ritual acts through characteristics and qualities, we can once again cite Grimes, who drew

[82] *Ibid.* 71.
[83] BERNET KEMPERS: 'Volkskunde' (1970).

up a list of what he termed 'qualities of ritual'.[84] The more of these qualities present in a concrete ritual act, the higher one could say its 'ritual
calibre' is. With these qualities we are dealing successively with often
formal characteristics or qualities. Briefly listed, they are:

Ritual involves performed, presented actions; that is to say that along
with words and thoughts, it is chiefly gesture, the act, that is central.
This involves stylised, formalised acts that moreover take place according to a fixed and thus repeatable pattern. Ritual is thus to be defined
briefly as 'specially designed', ordered acting according to fixed patterns.

Ritual has a robustly collective dimension; the acts are performed by
a group, a community, and that community is in turn bound together
by the ritual act. The pattern mentioned – the fixed order of a ritual –
is traditional, which is to say it is linked with past communities too.
There is always an appeal to the past. Myth especially plays a role with
regard to this 'traditional quality'.

Further, ritual actions have a strongly emotional dimension. Ritual
acting is acting that is not done superficially; it affects one deeply, is taken
seriously, is highly esteemed and deeply experienced. It is ultimately always
determined by the symbolic order, is symbolic acting, it points beyond itself.

Grimes briefly designated the latter two qualities or dimensions as
religious and functional qualities. Ritual and religion go together, and a
ritual is 'functional'. That last can lead to numerous misunderstandings,
seeing as the concept of function can be fleshed out in an extremely practical, instrumental or therapeutic manner. That appears to stand in shrill
contrast with the fundamentally purposeless and functionless quality of
ritual (see below). Such terminology can also lead to misunderstandings
by suggesting that a position is being taken in the debate on whether
rituals are primarily functionally anchored in social life, and that their
significance is chiefly to be connected with instrumentality and effectiveness in service of that social life (functionalism), or, at the other
extreme, that rituals only have meaning in themselves (symbolism). For
Lukken this discussion is reason for avoiding the word 'function' in his
latest book, previously cited, instead speaking of 'dimensions'.[85] For the
time being we will employ function and dimension alongside one another
without inhibition.

---

[84] GRIMES: *Ritual criticism* (1990) 13ff.
[85] LUKKEN: *Rituelen in overvloed* (1999) 47.

Dimensions or functions of rituality

A classic list of ritual functions or dimensions is closely connected with the qualities set out by Grimes which we have just noted.[86]

There is a discharge function. Rituals assist in channelling feelings and emotions. They help us through mediation and orientation. Rites and myths provide cohesion or order, can help us shape our outlook, for instance with regard to the past, or future.

There is also an ethical function. The deeper reality celebrated in rites, to which the play of the ritual refers, carries over into the rest of our activities. It is never without obligations; there is always risk. Ritual is the expression, source and norm for authentic human conduct.

The very important prophylactic function is closely related to the function of channelling mentioned above. Rituals help us get, and keep, a grip on chance, disaster, the ever-present contingency of life with which we are confronted. To an increasing degree this general function appears to again be playing a role in our rituality. In the life cycle rituals, at birth, marriage and death, with accidents, undeserved, sudden death, with senseless violence and disasters: these give every appearance of contemporary ritual repertoires being called upon to avert threats of every sort.[87] In research into rites there is more and more attention being given to this function, and the vexed concept of 'magic' is once again being thought through as it relates to rituality. Here and there in religious and theological circles there is even talk of the rehabilitation of magic.[88] Prophylactic ritual is no longer connected just with certain groups and cultures, as appeared from the adjectives such as 'agrarian', 'primitive' and 'popular' connected with it.

The expressive function is fundamental: rituals afford the possibility to express feelings, but also convictions.

There is a function of condensation; an extremely complex and complicated reality is compressed.

We already mentioned the social function when discussing qualities: a ritual is linked with a group or community, and rites also give this group individuality and identity. Nations, sports fans, associations and businesses constantly acknowledge this function. Here rites and symbols

---

[86] *Ibid.* 58-70.
[87] Cf. POST: *Het wonder van Dokkum* (2000) 154; see also Chapt. 5 in this study.
[88] LANG: *Sacred games/Heiliges Spiel* (1997/1998).

consciously or unconsciously play a key role, through songs, flags, ritual signposting in time and space.

With the final function, which might be called recreative, we touch on that in ritual which provides relief and contrast. In ritual that which is calculated, instrumental and functional is laid aside. Each ritual is a pause, a time of another order, acting at a different level. Ritual is conduct that is singled out, interrupting the rat race, a link with another time – true free time.

Rituals: repertoires and genres

As units of related rituals, the genres of ritual activities or ritual repertoires are closely connected with the general characterisation of ritual.[89] The spectrum of rituality can be divided in many and divergent ways. The parameters can be based on the repertoire itself when, for instance, feast rituals and commemorative rituals are distinguished, or based on the actors and participants, as when for instance collective ritual is distinguished from individual ritual, or, as will be developed briefly at the end of this paragraph for disaster rituals, public ritual is distinguished from private ritual. But there are also other typologies for the repertoire in circulation, such as place-linked rituals, rituals for averting danger, weather rites, etc. Still other genre divisions, such as the distinction between religious and non-religious rituals already mentioned above as a complicating factor, will be taken up in the subsequent discussion of the contemporary ritual context through examination of diagnoses and trends. At this point only a rather classic typology of ritual will be presented, in a general phenomenological sense. Various versions of this typology exist. Here we will give the short list from manuals, and a somewhat fuller list from Catharine Bell. Most briefly, four basic genres or repertoires of ritual can be distinguished: annual rituals, life rituals or rites of passage, crisis rituals and everyday rituals.[90] Bell works with a somewhat expanded division; in her standard work *Ritual: Perspectives and Dimensions*, she distinguishes six types (we will use 'ritual' and 'rite' interchangeably, while she expressly speaks of 'rites'):[91]

---

[89] The term 'ritual repertoires' was coined by ROOIJAKKERS: *Rituele repertoires* (1994).
[90] In a general sense we refer to LUKKEN: *Rituelen in overvloed* (1999).
[91] BELL: *Ritual* (1997) 94ff.

(a) life rituals, or rites of passage;
(b) calendar or annual rites;
(c) what she calls rites of exchange and communion; she devotes extensive discussion to these, which include for instance the complex sacrificial repertoire;
(d) rites of affliction and healing, under which she classes all sorts of prophylactic and apotropaic rites (i.e., those which offer protection and avert evil);
(e) feasts, festivals and fasts;
(f) political ritual, a repertoire also often denoted as civil ritual, comprising all sorts of rituals linked with courts and nations, expressly involving power, hierarchy and identity.

For our subject of rituals after disasters, it is interesting to observe how these really cannot be reckoned to any one particular genre. Of course, they are first and foremost crisis ritual, marking and approaching a shock, a crisis. But, on further consideration, rituals after disasters have something to do with almost all the genres. As rituals involving death, they touch on one of the transitions in life; as commemoration rituals they are part of the cycle of annually recurring rituals; as daily rituals they are among the small rituals at home (the lighting of a candle, cherishing a photograph, the often informal marking of the scene of the disaster, etc.). Further, as we will see, oblatory elements play a role in disaster rituals, and there are certainly also political dimensions.

There is still one more typology or genre division that affects the approach and structure of our study in a very concrete way. There are distinctions made among public ritual repertoires and private, more personal ritual repertoires. Through the coupling of ritual and disaster we intend here, we are concerned chiefly with public rites such as mass silent processions, large memorial services and such. Their public nature is expressed primarily through the role of the media. Naturally, a disaster also is accompanied by an extensive, more private ritual repertoire, such as the funerals of individual victims and the memorial rites practised by their next of kin in the home setting. Sometimes in the case of disasters the line between these two repertoires is difficult to draw clearly. Funerals of victims become mass events. Most frequently however there is a two-track situation: public memorial rites alongside more closed family and personal rites. A noteworthy tendency in this connection – and one which testifies to the fluent boundary between the repertoires – is that the media to an increasing degree seems to have an interest in these more closed ritual acts. A factor contributing to this is undoubtedly that a rather general category such as 'a blow' or 'calamity' can in this way be personalised and given a human face.

Aspects and themes

Following on our pluriform discussion intended to identify qualities defining the concept of ritual, there are still a series of relevant basic dimensions and aspects of rituality.

Sacrality tendencies

It is also important to briefly bring ritual into connection with what are termed sacrality tendencies. We have already encountered this in Grimes's triple characterisation (ritual, spirituality, religion).[92] When, briefly referring to the long tradition (chiefly in the religious disciplines) of study of cultus and culture, we draw up a balance, we can affirm that there is a non-specific, basic sacrality rooted in man and culture.[93] Rituals are in many respects closely connected with this sacred dimension, but in particular with the sacrality of place, time, persons, things and objects. Despite clear desacralising tendencies (to which Christianity made – and makes – an important contribution), there seems to be a general, anthropological, cultural *persistence du sacré*:[94] there is always a sacred reference to forces, powers and dimensions that surpass us, a reference to the transcendent through which we can rise above the banality of the ordinary. In this context one can aptly speak of the 'sacred milieu'.[95] There are certain privileged segments and moments where this reference pushes forward, as it were. These include the rites of passage, confrontations with new life, love and death. These also include confrontations with the contingency of our life as this is radically experienced in disasters (see above for our definition of a disaster).

It has been frequently pointed out that these tendencies surrounding sacrality are extremely complex and dynamic precisely for modernity.

---

[92] GRIMES: *Deeply into the Bone* (2000) 71.

[93] In summary see POST: 'Speelruimte' (2000) with extensive bibliography; see particularly ENGLERT: 'Les valeurs sacrées' (1999). Cf. RAPPAPORT: *Ritual and religion* (1999) particularly Chapts. 9 through 14.

[94] See ENGLERT: 'Les valeurs sacrées' (1999).

[95] *Ibid.*

Surveying and testing the sacred milieu is a difficult task, but one indispensable for achieving perspective on ritual acts.[96]

Making further distinctions among the basic dimensions of sacrality is important for sounding out the general sacral milieu.[97] With R. Englert we can indicate the basic structure of the sacral order through four dimensions, each with certain qualities.[98] The dimensions or functions of ritual set out above will be easily recognised here.

(a) Symbolic dimension. This involves the quality of establishing identity and profiling. Group identity is shaped through rites and symbols, through reference to sacred values and images. Within groups and subgroups that is done through the cult of brands, fashion and trends, for instance, in which constant sacral references are to be found: Levis addresses us saying, "Thou shalt wear no other jeans than mine!"

Persons, heros and idols play an important role here. They are linked with the identity of the group. Sports or pop music stars stand for particular group cultures, as do certain saints for a nation (for example, St. Patrick and Ireland).

(b) Cultural dimension. The cultus is fundamental for the sacral order. The sacral is always mediated, via symbols and symbolic acts, and via persons, intermediaries and 'advocates'.

(c) Ritual dimension. The general dimension of the cultus receives concrete form in the ritual as ordered, structured acting. For our purposes, the cultural and ritual dimension can be taken together.

(d) Mythic dimension. As a final basic structural element in the sacral order, there is its anamnestic quality. Rituals that give the cultic dimension concrete form in stylised action generally have a supporting narrative structure. In rites and symbols an old story becomes a present reality, with an eye to the future. In this way the past, present and future are bound together into a meaningful whole. Myth provides connection or order in the enormously broad and compartmentalised ritual repertoire. Many scholars in the humanities have identified a yearning in our culture for such anamnestic qualities and the connection and cohesion they introduce. We see in our culture an assiduous quest for narrative structures of this sort. Television series always have

---

[96] Cf. POST: 'Interference and intuition' (2000); IDEM: 'Programm und Profil der Liturgiewissenschaft' (2002); IDEM: 'Rituell-liturgische Bewegungen' (2002).

[97] See the apposite development by ENGLERT: 'Les valeurs sacrées' (1999) 408-415.

[98] ENGLERT: 'Les valeurs sacrées' (1999).

a basic connecting narrative structure of this sort, with each episode carrying forward, and being carried forward by the story, transparent and stable.

With regard to our exploration, this dimension, as it deals with disaster ritual, will offer us a perspective for evaluation. People appear to consciously or unconsciously judge ritual on this basis: what is it about? What is the content? It is often the anamnestic, mythic dimension that is being referred to when people speak about authentic or relevant ritual as opposed to empty, rhetorical ritual.[99]

Integral

It is rather generally acknowledged that justice can only be done to ritual if an integral perspective is maintained. One must take seriously the general human givens with regard to ritual. Every consideration of ritual and symbol involves language and action, sensory and physical and verbal and non-verbal elements. Thus all the senses, and the *artes* connected with them, are literally involved in ritual.

Complex: polysemic and multi-layered

Ritual is a constructed system; one might speak of a cluster of signs and symbols. Such a cluster has its own language, syntax and grammar, and, in the same way that is also true for language, not every component is of equal rank. It is very important to see the order and coherence: which are the core symbols within the complex or ritual symbolic acts? This complexity makes a ritual ambiguous and open to connotations and associations. Together with the fact that a ritual is played ever anew – the previously mentioned important (and sometimes even definitive) aspect of performance – this assures that in its essence a ritual slips away from becoming fixed and controlled.

Yet this openness and elusiveness are restricted. The connection with symbols gives the ritual direction, for instance because of the existence of what are termed 'Ur-symbols', nearly archetypical symbols that present themselves as the core within certain rituals. These are universal symbols

---

[99] This point will be raised in the discussion of the repertoire of silent processions; see 3.5.

such as the sun, light, water, grain, the hand, a tree, woman. Particularly in the case of emerging rituals and in our repertoire of rituals associated with disasters, certain symbols and symbolic acts dominate by their presence: light, the colour white, flowers, photographic portraits, names, silence, silent procession.

Context and code, cultus and culture

Rituality is completely dependent on context, on existing 'cultures'. We conceive culture here very loosely, as an structure of contexts such as economics, politics and landscape. Ritual is always inculturated ritual; it is always linked with context and culture. There is therefore always a sort of minimum of shared knowledge of the contextual codes necessary for ritual symbolic play. These codes are acquired in a culture, consciously or unconsciously, through growing up in it, and indeed participation in rituals is often one the prime sources. When people from one culture go to another one, they are constantly confronted with this fact. Gestures, colours, acts and clothing often have entirely different and unexpected meanings. Corporate managers, but also soldiers in peacekeeping forces who are sent out to Asia or Africa receive courses to enable them to appropriate the codes, so that they do not behave too disruptively in communications and actions.

Inculturation

Because contexts are continually shifting – and in our society this pace is quickening enormously – there is constantly a need for the inculturation of rituals.[100] Rituals must always maintain their connection with the surrounding cultural and anthropological milieu. For the rest, this connection does not always have to take the form of adaptation, but can also take the form of dissent! In our society there is the additional problem that the context is shattering and fanning out over series of sectors and subcultures, each with its own codes that are not understandable for people outside the group or sector. A certain generality of rituals

---

[100] The subject of ritual inculturation was worked out particularly through liturgical inculturation. A good survey is provided by LUKKEN: *Rituelen in overvloed* (1999) 122-143; POST: 'Interference and intuition' (2000) 54, note 15.

appears to be at risk as a result of this. In one secondary school class of 28 teenagers, very different group cultures can exist with rites and symbols that are based on their own peculiar, and for an outsider often unknown, codes.

Here we touch on the fundamental aspect of ritual inculturation. Inculturation looks at ritual in terms of its embedment in various sectors of a culture. The nature of this embedment can be quite divergent. There can be a high degree of integration. In the glorious period from about 1850 to 1950 there was in many European countries an extensive network of connections between certain dominant cultural sectors ('cultures') and the ritual with which communities of faith (Catholic and Protestant) expressed their faith. In many respects liturgy was the supplier of forms and the stock of ideas for rituality and culture.[101] That picture has since fundamentally changed. The complex and dynamic process of inculturation is defined by the pluriform manner in which ritual is dynamically connected with culture. Here we are actually speaking, at a general and almost programmatic level, about the interplay between cultus and culture. First and foremost, ritual is transcultural. There are ritual dimensions that appear to transcend a particular context or culture. Second, ritual is also contextual. It varies according to local historical, natural and cultural contexts. Third, ritual is counter-cultural. Rituals can be very subversive, recalcitrant and critical. It is precisely in ritual that opposition, protest and complaint can find a place and expression. Fourth, there is a cross-cultural dimension; this dimension makes it possible for there to be traffic back and forth among ritual traditions through borrowings and sharing. In our exploration of rituals associated with disasters we shall see how particularly the last two dimensions will explicitly come to the fore. Silent protests often have an undercurrent of protest and complaint, for instance toward failures on the part of social workers or governmental authorities. Disaster rituals often wrestle with the cross-cultural dimension: how, in a ceremony or commemoration, to give a place to sometimes very divergent ritual traditions and culturally defined repertoires. As we will see in the evaluation of disaster rites, ritual criticism in a general sense will assume the nature of questions about ritual inculturation.

---

[101] For this see HARTINGER: *Religion und Brauch* (1992); POST: 'Van paasvuur tot stille tocht' (1999).

Interferences[102]

As we will still need to work out, modern rituals are characterised by an unprecedented dynamism. Classic repertoires and genres, ecclesiastical, general religious and profane, run through one another. This has been spoken of in terms of the loss of borders, and, borrowing from wave theory, as interference. We prefer to employ the term interference to indicate the interplay of and cross-connections among repertoires. This preference is primarily inspired by the fact that the term aptly conveys the changes of context, quotations and borrowings in a general sense – with all their congruences, convergences and divergences – that are involved. We will see how disaster ritual is constructed ritual, where interference appears especially to play a key role.

Performance

We will separately repeat that rituality is acted, played. Just as music exists only if it is played, ritual exists only if it is enacted. That implies that rituality is dependant on performance. If the play is badly played, if the performance is deficient, an otherwise powerful ritual can be killed, reduced to a weak tincture of what is essentially a highly flavourful stock. Many ritual experts such as Grimes at this point refer to the contemporary tendency of distancing ourselves in ritual.[103] We often enervate ritual by not giving ourselves over to the play, but rather stand back from the ritual, adding our own static to it, explaining it, keeping aloof from the sensory elements in the symbolic play. We are often spectators to it; we talk about it, but do not taste it, smell it, let ourselves be carried away by it, replacing the baptismal pool with sprinkling the child's head. We cherish ritual at arms length: commentary on the side, making photographs or video tapes to view the ritual at a distance in time and place.

In the further discussion of the contemporary ritual context we will return to this point of distance, and the closely related point of the physical and sensory nature of ritual, also already mentioned. Exactly here, it will appear, we have themes with which we can catch and characterise current tendencies.

---

[102] For the use of this concept see: above p. 10; POST: 'Interference and intuition' (2000); IDEM: 'Van paasvuur tot stille tocht' (1999).

[103] Cf. GRIMES: *Deeply into the bone* (2000); zie ook: POST: *Het wonder van Dokkum* (2000).

Ritual: adequate, functional or gratuitous?

A final theme that we will deal with separately is the functionality or instrumentality of ritual. Here, in connection with ritual, it can be asserted that in both practice and theory questions are being posed more and more about the tension that exists between the peculiar, specific nature of ritual action, which is not primarily directed to utility or effect but to expression and condensation (see above), and non-ritual action that is primarily instrumental and effect-oriented.[104] In the critical-normative sense Grimes links this with the space (both figurative and literal) ritual is allotted in our Western culture, and the distinctions that we have begun to introduce among what actions do, bring about, and mean. The context of doing – effective, goal-oriented actions – dominates through technology, biology, chemistry, physics and economics, while the space for meaning is marginalised (art, religion, philosophy). Ritual appears to be given ever less space as a characteristic form of expression, and is being pulled increasingly into the camp of effective, instrumental acts.

As a sort of basic code, ritual is counted as part of the category of uselessness, the same domain to which the arts belong. Rites are purposeless and beautiful. They do not belong to the category of utility, function, purpose and profit. Today our rites appear to be more and more judged for their purpose, use and point, while rituality is in essence purposeless and without point, but – note well! – not without meaning. Ritual action is idle, is like the play of a child, the movement of angels, juggling with clouds.

Here we encounter not only the aesthetic dimension of ritual (in disaster ritual we will see how poetry and music often are the language of the ritual), but also the aspect of the degree to which the need for ritual and coping or processing trauma are related.

---

[104] I raised this point several times in connection with the previously mentioned study by MENKEN-BEKIUS: *Rituelen in het individuele pastoraat* (1998); Cf. POST: 'Rijke oogst' (1999) 104; also: IDEM: *Het wonder van Dokkum* (2000) 153ff.

2. DUTCH DISASTER RITUAL (1990-2001): A SURVEY OF THE REPERTOIRE IN INTERNATIONAL CONTEXT

2.1. STRUCTURE

In the second chapter we will first offer a general history of the major national disasters that have taken place in The Netherlands since 1990, and specifically the ritual repertoire which accompanied them.[1]

As we assume that the rituals were not all new or unique, but are linked with others in the recent past here or elsewhere, a search will then be made for other disasters and other rituals that may have been of influence. First we will examine several comparable situations in The Netherlands over some years prior to 1990. Then we widen our search to Western Europe and beyond it, and list those disasters that are most plausibly candidates for having been influential, either by the nature of the disaster, or by extensive media attention.

Having moved from ritual after disasters in The Netherlands to ritual after disasters in the surrounding countries, in 2.3 we study the contiguous ritual that developed around the dramatic deaths of internationally famous persons. With regard to our specific focus on The Netherlands, another very characteristic area of contiguous ritual is also studied: the whole of collective rituals after the violent deaths of young people on the street, in entertainment venues and as victims of sex crimes. The greatest attention is given to the period of 1996 and 1997, when the disparate elements of mourning rituals after disasters, collective expressions of sympathy and protest after senseless violence, mass processions and mass commemorations appear to crystallise into a more or less fixed scenario for collective conduct in mourning.

In 2.4 the various elements are brought together in a tentative synthesis, and a first characterisation is attempted. This characterisation anticipates both the thematic discussion of specific cases later in the book in chapters 3 and 4, and our balance and perspective in chapter 6.

---

[1] Unless accompanied by the name of the country involved, all places mentioned in this chapter are in The Netherlands.

In general, through the whole of this chapter we will work descriptively. We proceed from the phenomenon as it presents itself to us, and as it has been preserved in primarily journalistic sources.[2] Both personal narratives and critical reflections are omitted here.

2.2. CHRONOLOGICAL SURVEY OF RITUALS AFTER DISASTERS SINCE 1990

We will circumscribe our history of disasters in The Netherlands by first limiting it to the period 1990-2001, and second by employing the criteria established above for what will here be considered a disaster. As a matter of principle, on no occasion in this book will the number of fatalities be used as the criterion. Although for instance the world-wide annual survey of disasters in the *Encyclopedia Britannica* employs the criterion of ten or more dead, in the context of Dutch disasters we will be using other criteria as well as the number of fatalities. In any case, in statistics the number of fatalities very quickly emotionally eclipses the number of seriously burned survivors, though the latter is usually larger. The 'major' national disasters that are discussed in our study however do fulfil that quantitative criterion. Disasters such as that in Enschede (explosion in a fireworks factory in a residential neighbourhood, 2000) and Volendam (fire in a cafe, New Year's Day, 2001), show that not only the number of dead determine the extent of a disaster, but that the 'size' of the disaster also has to do with the degree of disruption, the loss of homes and property, and the way in which the wounded will be scarred for life.

On the international lists we find the following reported as Dutch disasters: a chain-collision on the motorway near (Nov. 6, 1990); a fire in a boarding house in The Hague (mid-September, 1992); air crashes in the Bijlmer (Oct. 4, 1992), at Faro, Portugal (Dec. 21, 1992), near Eindhoven (July 15, 1996) and above the Waddenzee (Sept. 25, 1996); the firework explosion in Enschede (May 13, 2000) and the cafe fire in Volendam (Jan. 1, 2001). The 'silent' disaster[3] at Bovenkarspel, also

---

[2] Our central sources have been the archives of the most important Dutch daily newspapers, the *Algemeen Dagblad, de Volkskrant, NRC Handelsblad, Trouw* and *het Parool*, consulted on line through the Krantenbank. Regional papers were consulted in the cities of publication, or with the assistance of the archives of the Dutch Press Service. Audiovisual material was provided by the Netherlands Audiovisual Archive in Hilversum.

[3] This term is used in the article by SLIJKERMAN: 'Legionella, een 'stille ramp'' (1999).

termed the Flora disaster (beginning February, 1999), is a clear border-line case in this list: by Dutch standards, the number of fatalities as a result of this legionella infection was high – more than 30 – but the extent and cause became clear too late for it to be experienced as a disaster from the beginning. In addition, there is a category of disasters in which a number of Dutch residents were directly involved, such as the air crash near Paramaribo, Surinam (June 7, 1989) or the earthquake in western Turkey (Aug. 17, 1999).[4]

Placing the list of Dutch disasters in international perspective, then in Western Europe over the past fifteen years we find (among others) the sinking of the Herald of Free Enterprise (Zeebrugge, Belgium, Mar. 6, 1987), the bomb explosion on the aeroplane above Lockerbie, Scotland (Dec. 21, 1988), the sinking of ferry boats in Italy (Leghorn/Livorno Apr. 10, 1991, and Brindisi, Mar. 28, 1997) and the Estonia off Finland (Stockholm/Turku/Tallinn, Sept. 28, 1994; see 4.1, below), the train derailment near Eschede, Germany (June 3, 1998), the disco fire in Göte-borg, Sweden (Oct. 30, 1998), the crash of a Concord supersonic trans-port near Paris, France (July 25, 2000) and the sinking of the Russian submarine Kursk (August, 2000).

Outside of Western Europe major disasters of all categories took place, which people in The Netherlands shared through news reports on radio and television, and through longer or shorter articles in national news-papers. As a random selection of the largest international disasters of recent years we can list the chemical poisoning at Bhopal, India (Dec. 2, 1984), and the earthquake at Kobe, Japan (Jan. 17, 1995).[5] The attacks on New York and Washington D.C. on September 11, 2001, form a sort of 'outside category' (see 4.2 below for this).

When, in the context of rituals after disasters in The Netherlands, we focus specifically on those disasters in this survey that received sufficient attention in Dutch news media to be considered as possible sources for mourning rituals to be quoted and imitated, then it is striking that a sunken ferry boat in Bangladesh, the Philippines or southern Africa is

---

[4] Many Surinamese live in The Netherlands; the country was a part of the Kingdom of The Netherlands until 1975. The Netherlands is also home to many Turkish immi-grants.

[5] There is discussion possible over the question of whether terrorist attacks should be counted among disasters. If so, then we must also list the attack in Oklahoma (1995, 168 dead) and the recent attacks in New York and Washington, D.C. (2001). See our Chapter 1.2.1.

only good for a simple mention, while in the case of aeroplane accidents in North America, for instance, the collective mourning rituals or commemorative services also often receive some attention. This factor of scope or impact we will here term 'perspective'. This is the case in an almost exemplary way for the attack of September 11, 2001, in New York.

A second factor in the exploration of the route along which possible interference would arise seems to lie in the subcultural character of the group involved. Thus it appears that the stadium disasters (Bradford, England, May 11, 1985, Brussels, Belgium, May 29, 1985, Sheffield, England, April 15, 1989 and Corsica, France, May 5, 1992) form a subgroup, just as do disasters at discos, cafes and pop concerts, with their homogenous youth audiences. Both subgroups involve subcultures of predominantly young people.

On the other hand, the heading of natural disasters is hardly a category of interest for us, viewed in terms of the ritual repertoire, because floods (for instance, northern Italy, November 4 and 5, 1994, northern Spain, Aug. 8, 1996, and central Europe, summer 1997), earthquakes (central Italy, Sept. 26, 1997), storms (west coast of Spain and France, Jan. 23, 1998) and landslides (southern Italy, early May, 1998) often claim their fatalities at great distances from each other. It appears a certain unity of place and time is necessary for the phenomenon of 'ritual density' ('condensed' ritual activity, which reaches a 'critical mass' in one time and place), and that this was not a factor in the natural disasters within Europe which were studied.

A fourth factor which appears to play a role is the cohesion of those involved. When a neighbourhood (such as the Bijlmer, the section of South East Amsterdam where an El Al air freighter crashed in 1992, or the Roombeek neighbourhood in Enschede where the fireworks factory exploded in 2000) or a travelling group with a common background (such as the fanfare corps in the Hercules crash at Eindhoven in 1996) is concerned, there is a collective identity involved as well as the shared time and place. For example, it would appear that after major traffic accidents on the motorway near Breda (chain collisions November 6, 1990 and May 19, 1992) the site of the accident itself took on little ritual importance. This impression however may be incorrect, because at that time the press had not yet picked up on the phenomenon of displays of grief at the site of traffic accidents. For the rest, this is also true for the train derailment near Hoofddorp (Nov. 30, 1992), while at the same time the press, in its customary year-end summaries, was terming 1992 a 'year of disasters'. At the moment that the annual reviews appeared in the newspapers the air crash in Faro, Portugal (Dec. 12, 1992), had come as the last of the sad series. We will term this factor of collective identity 'cohesion'.

As a fifth factor in the process of forming a ritual repertoire around disasters, we should now, looking ahead, list two areas that do not strictly belong to our topic: the collective ritualisation after the sudden and/or violent death of international celebrities, and the collective ritualisation after what is termed 'senseless' violence, apparently random street violence. The latter area appears to be of particular importance when it involves young persons who are the victims of street violence, violence in entertainment venues, and when minors are murdered after sexual assaults. This will be termed contiguous or adjoining collective ritual.

As an entirely unique, sixth factor in the process by which the ritual repertoire accompanying disasters arises, we must here mention the multicultural nature of the community involved. In The Netherlands this was especially visible after the disasters in the Bijlmer and at Enschede, but also in the commemorations of the air crash at Paramaribo, and after the earthquakes in Turkey. The rich spectrum of mourning rituals in the context of collective commemoration will be the topic of a separate discussion later in this book.

As a seventh and final factor, we would mention the general context of emerging rituals, rituality arising around memorials and in particular around mourning and grief processing. By this we refer particularly to the larger context of innovation and self-chosen ritual surrounding dying and death. Study of collective mourning rituals appears to constantly uncover lines running between the private and the collective domains. We term this interplay the wider cultural context of ritual innovation, which again is connected with what we previously termed ritual interference.

We will use these seven tendencies or parameters as a grid in the discussion which follows.

The Bijlmer disaster (1992)

For The Netherlands, 1992 was indeed a year of disasters. In April Limburg was rocked by an earthquake; in July there was a severe explosion in a tar factory in Uithoorn; in September a rooming house in The Hague was totally destroyed by fire; in October an aeroplane crashed into a highrise apartment building in the Bijlmer; in November an intercity train to Vlissingen derailed near Hoofddorp; and at the end of December a plane of the Dutch airline Martinair was involved in a crash at Faro, Portugal.

In this book our study of the origins and growth of the emerging ritual repertoire after disasters begins with the Bijlmer, although it is clear that for the Surinamese community in The Netherlands there were parallels with the June 7, 1989, air crash in Paramaribo. Not only had many of the residents of the Bijlmer been directly involved with the victims of that crash, but the fatalities were commemorated in the Bijlmer at that time, and on an annual basis thereafter. Photographs of this commemoration still hang in the Kwakoe Surinam Cultural Centre, a site in the Bijlmer where many of the Surinamese affected by the 1992 crash gathered after that event. During the memorial service for the victims of the Bijlmer disaster in Amsterdam's convention centre, in one corner 171 candles were lit for the victims of the earlier disaster.

Those affected in the Bijlmer in 1992 had however an extremely mixed background. In addition to Creoles of Surinamese background there were many East Indians, Dutch, Moroccans and Ghanaians. The Bijlmer's diverse multicultural population exhibited mourning practices that were new to many Dutchmen. While after some time voices were raised that the disaster plan was 'too white' in all sorts of ways, and people were evidently insufficiently prepared for, or lacked experience with ways of processing grief outside of Dutch culture, on the surface it appeared as if on the contrary both participants and spectators experienced the non-Dutch elements in the public mourning ritual positively. At the time only a few voices were raised to say that one element had been absent from the impressive memorial service: the dead crew of the El Al freighter were hardly mentioned.

The collective mourning ritual after the Bijlmer disaster displays a succession of steps that later became nearly 'classic': (a) the event being termed a disaster and the official proclamation of the accident scene as a 'disaster area'; (b) visits from dignitaries; (c) spontaneous tributes (a sea of floral tributes, candles, stuffed toys, notes of condolence and drawings); (d) condolence registers and obituaries for victims who were in some way special; (e) ecumenical services in various centres near the disaster area; (f) a silent procession from a common assembly point to the ruins (broadcast live); (g) a commemoration for the dead in the Amsterdam RAI, a large convention centre (broadcast live on radio and television); (h) flying flags at half mast, tolling church bells, prayers in churches and mosques, and observances of one or more minutes of silence; (i) the ritual marking of the scene of the disaster; (j) erection of a monument; and (k) annual memorial gatherings.

Spontaneous monuments also appeared near the disaster scene. The silent procession, which began near the Community Centre and ended near the rubble, was no funerary act; the dead had already been buried or cremated individually. The procession was a collective memorial and homage; there were songs for the dead, drumming and dancing. The Ghanian community appeared in red, the Surinamese in black and white. Through the silent procession, in which representatives of the governments of The Netherlands, Surinam, the Dutch Antilles and Ghana participated, the unofficial site for floral tributes near the disaster scene became the scene for the official wreath laying. Organisations of victims from other previous disasters, such as that at Lockerbie, expressed their sympathy. After the silent procession a large commemorative service was held in the RAI, watched on television by about 3.5 million viewers in The Netherlands and Surinam.

Around the place where the spontaneous memorials had risen a park area was created, where a tree of hope, a mosaic carpet of tiles with personal interpretations and memories, and the 'footprint' of the apartment blocks destroyed form ritual centres for individual commemorations, and for the annual memorial that is accompanied every year with a silent procession to this memorial site, where kites (preferably silver-coloured, with the image of a hummingbird) and balloons (43 for the identified dead, and one for all the nameless victims) are released, the band of the Salvation Army (which was involved in disaster relief at the time) plays, and flowers and wreathes are again laid.

The Faro disaster (1992)

While discussions were still under way between the residents, next of kin and others involved in the Bijlmer disaster and various organisations and agencies regarding a lasting monument for the victims, on December 21 of the same year The Netherlands was once again struck by an air disaster – this time in Portugal, but involving a Dutch aeroplane with primarily Dutch passengers on board. On December 30 a memorial service was held in hanger 32 of Martinair airlines at Schiphol, the Dutch national airport at Amsterdam. Twenty-nine coffins were arranged in one corner, each with a pink and a white bouquet, from the airline and the travel bureaus, respectively. Other victims had already been buried or cremated after private ceremonies. Among other attendees at the memorial service were wounded survivors of the disaster who had been brought by ambulance or in wheelchairs, and a dog which had also been travelling on the aeroplane involved. In addition, members of the Dutch royal family and representatives of the Dutch and Portuguese governments were present. An honour guard was formed by the full crew of a Boeing 767 that had landed at Faro shortly before the DC 10 involved in the accident. On a table 54 candles burned, one for each fatality. In the hanger, which had been converted into an auditorium with dark velvet drapes and green plants, the flags hung at half mast. Six individuals spoke, among them the President/Director of Martinair, a woman representing the travel bureaus, and three clergy. A poem was read, a large choir sang, and two minutes silence was observed.

It was an austere and quiet gathering that lasted barely an hour. The central Dutch non-commercial channel, the NOS, provided a live broadcast; other media were excluded. There were no great displays of emotion, although while filing past the coffins most mourners were overcome near the three children's caskets. There was some consternation regarding the appearance of the dog belonging to the passenger Pamela Lewis, whose presence was not only justified by the fact that he had been on the plane involved, but particularly because his owner felt she owed her life to the animal; because of the dog she had been forced to sit in another seat on the plane than the one assigned her, and the passenger with whom she had exchanged seats was killed in the crash.

Perhaps because the accident had taken place in bad weather and outside Dutch territory, the protest element remained in the background in this service. The tenor of the addresses principally involved inadequacy – not only technical and human failings, but also the way words fell short when confronted with an event of this sort. Just as with the Bijlmer disaster, the sensationalism of the press came in for criticism. The inevitable disaster tourism, which we were here spared because of the distance, was deliberately controlled as a matter of policy in following disasters by declaring the scene of the accident as a disaster area.

The Hercules disaster (Eindhoven, 1996)

The next major disaster again involved an aeroplane crash. The disaster on the military air field at Eindhoven (July 15, 1996) has since then primarily been known as the Hercules disaster, from the Hercules military transport involved. Although all the victims received private burials or cremation, there were two collective mourning ceremonies held, one in Eindhoven (for this see below, 3.2) and one in Brussels (the crew were Belgian, the passengers Dutch).

The most striking part of the service in Eindhoven was the performance by a fellow musical group, the Budapest Chorus, from Hungary. Several clergy spoke, the poem read by the Humanist advisor making the deepest impression. In the following chapter this case will be explored further.

The observance in Brussels was striking for its military character: preceded by a military parade in which the marchers wore black armbands, there was also a tribute in the form of a fly-past by the Belgian Air Force in which 74 planes flew over Brussels, the seven Hercules transports in it forming the traditional 'missing man' formation (an empty spot in the formation symbolically indicating the 'hole' in their midst). The four Belgian crewmen were posthumously honoured by Belgium's Crown Prince Philip, who placed the medals on their coffins.

In various places in The Netherlands flags were flown at half mast, among them Vught, where the theatre De Speeldoos had been the home base for the band who were the victims. Some time later a monument was also unveiled: an aeroplane beneath a music staff with 34 notes.

Dakota disaster (Waddenzee, 1996)

There was still another aeroplane accident in the same year, this time involving an antique World War II Dakota transport that had taken off from the airport on the island of Texel, which lies to the north of the Dutch mainland (Sept. 25, 1996). On board were the crew and personnel from a construction company and civil servants from the Province of North Holland, together taking a day's excursion. The plane crashed onto a sandbank in shallow water; both the bodies and personal possessions were recovered with difficulty, and brought to the nearby naval base at the port of Den Helder by boat. The arrival of the two boats with the victims was observed with the familiar marine traditions. For instance, watch was maintained at the head of the harbour until the two boats with bodies came in: "That is how it is done in the naval city of Den Helder. We only go away when everyone is 'home' again".[6]

---

[6] As quoted in *NRC Handelsblad* (October 1, 1996), in an article by BEUNDERS on professionalising disaster reporting: 'National mourning becomes a "media event"'.

In the historic St. Bavo church in Haarlem, the capital of the province of North Holland where the accident took place, the next of kin and colleagues of the victims remembered the dead. In Ouderkerk aan de Amstel, the victims from the construction firm in Ouderkerk were separately remembered in the St. Urbanis church. Thirty-two candles were lit at both services. Army and naval chaplains spoke at the services. The service in Haarlem was broadcast live.

A month later the next of kin were afforded an opportunity to visit the place where the aeroplane had crashed into the sea. Many of them had let it be known that they wished to visit the spot. The place was marked with a yellow buoy. During the memorial service at sea a small fleet of six fishing ships with their flags at half mast were tied up together. When their engines were shut down a silence fell over the water. After some words from a naval chaplain the small boats sailed past the buoy. Flowers were scattered in the sea as a greeting.

Precisely a year later a monument was unveiled in the garden of the provincial government building in Haarlem. It consists of a basalt plinth bearing a glass plate with the names of the victims sandblasted on it, flanked by a bronze sculpture that is composed of wings sweeping upward. A monument was placed at the airport at De Cocksdorp, on the island of Texel, at the same time: a Dakota cast in bronze, flying above a stainless steel silhouette of the island.

Flora disaster (Bovenkarspel, 1999)

Only after several weeks did it become clear that various patients who were being admitted to hospitals in various places around The Netherlands with a serious form of double lung illness had in common with one another a visit to the West Friesian Flora, a large regional garden exhibition in Bovenkarspel, in February, 1999. When it was discovered that these were cases of infection by the dangerous legionella bacteria, also called legionnaire's disease, the alarm bells went off: the illness can only be treated if recognised in time. For many it was already too late. When the Flora was definitively identified as the source of the infection, the situation was quickly labelled the Flora disaster.

During the investigation the flags by the Flora offices and the municipal building flew at half mast. Condolence registers were opened at various places. The Flora Legionnaire's Disease Foundation held meetings where the victims' next of kin could share their grief, experience, and especially questions with one another. Upon request, at the close of these sessions a minute of silence would be observed.

On June 28, four months after the Flora, what was called a reflection gathering was held for patients and their relatives and the next of kin of victims, in a sports centre in nearby Grootebroek. The Minister of Public Health and other representatives of the national and provincial governments spoke there. It was an evening of condolence, at which candles were lit for each of the dead victims and their names read out one by one. They were remembered in a moment of silence. The gathering was deliberately not called a memorial, because the affair was far from closed; many victims were still in hospital. Here too there were many flowers and flags hung at half mast. The West Friesian Men's Choir sang, poems were read and words of remembrance spoken.

After long discussion the decision was made to proceed with erecting a monument: 28 trees for the fatalities. Bushes around the trees symbolised those who had been, or were still ill. Together the trees and bushes form a park, where a basalt monument in the form of an open book, with a memorial text and the poem 'De gestorvene' (The departed) by Ida Gerhardt, a prominent Dutch poetess, commemorates the victims.

Firework disaster (Enschede, 2000)

The next national disaster, the fireworks explosion at Enschede (May 13, 2000), was of a totally different nature, but viewed in terms of emotional impact and ritual it would seem a direct parallel with the Bijlmer disaster in Amsterdam. With each of the intervening disasters one saw that various groups of fellow-sufferers from elsewhere in The Netherlands or in other countries were either represented or sent flowers or an expression of sympathy; in Enschede indeed requests for sharing personal experience went out to groups such as organisations of the next of kin from the Bijlmer disaster.

Among the parallels are the fact that here too a specific section of a city was involved, in some cases several members of families were killed, and homes and property were left in ruins, often unrecognisably charred. The similar social status and the multicultural aspect of the neighbourhood involved must also be noted, with relatively large numbers of victims of non-Dutch background, although this was much less obvious from the collective mourning rituals than had been the case in the

Bijlmer.[7] In addition to several condolence registers, a sea of flowers, a spontaneous monument, a visit by the royal family, a silent procession, a public memorial service, flags at half mast and a minute silence, here there were also unique elements such as the reading of each name separately, a series of condolence concerts, and alternative methods of collecting relief funds. When the neighbourhood involved was quickly sealed off with a triplex hoarding, this became a sounding board for emotions. Not only were flowers placed and candles lit at its foot, but handwritten texts of sympathy, condolence and protest appeared on it. Here too the funeral services and cremations took place in a relatively private sphere, as much as possible shielded from the press and those who were not close relatives. Three bodies were flown to Turkey for burial, at which representatives from the Dutch government and the municipality were present.

New Year's blaze (Volendam, 2001)

Finally, in Volendam, where the victims of the cafe fire (Jan. 1, 2001) formed a special group, namely that of young adolescents (the youngest victim was thirteen) from one small, tight Roman Catholic community, we saw in the news reports how the separate victims were each given their own wake, but in the course of the week were all buried next to one another in the same section of the churchyard behind the Vincentius Church.[8] It took some time before the scene of the fire in Volendam became a spontaneous floral monument; here it appeared that the school and church were the ritual centres rather than the site of the disaster itself. only when preparations were being made for a silent procession were steps taken to create a stage in front of the Cafe De Hemel on which a large quantity of flowers could be placed. In the course of a week-and-a-half there were flowers and notes that appeared at the hoarding with which the burned-out cafe was fenced off, but not in the great numbers that had been

[7] For example, on May 22 a condolence notice was published in Enschede on behalf of the Surinamese community: "Our resilience is tested again. The Surinam Airlines disaster and the Bijlmer disaster claimed victims from among our families. Now the fireworks disaster in Enschede has again hit us terribly hard." One Surinamese family lost five members; a Turkish family was left mourning three members.

[8] A former fishing village on what used to be the Zuiderzee, Volendam has traditionally been a small, tightly-knit Roman Catholic community. For years the village has been an important tourist attraction, with many foreign tourists coming up to the village from Amsterdam on excursions daily.

seen elsewhere. It is reported that these came primarily from outside the community, and that the residents of Volendam themselves, including the young people, either stayed indoors or sought out the school or church.

The silent procession, here termed the 'Procession of Solidarity' on the way to a 'Gathering of Solidarity', was also somewhat distinct from its predecessors. It was led not by dignitaries, but by young people: relatives, friends and classmates of the victims. They carried propane lanterns, without open flame. Along with the Crown Prince, there were representatives from the government, as well as Cardinal Simonis, the acting bishop of the diocese of Haarlem (vacant at the time) and the auxiliary bishop. The procession ended at a stadium where a collective memorial service was held. There were spoken portions, but also singing; in addition to the hymn 'The Lord is my Shepherd' and the *Ave Verum*, there were youth songs. The memorial was not devoted only to the (at that time) ten fatalities, but also to the dozens of seriously burned young people who were still in intensive care units at various hospitals, and before whom lay a very long road to recovery, with many operations. Several of them were to die from their injuries later.

In Volendam too there was direct contact made with fellow-sufferers from a comparable disaster, the disco fire in Göteborg, Sweden, two years before, at which there were not only many fatalities, but also many young people literally scarred for life. As of the time of writing there are still regular contacts and exchanges being carried on among the victims and next of kin from these two disasters.

2.3. CONTIGUOUS RITUAL REPERTOIRE

The disasters discussed above reflect a selection which is based not only on the number of fatalities and seriously injured individuals, and those affected in other ways, but also on the manner in which the events were followed by the media and how the disasters live on in memory, for instance by means of annual commemorations, monuments, and so forth. This does not detract from the tragedy of other collective disasters in which others were involved at the same time. For example, in the weeks after Amsterdam's Bijlmer disaster there was a letter to the editor which noted that the media hype around the disaster left a bitter taste for the author. Shortly before (Sept. 28, 1992) there had been an aeroplane crash in Nepal in which, among others, fourteen Dutch citizens had lost their lives, including the son of the letter writer, and no more than perfunctory attention had been given to that disaster.

On the other hand, there are also next of kin who consciously seek anonymity after a disaster. In a church in Laren, in the central Netherlands, there is a large vase on which the victims of the Faro disaster are commemorated: the names of the victims, and seven stars for those dead whose next of kin would rather not have the name kept in public sight. Still another possibility is represented by the fire in De Vogel, the boarding house in The Hague, about which little was to be found in the news media at the time, possibly because the fatalities did not clearly 'belong' to any group, or could not be identified with, not even by their neighbours, much less by Dutch citizens in general. But even in the case of a major international disaster, such as the aeroplane bombing over the Scottish town of Lockerbie in 1988, it is only later, following a similar disaster in The Netherlands, namely the Bijlmer crash, that we find any special discussion in the Dutch press about the manner in which the Lockerbie dead were commemorated.[9]

When people in The Netherlands are asked to name some major disasters before 1990, most remember the Great Flood of February, 1953, and the aeroplane disaster at Tenerife in which a total of 538 people died, of whom 248 were Dutch.[10] The role of the then current news media was critical. After radio came television, and after cable television with transmitters around the world came internet as an important medium and forum. A culture of commemoration is no longer limited to the place itself; it is precisely the electronic superhighway that links many at the moment of a disaster. Digital condolence registers are opened, digital candles lit, and digital roses offered. It is interesting that objects such as flowers, candles, sympathy notes, photographs and personal memorabilia left at the site of a disaster are associated by many with southern vacation destinations such as Italy and Spain, where visitors often saw such temporary shrines along the road side.

It might seem that with the mourning and memorial rituals after the Bijlmer disaster, the repertoire was simply there, that it had already been formed, and that thereafter only the details were varied with the different disasters. Yet a clear development can be observed. In order to get an idea of this it is necessary for us to shift our examination to major disasters which had taken place in other countries prior to the Bijlmer dis-

---

[9] Such as in the *Algemeen Dagblad* for October 10, 1992. Later, in the period 2000-2002, the disaster again attracted major international interest through the trial that was held on Dutch soil according to Scotch law, on the former military base at Zeist, involving two suspects extradited from Libya.

[10] Cf. REIJNOUDT & STERK: *Tragedie op Tenerife* (2002).

aster. We will also have to shift our focus in time back by five years or so. We then see, in countries surrounding The Netherlands, three stadium disasters, the first at Bradford, England, on May 11, 1985, a second at Brussels (often referred to as the Heizel drama), May 29, 1985, and the third at Sheffield, England, April 15, 1989. All three cases involved football fans. The unusually marked identity and loyalty of such fans was also expressed innovatively in personally designed mourning and memorial rituals. Fans have on more than one occasion requested mourning rituals that caused controversy in the football world, such as having the funeral procession pass through their favourite team's stadium, being interred under sod taken from the football pitch, etc. In Enschede a football jersey signed by the whole of the local football team was added to the sea of floral tributes. There was also a football as a grave gift, a recognisable link between the living and a mourned victim. In Volendam the collective memorial service was held in the stadium, a football player delivered the memorial address, and later a benefit fixture was played.

It is perhaps with the three football disasters that we can first see that modern creation of public heroes or martyrs which would later play a role in the silent processions in response to senseless violence on the street. In the cases of Joes Kloppenborg and Meindert Tjoelker, two young Dutch men who both paid with their lives for interfering with anti-social behaviour on the street, one can quite literally speak of modern martyrdom.

In any case, we find comparative material for the Bijlmer disaster in major international air disasters, such as those at Lockerbie (Dec. 21, 1988) and Paramaribo (June 7, 1989), and also after the crash of the Air India plane over Ireland (June 23, 1985), after the dramas in Ramstein, at the airshow (Aug. 28, 1988) and later with a military aircraft (Aug. 29, 1990). The air crashes at Zurich (Nov. 14, 1990) and Heidelberg (Dec. 22, 1991) must also be added to this list. From these it is noteworthy that there is increasingly more space for personal input in military mourning rituals.

Another category of comparative material is formed by a series of rail and tram accidents, such as those in London (Dec. 12, 1988), Rüsselsheim (Feb. 2, 1990) and Göteborg (Mar. 12, 1992). Several major ferry boat sinkings from that period (Zeebrugge, Leghorn) have already been mentioned. Oslo (Apr. 7, 1990) can be added to these. All received ample attention in the press, and at the level of policy the disaster plans implemented took into account – however minimally – the aspects of mourning and commemoration. Lessons were often drawn from the concrete situations of previous disasters. Now and then in a news report on television, or in a captioned photograph, there was indeed something to be seen of a ritual of parting, for instance the next of kin after a disaster throwing flowers into the sea at the spot where a plane had crashed or a ship sunk. The watery grave was visited collectively and flowers strewn in an attempt to pay final respects to the dead and, in the absence of physical remains, to allow death to become a reality. Heart-breaking scenes took place when a survivor could not let go of the flower and throw it overboard, as if the red rose was the loved one themselves and in letting go of the flower the loved one was definitively being surrendered to the sea. Recently we saw similar scenes at the site of the sinking of the later recovered Russian submarine, Kursk (August, 2000).

The role that the news media (and television in particular) played at the international level in shaping collective opinion, but also in the potential borrowing process or referral process within ritual repertoires, first became visible during the Vietnam war and the growing protest against it. In retrospect, this is also the case for the assassination and burial of president Kennedy (Nov. 22, 1963). Within the period we are discussing here we have particularly the sudden, violent death and burial of Olof Palme (Feb. 28, 1986), Yitzhak Rabin (Nov. 4, 1995) and Princess Diana (Aug. 31, 1997) which were brilliantly spotlit by the media. Although strictly speaking rituals surrounding the deaths of public figures, 'celebrities', do not fit within our subject, the parallel is legitimised by the flood of international media attention that turns the death of a popular media personality into a collective disaster. There is also clearly a contiguous ritual repertoire. For instance, the sidewalk in front of the cinema where Palme was shot quickly became a sea of flowers, with hundreds of paraffin candles. The same happened at the place where Rabin's life was violently cut short, and at not one but two places after the automobile accident involving Princess Diana: in Paris, at the site of the accident (a place which for that matter is still marked as such today), and in London, at various points around the city before and during the memorial service and burial which followed on the family estate. On all three of these occasions images of these public forms of participation in the mourning appeared in the newspapers and on television.[11]

---

[11] See for instance PERI (ed.): *The assassination of Yitzhak Rabin* (2000), in which parallels are also drawn between the role of the media after the violent death of Rabin and that of other prominent politicians such as Olof Palme and Indira and Rajiv Gandhi, respectively. For The Netherlands see, since then, the assassination of the politician Pim Fortuyn (May, 2002), with the explosion of public mourning, commemoration and protest rituals, which the media compared with that after the death of Diana.

The parallels are clear: through the news media these persons became more or less public property, and their shocking deaths therefore led to massive expressions of sympathy and protest. Especially television permits the viewer at home to empathise with the relatives and the invited dignitaries and with the anonymous public along the route of the funeral procession in such an intense manner that the whole event will leave behind a dramatic impression on many. When a similar drama then takes place in that viewer's immediate circle, or the larger community around them, such media events function as their frame of reference and as an example to which people can look, and from which they can borrow or imitate elements as they will. Through the reach of the medium of television and through the mixture of international guests prominently present in the cortege of the dead celebrity, such gestures of mourning become increasingly less private, less linked to any particular culture or country, or to any particular church or religion. Those – eclectic – elements which people have found stirring in one or another public funeral can be included and varied in the next. It is the public here who determine public ritual, one mass that quotes another, and there is a collective pool from which people draw. The funeral of Princess Grace of Monaco (Sept. 18, 1982) was another such media event.

The same process occurred in The Netherlands among the mass expressions of sympathy and protest marches after senseless street violence that drew considerable attention in the 1990s. We can watch the ritual repertoire around senseless violence grow to maturity during the period we have delimited: a more or less fixed programme that is ready for use if a young person dies from street violence, whether racist in nature or not, or from irrational aggression in cafes or discos, or after sexual assault, with which a large group of sympathizers – who for the most part have not known the victim personally – can commemorate the individual.

The first person in The Netherlands with whom the terms 'senseless violence', 'irrational violence' or street violence was associated was the Antillean Kerwin Duinmeijer, who died in Amsterdam in 1983 after a racist incident on the street. Among the ways his memory is kept alive are a monument in Vondel Park in Amsterdam, 'Mother Earth', the end point for an annual memorial procession which passes from the Dam to Vondel Park, and a website where anyone can still affirm their sympathy, not only for his undeserved death, but also with the struggle against all violence and all forms of racism.

In the case of Joes Kloppenborg, who was murdered in the Voetboogstraat in Amsterdam in 1996 after challenging anti-social behaviour
by a group of youths, there was also no silent procession organised directly
after his death, but since then his memory has been kept alive by a monument and by the 'Kappen Nou' ('Knock it off') Foundation, established
by his father Jan Kloppenborg, who has also appeared as a spokesperson
at later protests against senseless violence. The word 'help!' in neon letters is still to be seen in the Voetboogstraat above the site of the murder.
In recording the history of the silent procession as a regular component
in public response to senseless violence, it is important to note here that
in these cases it was only on the occasion of the erection of the memorial – both that for Duinmeijer and that for Kloppenborg – that a procession was organised, which is now termed a silent procession when
repeated as an annual commemoration.

Around 1997 a number of separate ritual elements seem to coalesce into
a more fixed and clearly defined repertoire, a sort of script. That was to be
seen for the first after the death of Meindert Tjoelker, who on bachelor
evening preceding his planned marriage was kicked to death when he dared
to intervene in an incident of vandalism on the street (Leeuwarden, Sept.
19, 1997), and was massively elevated to a symbol of all that is good. A monument was spontaneously created around the tree near the pedestrian bridge
on the Waagplein where the incident had taken place, with flowers, paraffin candles, drawings and cards, but also at the place where he would have
married a sea of candles appeared on the steps that he would have ascended
on his wedding day. A couple who did marry that day at that site placed
the bride's bouquet among them. Dutch and Friesian flags flew at half mast,
cafes and restaurants shut their doors, and people formed a 'human mourning ribbon around Leeuwarden', a 'silent circle'. Later he was given a monument: a book of remembrance with the broken rose that also appeared on
posters announcing actions. The tree, with a photograph of Tjoelker, was
not only a spontaneous monument, but also a modern pillory.

Later a similar pillory was created at Tilburg, in the province of Brabant, in the southern Netherlands: the tree in front of the cafe on the Pius-
plein where Justus Hertig was knifed to death after an argument in the
cafe. Paraffin candles placed on the street formed his first name. In that
same year, 1998, during a short period there were four young people killed
in incidents of street violence, and the abhorrence of such violence was
massively expressed. In the process streetlamp poles often took on the

form of pillories: sites for messages protesting and denouncing street vio-lence that took place near them, but also for protesting traffic conditions that contributed to a fatal accident nearby. When, for instance, a play-ing child was killed by a lorry, that too was experienced as violence.

The largest number of participants in a silent procession to that date were to be found in the commemoration for Froukje Schuitmaker and Marianne Roza, two fatalities in a music cafe in Gorinchem, in the west of The Netherlands near Rotterdam (Jan. 16, 1999). Thousands of white flowers in glistening cellophane were placed, and all over the country church bells tolled. The school Froukje had attended made it their first choice to work through their grief with one another as a school. Teachers and pupils together collectively visited the tiny street where the music cafe was located, but later many of the pupils, who distinguished themselves from other marchers by wearing a sunflower, walked in the silent procession. Members of the Gorcum Against Violence foundation participated, dressed in white T-shirts with the text "Does any violence make sense?" Some also wore pins with a ladybird as a symbol of protest against growing violence and weapon possession. Some wore a white ribbon or blue butterfly.

The organisation of the silent procession was chiefly an interplay between the mayor and clergy. The march began at the City Hall, passed through the narrow street where the girls had been killed, and ended in the Grote Markt. A minute of silence was observed, and in addition to the spontaneous floral tribute in front of the Bacchus music cafe, the fountain in the Grote Markt was also buried under flowers and other symbolic attributes. Candles were also lit in the reflection corner of the church after the march was over. For the rest, the first candle that was lit by the entrance of the music cafe was from the church's children's service, which had been taken from the church building to the sidewalk in front of the cafe less than twelve ours after the crime.

After the violent deaths of Marianne Vaatstra (Zwaagwesteinde, May 7, 2000) and Daniel van Cotthem (Vlaardingen, Jan. 14, 2000) there were likewise massive numbers who marched in silent processions. Such public gestures were not always appreciated by relatives of the deceased. For instance, after the murder of the child Nienke following a sexual assault in Schiedam's Beatrix Park (June 26, 2000), at the request of the family no silent procession or large gathering was held, although there were condolence registers opened and inevitably countless notes of sym-pathy and flowers appeared on the bridge in the park. In fact, 2000 was a record year with regard to silent processions. Among other places, smaller processions took place in Vught (taxi murder, July 20), The Hague (disco murder, May), Amsterdam (Recep Uzer stabbed to death at a cash machine in the Zeeburg neighbourhood; a tree was later planted and a commemorative plaque placed) and Lelystad (where in April a silent procession was held to the place where the body of Ankie Blommaert was found; there four torches were set into the ground and flowers placed in the reed border). Further to be listed is the procession organised in Utrecht for the murdered five-year-old Yasmina Habchi. (It later appeared that she had been killed by a neighbour boy.) Here the structure had to be adapted in two respects to satisfy Islamic customs: the procession could only take place after the mourning prayers had been said, and the procession could not end at the garbage tip where the body had been found.

Other processions are hardly remembered, such as that in 1992 in Hilversum, where the 15-year-old Hamito Quamar was shot to death by a neighbour in a fit of rage involving noise nuisance, and that in Adorp in 1996, where a father and his teenage son were killed at an unguarded level rail crossing. And although the owner of the dog Boris, from Drachten, shot to death in the park by the police for chasing ducks, believed that animals also had a right to such processions, organisers of other silent processions on the occasion of 'real' senseless violence objected. The procession was then transformed into a protest march against the violation of animal rights.

In light of all this, it would appear that the phenomenon of the silent procession has become a fixed component of expressions of public sentiment after disasters and senseless violence. But silent processions have also been organised to express sympathy and protest on other occasions, such as against the violence in the Molucca Islands, and following the execution of a Nigerian environmental activist. The first National Silent March against violence was organised on Sept. 28, 1999, in The Hague. A path of white roses was laid around the Hofvijver, in front of the Dutch Parliament. Silent processions combined with a minute (or two) of silence had for decades been held on May 4, Dutch Memorial Day, to commemorate the victims of World War II. As the *Volkskrant* observed, "With the ceremonies around the death of Tjoelker, the war has been transposed to the street, and Tjoelker has become a modern resistance hero."[12] We can see how elements of mourning ritual after disasters, following

---

[12] VAN RENSSEN: 'Achter de stille tocht', *de Volkskrant* February 6, 2000.

senseless violence, and from the traditional Memorial Day observances on May 4, have flowed together.

Furthermore, in writing the history of the silent procession in The Netherlands as a component of public mourning and mass protest, we must here refer to the phenomenon of the White March in Brussels (October 19, 1996), in response to the 'Dutroux affair'.[13] At the time the gruesome facts surrounding the kidnapped, sexually assaulted and murdered girls and the failures of the police and justice system had outraged many Belgians. The White March was a clear culmination of this. This silent procession – which really was a march against the silence and cover-ups – has been termed the 'greatest mobilisation in Belgian history'. Participant's motives were mixed: some wished to demonstrate their sympathy with the families of missing and murdered children, others marched with one clear demand, the fundamental reform of politics and justice. Even the peace movement had never been able to mobilise so many people. Among the other words used to describe it were the 'revolt of tears', the 'Calimero revolt' and 'the children's crusade'. Many participants were clad entirely or partially in white, or at least wore white ribbons, white caps, white scarves, or white T-shirts. Also, the colour of the flowers being placed was predominately white. White balloons were released and white flags and pennants were carried. It is notable that here those directly concerned, the parents of the girls involved, joined the march and addressed it. There were similar marches of support in The Netherlands, in The Hague and Maastricht, among other places.

As well as the unequalled mass character of the White March in Brussels, we must also here remark particularly on the consistently carried through symbolism of the colour white. In the media white was primarily interpreted as the colour of innocence (of the children) and of justice (which was scarcely to be obtained through the police and justice system). On the other hand, however, precisely in Belgium the use of white as a colour of mourning is not unfamiliar (for instance, in the funeral of King Boudewijn), and in the Bijlmer white was used (along with red, primarily among the Ghanaians) as a colour of mourning: white flowers, white ribbons, white balloons. A further inclination that occasionally manifested itself in the silent procession in Brussels, and also would play a part in other silent processions later, is what the *Volkskrant*

---

[13] For a primarily sociological analysis of the White March, see WALGRAVE & RIHOUX: *De Witte Mars: een jaar later* (1997); see also 3.5 below.

termed 'the demonisation of the perpetrator', in this case Marc Dutroux.[14] Although such later processions would also retain their peaceful character, in Brussels it was abundantly clear there was a perpetrator to point to. In the case of most other silent processions that situation has been much less clear, as police investigations were just beginning. But never does the public protest involve only the perpetrator; the police and justice system, the municipality, businesses, and especially tendencies in society were always put in the pillory too.

In addition to the White March in Belgium we perhaps must also mention here other public events which occurred during the period involved. One may recall the phenomenon of large marches in America, such as the Million Man March (1995), the Promise Keepers March (1996) and the Million Woman March (1997), although these mass marches were not in response to a disaster or a specific, violent death. Another contiguous phenomenon was the massive commemoration of the death of Elvis Presley, on August 16, 1997, at Graceland, in Memphis, TN, USA. Although every year numerous grieving fans visit his grave on the anniversary of his death, 1997, the 20th anniversary, was a top year. During the memorial week more than 150,000 visitors filed past his grave. On the 16th itself between 30,000 and 40,000 fans paid their respects, lighted candles in hand, and in addition to flowers there were spectacular floral arrangements in the form of a guitar, teddy bears and pottery angels left at the grave side.[15] The manner in which, for instance, John Lennon (in a special section of Central Park, NYC) and Jim Morrison (whose grave in the Père Lachaise cemetery in Paris has become a place of pilgrimage and cult object) are remembered should also be mentioned here.

Finally, in English-speaking countries during the same period we saw the phenomenon of school shootings, such as that in Hungerford, England (1987), Dunblane, Scotland (1996) and Jonesboro, USA (1998). These were later followed by shootings in a secondary school in Erfurt, Germany (2002). Here again the victims were adolescents or young children. Both the tokens of sympathy and the expressions of protest were massive: flowers, drawings, notes of condolence, and especially huge numbers of stuffed toys.

---

[14] In the article by VAN RENSSEN mentioned above (see note 12).

[15] See also the separate, extended discussion of the phenomenon of the silent procession in 3.5 of this book.

2.4. SYNTHESIS AND PROVISIONAL CHARACTERISATION

Although, from the international perspective, it is difficult to determine precisely when and where phenomena such as the silent procession, carpets of flowers, candles as tribute, stuffed toys and white as a colour of mourning appeared for the first time on a mass scale, and whether people in The Netherlands came to share in these as a result of media coverage, it is clear that we are dealing with a Western phenomenon characteristic of our times, which to be sure does have its own incidentals in each Western European and North American country (such as the parallel with the phenomenon of the annual Memorial Day ceremonies on May 4 in The Netherlands), but which in a relatively short time has become a familiar scene at mass commemorations.

In our historical survey we identified 1997 as the crucial year for The Netherlands. We would draw a line from the Promise Keepers March (Oct. 4, 1996), the White March (Oct. 19, 1996) and the 'Kappen Nu' Foundation of the father of Joes Kloppenborg, through the massive memorial for Elvis Presley (Aug. 16, 1997) and the funeral of Princess Diana (Aug. 31, 1997), to the collective expressions of mourning surrounding the death of Meindert Tjoelker (Sept. 19, 1997). While the massive turnout of participants for the silent procession in Leeuwarden could be seen as a precedent, it appears from the mass silent processions in Gorinchem, Vlaardingen and Zwaagwesteinde that the silent procession had become a fixed component of the ritual repertoire. With regard to this, it is noteworthy that in some respects collective rituals after disasters have 'followed' rather than 'led', but that historically the phenomenon of the silent procession appeared with disasters before it appeared with peaceful protests against violence. Could we conclude from this that there has been a gradual amalgamation of elements of the funeral cortege, World War I and II memorial observances, and protest marches?[16]

This brings us to shifting perspectives. Cameras bring royal marriages and funerals directly into our living rooms. Cameras connect mourning rituals in Monaco, Tel Aviv, Memphis and London with mourning rituals in the Bijlmer and Enschede. Cameras make the drama of Volendam at least as great as that of Lockerbie, not to mention the 300 Chinese who died in a disco fire in China shortly before the fire in the Volendam cafe. What determines the perspective? Mass mourning culture seems to be

[16] For what is specifically Dutch in this, see also 3.5.

primarily a matter of 'feeling personally involved', of appropriation, and less of global or quantitative perspective. Memorials for the dead of the First and Second World War, Auschwitz, Westerbork and Kristallnacht seem to be something for the older generations; cultural subgroups, including specific age groups, are busy forming their own memorial culture. That this is however less innovative and unique than is sometimes assumed has been demonstrated by our cross-connections among disasters, senseless violence and war commemorations.

Disaster rituals do not appear to be a hermetic realm. The role of churches as life buoys at the time of disasters, as tried and true purveyors of ritual scenarios, as experts in the area of sombre music, as a pool of idealistic volunteers or just as an open house at moments of collectively experienced need, appears to be far from over. The colourful visibility of forms of handling grief from foreign cultures also feed into memorial services, silent processions and funeral culture, providing new stimuli for their development.

If we place the public mourning rituals discussed above in the context of much wider developments in the field of mourning and coping with loss, of funeral and cremation rituals, then we see that our sub-territory perhaps does demonstrate parallels with the various ways of coping with death, but that at significant points it forms a definite entity. In general we can observe that in the case of sudden, violent or unusual death, not only the immediate family is overwhelmed, but that much larger communities publicly share in this death and wish to express this as a group. Precisely because the death comes unexpectedly, at an early age or in a disaster, and the death was not in any way whatsoever foreseen by the person themselves, it is necessarily others who have to give shape to the processes of mourning, burial, cremation and commemoration. This is in contrast to a tendency that we perceive today in the case of people who consciously prepare for their death for a longer time, such as AIDS and cancer patients. In their case one can speak of self-chosen ritual. Precisely because in the case of a disaster or a violent crime with a young and innocent victim this form of death always comes unexpectedly, a more or less fixed script – albeit as a civil initiative in which people feel that they themselves have a hand – appears to serve a purpose. Expertise is called upon from fellow-sufferers from other disasters, from clergy, from public authorities, from crisis managers and national support points for grief and trauma processing.

One thing we observe in the case of both expected and unexpected death is the increased participation of children; not only are they increasingly being involved in the death of members of their own family, but also the deaths of children are shared by children, whether that is on television or in the circle of their friends, classmates and children from their immediate community. Secondary school students also have to deal on a regular basis with the death of their peers, through accidents, suicide, and sometimes through street violence or a disaster. They are then involved in the design of sympathy advertisements, mourning rituals and possible commemorations. The churches also permit such personal input within their walls.

Still, it appears that death is precisely an area in which endless variation and experimentation is not possible. The expertise of churches in this field remains one of the manners in which ecclesiastical traditions are kept alive, and one of the reasons they continue to be sought out. In the case of disasters and violent death we see all sorts of hybrid forms involving tradition and innovation, church and state, the private and public domain. In the case of disasters we observe that most families opt for burial or cremation of the deceased member in their own manner, in closed circles, away from the eye of cameras. Some chose that – or at least agreed that – the collective factor, the accident which links their own dead family member with other dead, also be expressed in a collective service, and the individual burial or cremation takes place only after this. Sometimes the community structure is so tight that all can be buried in a special section of the cemetery, as was the case in Volendam. But sometimes there are no physical remains, and a symbol must take the place of the body, and symbolic action the place of an actual funeral.

The notes of condolence and drawings say it differently. Sometimes they are specifically intended for one person, and say something personal. Often, in addition to expressing words of comfort and sympathy they express something of hope, a faltering attempt in the person's own language and art to send something across to the black other side. Apart from the liberating effect that it can have for children to write or draw something of and by themselves, an awkward note or drawing is often an attempt to cross the gap, to reach out above the black hole.[17] Other spontaneous grave gifts also express a personal connection (a football, the team shirt or scarf) or a faith (little chinaware angels). Sometimes there are very personal gifts, of which only the giver can know the meaning.

It is not always those who walk at the front of the silent procession who will speak later at the memorial service. We are familiar with the fact

---

[17] For instance, in Enschede there was a note for the writer's deceased classmate, Cynthia Ransingh: "Cynthia, your hobby was drawing. Hopefully, where you are now you can still do that. God, let her draw. And be good to her."

that for the funeral cortege, from the home to the grave or the church to the grave, there was always a fixed order for those following the coffin. Although the silent procession is in many respects similar to the traditional cortege, with most silent processions in The Netherlands it can clearly be seen that the burgomaster takes a central place, flanked by important guests such as representatives of the Royal House and government. After them come clergy who may be present, together with the next of kin and directly involved. It is striking that relatives of the first degree often choose not to be present at such a moment. They are represented by a wider circle of family members and family friends. Those who are involved because they were fellow passengers or fellow residents are also found here. Behind them often come various institutions which organised the procession, as well as invited fellow-sufferers from similar disasters. Finally come the large group of sympathizers from the immediate community, but also those who have come from a distance.

The silent procession also forms a kind of bridge: the departure point is often a place that points to the community: a square, city hall, community centre or cultural centre. The terminus of the procession is generally the place where the disaster happened. Here, in the presence of the spot where it all took place, the dead are commemorated. Sometimes though the scene of the disaster is only a stop on the way to a stadium, a sports centre, or a public building where the official memorial service will be held. In this way the community and the individuals involved are linked with one another. The community speaks through the presence of the burgomaster. Generally his words include not only expressions of shock, but also statements of policy, promises that he will do all he can to determine what happened and why. Violated trust must be restored, and that obligation faces not only the burgomaster but is also borne by government ministers who may be present. The more personal and more poetic words at the place itself are spoken by others. Music and dance express grief, but also hope and solidarity. Generally several clergy are present, prominent at the head of the procession, or more modestly hidden in the procession. In England such a procession has been termed a 'compassionate procession'.[18] It could be that precisely in this procession of

---

[18] In her Christmas Message, 2000, Beatrix, Queen of The Netherlands, also used similar terms: "Grief makes one speechless. Well intended words do not get through. Comfort can then perhaps be conveyed by hugging someone in silence, and expressing sympathy in a gesture or simply in being there. In marching silently we find a communal form for expressing sympathy in solidarity."

compassion we have found a modern manner of expressing solidarity, a contemporary, secular form of belonging, even when believing is open to challenge from every side. Volendam opted for calling its silent procession to commemorate the victims of the cafe fire a 'gathering of solidarity'.

Finally, monuments mark the event in collective memory. Not only do they give a terrible experience a place in time and space, they form a fixed point to which those who lost loved ones or possessions can return. Moreover, a monument keeps alive both collective sympathy and collective attention. Those involved experience this as acknowledgement.

Surveying the whole of the ritual repertoire accompanying diasters, we can now attempt to reach a provisional characterisation. Here we have chiefly been occupied with their collective character. That this emerging repertoire is so collective in nature indicates an important development. Some dramatic events, including disasters, are apparently 'appropriated' in such a way that a compulsion to affirm sympathy arises in larger circles than just those around the victims. A gap opens up, often literally. The gestures that people make in an affirmation of this sort are an attempt to bridge this gap. Shock, despair, and violated trust are exorcised by temporarily forming a positive mass with one another. The ritual scenario which people call upon is a hybrid form that can tentatively be characterised with the term 'civil religion'. The borrowings involved point toward an international trend. Viewed in terms of ritual qualities, it is chiefly the collective, apotropaic qualities which stand out. The separate parts of the ritual repertoire do not appear to stand by themselves, but to be components of emerging rituality surrounding mourning and public protest.

3. CASE STUDIES I:
DUTCH CASES AND THEMES

3.1. Colourful Netherlands: The Bijlmer disaster (aeroplane crash, Amsterdam, 1992) and the multicultural dimension of disaster ritual (A. Nugteren)

Introduction

In the early evening of October 4, 1992, El Al flight LY 1862, a cargo transport carrying primarily flowers, perfume and electronic equipment crashed into the Bijlmer, a residential neighbourhood in Amsterdam. The Bijlmer, also known as South East Amsterdam, is a suburb at that time comprised of about 90% high-rise housing, built roughly between 1964/5 and 1970. It is home to a large number of nationalities. It also harboured many 'illegal immigrants' (i.e., foreigners without official residence permits). Ultimately there were 43 fatalities identified, most being immigrants from Surinam, the Dutch Antilles, Aruba, Ghana, Turkey and Morocco. Four hundred households had to be evacuated. Although there were fewer fatalities than initially feared, in the first days there was great alarm about the number of undocumented aliens who appeared on no list and would not be eligible for any relief. When it was promised that they could obtain legal status through a special disaster measure, it was difficult to establish who had right to participate in this programme. The nature of the disaster, in which bodies were burned beyond recognition or had to be dug out of the rubble, and the multicultural nature of the Bijlmer society, with many different rites and customs around death, made organising burials a complex process. On Sunday, October 11, 1992, precisely a week after the disaster, collective memorial rituals were performed, which were massively attended and broadcast live on television. An estimated 40,000 people joined in the silent procession, about 13,000 people attended the memorial service, and 3.5 million people watched the television broadcast.

When Mrs. Rita Rahman of the World Diaconate used the metaphor in an interview, that the hole which had been punched in the Bijlmer could perhaps at the same time be an opening for a better understanding of the long existing, inherent problems of the multicultural mix in South East Amsterdam, she expressed the hopes of many. But cynical

responses were also heard: apparently a disaster of this extent was necessary for The Netherlands to become aware of the daily reality of the multicultural society.[1]

Although on the Sunday when the victims of the disaster were commemorated with a silent procession and a memorial service people could
in no way foresee what prolonged aftereffects the Bijlmer disaster would
have, more than one of the speakers already noted that the solidarity
must extend beyond the day of the official mourning observances. On
the same day there were also carefully voiced warnings about the culturally determined complications of coping with grief in the absence of bodies. Although evaluations of the ceremonies on the memorial Sunday
were almost unanimously positive, there were still here and there sombre warnings with regard to how the disaster would be dealt with over
the longer term.[2]

Looking back now on the Bijlmer disaster, with later disasters and disaster ritual in mind, it is striking how 'mature' the memorial observances
in the Bijlmer seem, despite the fact that they stand at the beginning of
the explosion of collective mourning rituals over the succeeding decade.
Still, this concept of 'beginning' must be nuanced; for those directly
involved with the Bijlmer memorial there was after all the precedent of
the crash of a SLM (Surinam Airlines) passenger plane near Paramaribo
on June 7, 1989. Not only were many Surinamese from the Bijlmer
immediately related to victims of the crash at Surinam's Zanderij airport,
but in 1989 Amsterdam had seen its own mourning observances, held
in the same place where the Bijlmer memorial service took place (Amsterdam's RAI convention centre[3]), a commemoration repeated annually at
various other sites. In the Kwakoe Cultural Centre, where many gathered
in that first week of desperation in the Bijlmer, hang many photographs
of that official memorial.[4]

---

[1] There were also sardonic remarks about the disaster being 'a crash course in Bijlmer
studies'.

[2] For instance, with regard to disaster tourism, the remark was heard, 'Never before
has the Bijlmer seen so many whites'.

[3] The RAI is a huge Amsterdam complex for large-scale events such as exhibitions,
trade fairs, pop concerts and international conferences. It will henceforth be refer to as
'the RAI'.

[4] See, among others, the article 'God houdt niet van de Bijlmer' (God doesn't like
the Bijlmer), *NRC Handelsblad*, Oct. 10, 1992, which is accompanied by a photograph
of that memorial observance.

What was completely new about the collective mourning ceremonies in 1992 was the heterogeneity. No less than 500 organisations were involved in the planning of the memorial, 36 nationalities and an unspecified number of religious denominations. The Comité Rouwplechtigheid Bijlmer (Bijlmer mourning ceremony committee) was formed posthaste. While the official components of the ceremonies were planned as public rituals, in the preceding week there were diverse, more closed gatherings of which there were sometimes brief televised reports, such as one at a Pentecostal church which met in a space under a parking garage, and a group of Ghanaians who sprinkled the disaster scene with alcoholic spirits. There were further gatherings in various church buildings, cultural centres, the sports centre, and in homes. The authorities had given permission for holding such smaller, group-related ceremonies, with the exception of a torchlight procession which the Ghanian community had requested. The flames of the torches would have evoked too many painful associations for Bijlmer residents.[5]

The centre of the disaster site, immediately declared a disaster zone and fenced off, was no longer accessible when the rescue and recovery efforts began, but the huge, V-shaped chasm at the ends of two adjoining high-rise apartment blocks was visible to everyone. From the first day flowers were hung on the fence, and sympathy notes and cards were stuck among them. One protest banner appeared, but the rage only came later. Queen Beatrix visited the site, and was present at a church service. Mayor Van Thijn was interviewed daily about the situation, the number of possible victims, and progress in recovery efforts. There was great ferment about not only the number of missing persons, but also about the number of undocumented victims, whose names did not appear on any official lists. Ultimately the official death toll was set at 43, with about 45 injured. Very quickly parallels were drawn with the Lockerbie crash, in which in 1988 a passenger plane came down onto a Scottish town. That disaster claimed 270 lives, among them 11 residents of the town. On October 10, 1992, the *Algemeen Dagblad* published "Lockerbie weet te gedenken" (Lockerbie finds a way to remember), an extensive report on the way that the victims there had been commemorated. On October 14 an article entitled "Amsterdam kan leren van Britse aanpak nazorg" (Amsterdam can learn from British approach to aftercare) appeared in

---

[5] Similarly, in 2001, after the Volendam cafe fire, it was decided to use propane lanterns for the silent procession, rather than torches or candles.

het Parool. In all the solemnities after that there would be one candle, one balloon or one blank name space, intended for all the unidentified victims.[6]

The silent procession

The official portion began in Amsterdam around 11:30 a.m. on Sunday morning, October 11. Throngs of people from the immediate area, but also from other parts of the city and from the whole country, streamed in: men, women and children. The procession was organised in such a way that at the sports centre that formed its starting point a solemn beginning could be held, with among other things a trumpet call sounded by the Salvation Army Band, songs by the children's choir from the Rozemarijn School, and an address by Burgomaster Van Thijn. He noted that there would be no further speeches at the end of the procession, to give everyone the opportunity to mourn and remember the dead in their own way. After he had called upon everybody to join in a procession "that will perhaps be the most difficult of our lives", the mass slowly began to move.

It is notable that the dignitaries (in addition to the Burgomaster, the Dutch Prime Minister, the Ghanian and Surinamese Ambassadors and the Prime Minister of the Dutch Antilles) walked in the midst of the public. Along the route various stages were set up where groups of all sorts played or sang, and also in the body of the procession there were here and there separate groups of people who sang, danced or drummed. The Ghanaians were conspicuous with their red ribbons and black-shrouded drums, the Creole Surinamese, chiefly women, through their deliberately chosen clothing combinations of black and white. Many carried with them wreathes, flowers or balloons (chiefly black).

On arrival, the Mayor laid the first wreath at the fence surrounding the disaster site. A wooden platform – which was hastily expanded – had been constructed to receive the tributes. Everyone placed the wreaths or flowers there with their own hands. Some stayed there a time, others moved on their own initiative to the RAI, where 9000 visitors were expected in the main hall, and where in several other conference halls large video screens had been set up to accommodate any overflow attendance.

---

[6] All the unidentified victims were buried in one mass grave, because the bodies had to remain at the disposal of the authorities.

The memorial service

Among those seated in the first row were Princess Juliana (the former Dutch Queen), Crown Prince Willem-Alexander, Burgomaster Ed van Thijn, J. van Kemenade (the Queen's Commissioner for North Holland), Prime Minister Ruud Lubbers and Vice Premier Wim Kok, as well as the President of the Republic of Surinam, Ronald Venetiaan; the ambassador of Surinam to The Netherlands, C. Ramkisoor; the Prime Minister of the Dutch Antilles, Maria Liberia-Peters; the Minister Plenipotentiary of Aruba, A. Tromp-Yarzagaray; the ambassador from the Republic of Ghana, A. Ntim Abankwa; and a minister from the Israeli cabinet, Y. Kessar.

The memorial service began in the RAI just after 3:00 p.m., and was opened by Gerda Havertong.[7] She was the mistress of ceremonies for the whole duration of the programme. Sometimes she merely announced the next speaker; sometimes she also expressed the mood of grief and condolence in several words of her own. In her opening words she recalled to mind the previous Sunday, the muffled explosion, the fireball, and how a residential neighbourhood suddenly became a disaster zone.

– First to appear was a percussion group 'from six cultures' with 'drum rituals surrounding death'.

– The first speaker was Mrs. Meijer-Cratz, chairwoman of the Bijlmer Mourning Ceremony Committee. In previous interviews she had given an impression of the complexity of her task of organising mourning ceremonies in which so many interests and traditions had to be given a place. At the RAI she read an evocation of 'the moment that it happened, when the evening was still young', in the form of a poem.

– This was followed by Ghanian music. The women of the 'Resurrection Singers' gospel choir were glad in green, with white collars, the men in wine red with white collars.

– Next came the address by Burgomaster Van Thijn. He also called to mind the evening of the disaster. He spoke of solidarity ('our Bijlmer'), but also recalled the uncertainty, worry, the painstaking progress of the rescue crews for whom 'every sign of life counted'. That ultimately the number of expected fatalities was reduced from 250 to 43 was a cause for relief, but the affliction remained great. He also referred to the need for aftercare when the disaster would again be forgotten by outsiders.

---

[7] Actress, known in The Netherlands primarily for her appearance in the Dutch version of 'Sesame Street', and herself a native of Surinam.

– Next came the appearance of a black soloist, Henry Muldrow, with
two songs, 'There is a Balm in Gilead' and 'Deep River'; he was accompanied by guitar.

– The next speaker was Prime Minister Ruud Lubbers. He too recalled
the Sunday evening, 'the hell on earth', the fire sea, the inferno. He
informed the gathering that he had never before received so many messages of condolence from other countries as after this disaster. He referred
to the services that had been held in churches, mosques and synagogues.
He himself read Psalm 22: 'Be not far from me' (vs. 11). He paused to
consider 'colourful Netherlands' and how many came here in hope from
other lands to build a better life: 'it gnaws and pounds in us'. He too
warned for 'tomorrow, the future' and how easy it was to forget even a
drama like this when public attention would move on to other things.

– The following speaker was Mr. Toon Borst, community worker in the
Bijlmer and himself a resident of one of the buildings that had been hit.
He called to mind his recent trip to Surinam where he had visited the spot
where three years before the SLM plane had crashed, and the monument
there of six white granite blocks with the names of the 171 victims. He
also called to mind the evening of the disaster, by remembering that just
at that moment his son had called to him saying that the football match
was starting on television. 'A chasm has opened up in all of us'. He recalled
the old woman from Romania and her two dogs, the children who played
on the lawns in front of the flats, who he would never see again.

– Next came a Hindustani song, 'Akash' (Space), sung by Nsiah
Krishna, wearing a cream-coloured silk sari, accompanied by an ensem-
ble with sitar, tabla, tamboura and harmonium.

– President Venetiaan of Surinam then spoke. He extended his sympathy to the victims and emphasized how involved people in Surinam too
were in this disaster.

– Following this Lidwina Booi sang the song 'Despedida' (Farewell),
accompanied by black guitarist Julian Coco.

– Then it was the turn of the Prime Minister of the Dutch Antilles,
Mrs. Liberia-Peters. Among other things, she raised the issue of final rest-
ing places: in the Antilles, not in Amsterdam.[8] She delivered a prayer
emotionally, partly in Papiamento. She received applause.

---

[8] If desired, bodies were flown back to the country the person had come from, with
insurance and the municipality covering the cost, along with travel costs for two family
members. If the burial or cremation was in The Netherlands, these institutions would
pay for two family members to travel here.

– Immediately thereafter the Minister Plenipotentiary of Aruba, Mrs. Tromp-Yarzagaray, spoke, among other things conveying the feelings of the Aruban Prime Minister, who himself could not be present.

– Then followed the cantor of the Jewish Community of Amsterdam. He sang a psalm in Hebrew, accompanied by a harpist.

– Then Rabbi L. van der Kamp said the Yizkor and Kaddish, Jewish memorial prayers.

– Minister Y. Kessar spoke for the government of Israel, in English, and remembered the four Israeli victims, the three crew and the only passenger.[9]

– Next a Ghanian percussion group appeared, with singing, drumming and clapping in rhythm. It is striking that from this moment the applause that had followed Mrs. Liberia-Peters words in Papiamento was repeated, as it would be for the address by the Ghanian ambassador and the song from the Islamic Men's Choir.

– The Ghanian ambassador to The Netherlands, the Hon. A. Ntim Abankwa, expressed his sympathy for all the victims and referred in particular to the many among them who had come to The Netherlands to seek success here. Among them the anonymous victims, the 'illegal immigrants', deserved special sympathy.[10]

– Then Imam Omar, of Amsterdam's Al-Kabir mosque, recited a portion of the Koran.[11]

---

[9] Some newspapers raised questions about this lone passenger. It appeared to be an exceptional situation. This woman's parents received some attention in the press, but the background of the three crew members remained vague. In Tel Aviv they were honoured by two formations of five aeroplanes each making a fly-past above the seafront.

[10] At first people spoke chiefly of "a big hole in the Amsterdam municipal registry", but it quickly became clear that many of the victims, both fatalities and homeless, were not on the register because they were living in The Netherlands without official permission. That led to the promise from the Secretary of State responsible that they would be considered for a residence permit on humanitarian grounds. It was particularly the churches in the Bijlmer which, from the first moments after the disaster, opened their doors for these now doubly-homeless people. The Protestant congregation 'De Nieuwe Stad' (The new city) proudly termed itself the 'First Aid Church'.

[11] Although the Islamic input in the memorial service was modest, during the whole week Amsterdam's mosques had been active in receiving those involved. Many mosques in The Netherlands also organised extra prayer services. Organisations of Surinamese, Moroccan and Turkish Muslims worked together in these. Later the Taibah mosque, near the Kraaiennest subway station in the Bijlmer, would function as the starting point for the annual memorial procession.

– Following this, the poet Jamal Khamis read in Arabic a poem he had written, 'Fear descends'.

– This was immediately followed by a performance of the Islamic Men's Choir, from the Bijlmer.

– The next speaker was Mr. R. Janssen, chairman of the local council for South East Amsterdam. He evoked the image of how the Bijlmer, like no other place in The Netherlands, was linked by so many threads with the rest of the city, country, and world. He also referred to the sense of community in the Bijlmer, and promised the deployment of professional social workers and volunteer community workers. The gaping hole could not be closed, but there must be a search for forms of collective and individual comfort and reconstruction.

– An announcement from Gerda Havertong introduced a performance by the Royal Concertgebouw Orchestra, under the direction of Riccardo Chailly. They played the 'Eroica', the funeral march from Beethoven's Third Symphony.

– The observance closed at around 5:30 p.m. and the crowds streamed out of the convention centre.

The monument

After this account of the mourning ceremonies on the Sunday after the disaster, there follows now a short description of the gradual development of the memorial monument in the Bijlmer, a place where to this day fresh traces of memorial rituals can be found, and the spot at which the annual memorial procession ends. This digression to a later point in time is here justified by the fact that the site of the 1992 memorial rituals more or less spontaneously grew into what it now is, the centre of a memorial park. Not without reason, it has been referred to as a 'growing monument'. Management and maintenance have recently been transferred to the hands of the Beheer Het Groeiend Monument (Stewardship of the growing monument) Foundation.[12] 'The tree that witnessed everything', a tree which remained standing at the scene of the disaster, is the heart of this monument, and it is this tree that became the ritual centre, not only for the annual commemoration, but also for the 'Bijlmer feeling' itself.

---

[12] See VAN BOXTEL: 'Het monument is van iedereen' (1999) 3.

The foundation which now administers this monument has also adapted a memorial protocol through which journalists are now kept in the background. The first place in the annual wreath laying is for representatives of the local council, the second for next of kin and others directly involved, and only third for representatives of the municipality, national government and politics.

Not only does the monument grow, but in particular, it blooms. Around the tree a wooden stage has been built on which pots and vases with plants and flowers are placed, where notes and poems sheathed in plastic sleeves are left, and where all sorts of individual tokens of involvement are laid, hung or tacked up. The residents incorporated their own feelings, and sometimes their personal experiences, in the surrounding mosaic carpet.

The tree figured only slightly, if at all, in the official memorial described above. Only later, when the fences were removed, did this tree develop into a spontaneous monument. It was classmates of the 18 young children who died in the disaster who made this tree into a focus for remembrance, when the organisations still needed a long time to plan the landscaping around the residential towers involved. They hung notes, drawings and balloons in the branches, left plants and flowers there, tacked photos to the trunk and sang songs around it.[13]

Analysis and characterisation

When we consider both elements in the memorial Sunday in Amsterdam, the silent procession and the service of mourning in the RAI, several matters stand out.

(a) The use of the term 'silent procession' for the march from the sports centre to the scene of the disaster appears to have been self-evident. Everyone used this term, sometimes varied with 'memorial procession'. Now and then one could detect some discomfort at connecting the idea of silence with the – to Dutch standards – sometimes exuberant expression of mourning by Surinamese and Ghanaians. When the organisers were asked about this, they pointed out a misunderstanding: in all cultures grief makes people diffident, but sometimes raw emotions arise to which expression is given.

---

[13] See, among others, SPEE, ROOS, FIDDELAERS: *Veelkleurig verdriet* (2000).

(b) The silent procession, the content of which was deliberately left open in order that everyone might express their grief and sympathy in their own manner, was only minimally directed. The procession left from a common assembly point, the sports centre, for the scene of the disaster. Along the route there were various stages with presentations. The dignitaries mixed with the crowd. Small groups danced, sung and drummed during the march. After the burgomaster had laid his wreath, others placed their bouquets and wreathes at all sorts of places along the fence. From a typological and historical perspective, this was a more massive, looser variant of the memorial processions that were familiar in The Netherlands prior to 1992 from Memorial Day rites focused on the dead of World War II.

(c) The protest element was almost entirely absent; even the one banner that was carried was only an expression of mourning and certainly not an indictment. The protest would come later.

(d) The memorial service was carefully directed. Not only were elements such as 'first language' (prose) and 'second language' (poetry) taken into consideration, but verbal language was continually alternated with musical language. Not only Dutch was heard (in many ethnic accents), but also English, Papiamento, Hebrew, Arabic, Sanskrit and Portuguese. There were approximately as many female speakers and musicians as male, and in their total they approximated the cultural mix of the Bijlmer population. Religious expressions were not avoided, but they generally remained in the background.[14]

(e) The only ritual awkwardness to be mentioned here involved not the organisation or the personal input of those who carried out the programme, but arose among the audience itself. Half way through the service there was spontaneous applause after the Papiamento section of Mrs. Liberia-Peters's emotional speech, an understandable acknowledgement and recognition. The applause was repeated a couple of times thereafter,

---

[14] In general, Dutch churches did not appropriate the events in the Bijlmer as God's punishment or God's will. For instance, in *Trouw*, Oct. 10, 1992, one found: "Church magazines generally react only at second or third hand to what newspapers regard as big stories. But in any case, this week they showed they had heard the explosion in the Bijlmer. Ed van Straten advised his readers in the *Algemeen Doopsgezind Weekblad* [General Baptist Weekly] that they should leave God out of this. His Name should be spoken only to express thanks for having survived, as the Ghanaian woman did, who thanked God because she and her children had been brought through this alive." This is not in contradiction with the doubt that was sometimes expressed in the Bijlmer itself, "God doesn't like the Bijlmer"; see *NRC Handelsblad*, Oct. 10, 1992.

as if people felt that one round of applause required that they applaud others too. The painful question of whether or not one should applaud is familiar from concerts in churches, after emotional speeches at a graveside, and with other mixed forms of the sacred and secular domains. A comparable discomfort arose when the Concertgebouw orchestra performed at the close of the mourning service.

(f) In later public mourning rituals after disasters, funerals, silent processions and collective memorial services continued to be linked with one another in various ways or, on the other hand, were separated. In the case of the Bijlmer disaster, in some cases bodies were never recovered, or only body fragments were found for identification purposes. Some bodies were awaiting transport to other countries. Therefore there was no idea of a collective funeral, and thus no collective cortege; the procession was a semi-independent mourning rite, such as we are familiar with from the Dutch Memorial Day observances. The term 'detached ritual' appears apposite here.

(g) At the same time there was identifiable adaption of ecclesiastical ritual, because there are parallels with traditional funeral corteges, from the home to the church and church to cemetery. It is noteworthy that the later annual memorial processions in the Bijlmer have used the Taibah mosque as their point of departure, and not the sports centre of the first procession.[15]

(h) Although strictly speaking the disaster with the SLM aeroplane in Paramaribo does not fit within our study – not only did the crash take place outside The Netherlands, but it is also outside our self-imposed time frame, namely in 1989 – there are clear parallels. The SLM disaster involved primarily Surinamese living in Surinam and The Netherlands. Many of those involved in the organisation of the mourning ceremonies in 1992 had been directly involved in the mourning services in the RAI in 1989, and were still involved in the annual commemoration for the SLM victims. The scale of the Bijlmer disaster was different: there were fewer dead to mourn, but the whole of The Netherlands mourned with them. The live television broadcast was watched by nearly half of all Dutch adults, and could also be followed live in Surinam and the Dutch Antilles.

---

[15] After the disaster the sports centre was identified as a location with the capacity to receive a large number of people, as necessary. On the day of the silent procession it functioned as the assembly and stepping-off point. A week later it was the site of in interreligious memorial service which was intended primarily for Bijlmer residents themselves.

(i) Despite this, there are hardly any culture-specific elements from Surinam that can be pointed to as having defined the public mourning ceremony. They were present, but not dominant, only there as part of a mix with other elements. For instance, a group of Surinamese women sat in the audience during the memorial service, by their attire clearly recognisable as designated mourners, but in the mixed service they had no function. The same was true for other group-lined expressions of grief. In the week preceding the official ceremony the television now and then showed brief reports of various denominational gatherings. For instance, a church service was organised in the Roman Catholic chapel in the Begijnhof in the old centre of Amsterdam, a 'service of consolation' was held by the Moravian Brethren and the Evangelical Lutheran congregation, and the Eucharist was celebrated in 'De Nieuwe Stad'. From interviews it appears that in the course of dealing with their grief, many Surinamese later developed their own 'back room rituals'.

(j) Parallel with the collective rituals in Amsterdam, we can also list the tolling of church bells especially for the Bijlmer that Sunday; many flags were flown at half mast; and there were special prayers of intercession made in the churches during their Sunday services. In Amsterdam that evening the Concertgebouw Orchestra played a memorial concert, observing a minute of silence.[16] In Willemstad, Curaçao, a mourning service was also held, and flags were flown at half mast.

(k) Although in the days following the Sunday memorial the reactions heard and read were mostly positive, people in general found that the Dutch commentary broadcast live with the various ceremonies was insensitive and distant. The Netherlands appeared impressed with the comfort gained through the multicultural mourning rituals – 'The Netherlands at its broadest' – but a bit ashamed of the businesslike commentator's voice accompanying the television images, and of the ignorance and awkwardness of Dutch interviewers. Later there would be criticism from non-native Dutch circles of the predominantly 'white' disaster response. Apparently Dutch journalists and social workers were not yet really attuned to the multicultural society.[17]

---

[16] The programme included the 'Adagio for Orchestra' by Otto Ketting and the 'Marcia Funèbre' from the Third Symphony by Ludwig van Beethoven. Midway through the concert the concertmaster, Jaap van Zweden, spoke briefly and requested a minute of silence.

[17] Various articles appeared on this later, such as ALWART, MACNACK, PENGEL-FORST & SARUCCO: 'Rouw en rituelen na de vliegramp' (1993); DE JONG & VAN SCHAIK:

'Colourful Netherlands'

In later commentaries, people showed themselves pleasantly surprised at the sensitive words of the then Dutch Prime Minister Ruud Lubbers. Regarding 'colourful Netherlands' he said,

Many, very many, of those affected came to our country from elsewhere – from Surinam, from the Antilles, but also from other countries. Colourful Netherlands. Today we all recognise our link with the victims, with their family members, their friends and acquaintances. Thus the accident, the disaster, is also a message for us, that we share the grief and cares of our fellow countrymen, that we will continue to share them. Only through all this grief and misery can a colourful Netherlands become a reality.

He ended this portion of his speech with words that had the character of a prayer, the prayer with which he had also opened his address:

It is again Sunday in The Netherlands. This morning many, very many, here in Amsterdam, in the Bijlmer, in the whole of the country, went to church to pray, to share the grief in churches, or shared it in mosques or synagogues, or just at home, or outside in silence on the street. Sunday, the Lord's Day. But the words of Psalm 22 are also true for Allah and Jahweh:

> Be not far from me,
> for trouble is near,
> for there is none to help.

My God, why? What unfathomable sorrow! Come to our aid! Help those who have lost their loved ones. Give strength, a sense of your presence.

The address by Mrs. Liberia-Peters was also permeated by a deep religiosity. That heads of governments would profile themselves in this way appears to have made a deep impression with their fellow believers. These were indeed words in which the pain and shock could be heard, and which responded to it with no easy certainties.

Although later in this chapter, in the analysis of the memorial service in Eindhoven after the aeroplane crash there in 1996 (see 3.2, below), it will

---

'Culturele en religieuze aspecten' (1994); HAMERSMA: 'Naamloze vermisten' (1992); VAN DUIN: 'Een beschouwing van het 'rampjaar' 1992' (1993); WOUTERS: *Er valt een gat...* (1993). Following the disaster in Enschede the experience gained from the Bijlmer was called upon, in the person of The Rev. Mr. Ruff, a Moluccan clergyman of the NaBij Foundation (*Na*bestaanden *Bij*lmerramp = Next-of-kin Bijlmer disaster), and others.

be seen that the use of Biblical language in collective mourning observances may encounter resistance from some, here it is the inclusivity, and not the choice of words from a Psalm by the Prime Minister, that is our subject.

Lubbers did not invent the term 'colourful Netherlands'. It is a term that already had wide currency when he used it in his address. It is possible that with this term he was making a conscious connection with that earlier disaster at the airport at Zanderij, Surinam, where many members of a Dutch-Surinamese football team, the 'Colourful Eleven', were among the fatalities. It is also possible that he saw the situation in the Bijlmer on that Sunday in 1992 entirely on its own. But he created links that called up positive associations, despite 'this grief and misery'. The Rev. Douwe N. Wouters, who published a book based on his experiences after the Bijlmer disaster, writes,

'Colourful Netherlands' suggests that the arrival of people of colour in The Netherlands has enriched the society. 'Colourful' has its own attractiveness, over against 'colourless' or 'monotone' – that is to say, white. The Prime Minister also left no doubt about who he had in mind. He specifies the very many who had come from Surinam, the Antilles and many other countries. Their coming has enriched the composition of the original population. Such an assertion can only have a salutary influence in a time characterised by increasing hatred of foreigners. It is not necessary to list examples of countries which have been torn apart by racial troubles. In the present situation it is indeed more difficult to list places where peoples of different backgrounds live together peacefully and acknowledge each other's ethnic identity… Against the background of smouldering racial delusions the selection of this term by our Prime Minister was all the more remarkable. 'Colourful Netherlands' indicates that a diversity of colour is one of the things that defines the present identity of The Netherlands.[18]

It is apparent, however, that the connections that Lubbers made in his address do not involve only various skin colours. He made an explicit reference to cultures and religions. With the term 'colourful Netherlands' he was referring not only to a multiracial Netherlands but especially to a multicultural and religiously pluralistic Netherlands. Grief drives people apart, but grief also links people together. What was important on the memorial Sunday in Amsterdam was not the differences, but 'our Bijlmer'.[19] Whatever the rhetoric of such a term is worth – and what it

---

[18] WOUTERS: *Er valt een gat...* (1993) 140.
[19] As in the words of Burgomaster Ed van Thijn, in his address in the RAI.

later appeared to be worth when the difficult negotiations between those involved and official institutions dragged on for years – for the duration of that one day what was important was 'our Bijlmer'. The colourfulness of The Netherlands appears to have something enriching for Amsterdam. At the same time, it must be clear that such a one-day *communitas* is not free of patronising, even neo-colonial aspects – all those 'others' bring their tribute to colour into our colourness, especially when it comes to mourning rituals![20]

A realistic assessment of human behaviour may counsel reserve with regard to the actual degree of solidarity, but this must not however keep us from viewing three aspects of the Bijlmer memorial in general as successful. There was a well thought-through mixture of elements without it coming across as artificial. It appeared to have struck the right tone. In the light of emerging rituals – with regard to which Grimes is by no means the only one to point out that much new ritual is 'not yet dry behind the ears' – it must be acknowledged that particularly the memorial service came across as remarkably 'mature'. There was a lot happening, it was a varied presentation, but there was a confident alternation of individuality and unity, of first and second language, of verbal language and musical language.

Comparatively speaking – that is to say, comparing the Bijlmer rituals with the mourning repertoire surrounding later disasters in The Netherlands – it can be said that the authorities were not dominant, either organisationally or in the performance. The silent procession was not hierarchic in structure, as later in Enschede, but on the contrary was left remarkably free. The stepping-off point was a sports hall, not a city hall. Everybody was mixed together. Everyone placed their flowers in their own way.

The large memorial service was, on the other hand, extremely structured. Speakers and musicians kept to the time schedule. There were no angry words directed toward Schiphol airport and its continued expansions,[21] nor toward Dutch asylum policy, nor the City of Amsterdam. However, no representatives from the airlines were included in the official programme. The only reference to the cause, or the 'perpetrators' or 'guilty parties', if one prefers, lay in the discreet presence of the Israeli

---

[20] As in the quote from Thomas, in his book *La mort Africaine*, from an 'old, wise man' from Chad, who says, 'Les Blancs connaissent toutes choses. Une seule affaire leur échappe: la mort.' (cited in DE JONG & VAN SCHAIK: 'Culturele en religieuze aspecten' (1994) 302).

[21] The neighbourhood affected, the Bijlmer, lay under one of the incoming flight paths for this, the most important Dutch airport.

cabinet minister, who memorialised his four dead countrymen, the three crew members and their one passenger. With the first memorials for later aeroplane crashes (Faro, Waddenzee and Eindhoven) the ritual role of the airline sector would be larger.[22]

There were no candles, no list of names was read, and no stuffed toys were placed in those first days. The flowers came in all the colours of the rainbow. The balloons were generally black. The silent procession was held during the day, not in the evening. The monument at the site of the memorial rites developed spontaneously, and was built up around the tree by the residents themselves. It was not something from the studio of an artist, but a tree that stood there already, a tree that gradually became a natural focus.[23]

This is the official account, the version which was made public. The story of the individual processes of coping with the disaster can be found in bits and pieces, scattered through an enormous number of reports and articles. From these it appears, among other things, that the evaluation given by The Rev. Nico ter Linden, "everybody feels better for it", while it is perhaps the case for many, is not true for all, as asserted.[24] Letters

---

[22] Later, once the process of investigation into the cause and responsibility had begun, it appears that the next of kin and survivors generally preferred to organise the annual commemorations 'among themselves', without dignitaries (verbal report on the commemoration in Eindhoven after the Hercules disaster of 1996).

[23] In this section, with the emphasis on multiculturality, it is perhaps fitting to recall the many such 'trees of remembrance' or 'memorial trees' around the world. Later on, such trees would be planted after disasters in The Netherlands, as was the case after the *legionella* disaster. Mention should also be made here of the action by the Dutch Cancer Fund to plant a tree for every deceased cancer patient in a large park (the 'Cancer Woods'). Elsewhere in the world such trees are often not intentionally planted as part of a memorial site, but a memorial cult arises spontaneously around an existing tree, in about the same way as around a streetlight pole after a traffic accident. The tree in the Bijlmer, 'the tree that witnessed everything', is an example of such a spontaneous monument.

[24] In the article 'De kerk als reddingsboei bij rampen' (The church as life buoy in disasters), in the *Algemeen Dagblad*, Oct. 10, 1994, Ter Linden says, among other things, "Certain stimuli demand a religious response. Even with secularised people who are not schooled in religious perceptions, under particular circumstances such stimuli can lead to religious acts or feelings. At a wedding you can perform funny sketches; in the presence of death you are struck dumb. It is not easy to organise something. But there is always a church service available... With the Bijlmer disaster half The Netherlands was sitting in front of their television. The broadcast of the silent procession and the mourning service had high ratings. But, in the last analysis, it was also a very comforting happening... The Prime Minister did not speak there as a priest. That is why we had the imam, the clergyman, the choir for the Ghanaians. And everything taken together, everybody feels better for it."

to the editor which were published in various national newspapers also contain critical notes. Moreover, experiences of social workers of ethnic background demonstrate that while collectively experienced sympathy did afford great comfort, various culturally defined ideas and practices surrounding death were complicated by the nature of the disaster: the absence of some bodies; bodies recovered only in fragments; some dead having no official status, even no name.

In the article by De Jong and Van Schaik, "Culturele en religieuze aspecten van rouw- en traumaverwerking naar aanleiding van de Bijlmerramp" (Cultural and religious aspects of grief and trauma processing on the basis of the Bijlmer disaster), four such culturally defined complications are listed: (1) the fear of spirits when the deceased meets their end suddenly or violently, or when the burial is not carried out in the culturally specified manner, or if the body is not found whole, or when several immediate relatives can not be present; (2) the closing rituals when the period of mourning ends; (3) the physical closeness of the deceased, and the advice, often imposed by authorities in the Bijlmer, not to view or touch the body; (4) rituals to break the old connections with the deceased, such as, for instance, by destroying his or her personal possessions, by no longer speaking their name, or by moving house.[25]

Precisely when death is so sudden, and seems so unbefitting and senseless, when it comes so literally out of the thin air, people often reach back for old identities, and old rituals, such as Winti.[26] Typical expressions of this would be the remarks, "Christianity is my front room and Winti is my back room", and "I pray to Mary if things are going well and I pray to mother Aisa if things are not going so well".[27] Forces and powers from Africa were also experienced in the midst of the concrete of the Bijlmer. Such 'back room belief', which after the Bijlmer disaster expressed itself in many personal 'back room rituals', was not really made present in the public memorials. Moreover, many lost their homes, and

---

[25] DE JONG & VAN SCHAIK: 'Culturele en religieuze aspecten' (1994).

[26] Winti is a cult found among the Creole population in Surinam, among others, in which the belief in supernatural beings is central. The cult arose from religions and cults which were brought along by black slaves from West Africa. In contrast to other Afro-American religions and cults, the Winti cult has hardly any Christian elements.

[27] Cited in WOUTERS: *Er valt een gat...* (1993) 172.

their personal possessions. The remains of the two apartment blocks were sealed off, and only with special permission and under special accompaniment were some later allowed back to collect personal possessions. In total, 400 households were evacuated. In this upheaval the customary personal rituals could not be carried out in the manner in which people would have performed them under normal circumstances. This raises the question of to what extent the very innermost circle of those affected really benefited from the large-scale, structured memorials, and if such mass rituals are not a self-justifying exercise on the part of the wider community.

Multicultural mourning rituals

In The Netherlands the mourning rituals of various ethnic groups had played a role at the level of policy for quite some time. Jewish cemeteries had for centuries been a visible manifestation of 'other' religious customs in this area. Although even prior to 1960 small groups sporadically insisted on carrying out their own mourning rituals, the complications that could arise from this only came to light after the first wave of immigration. Numerous memoranda suggested that attention be given to the importance of their dead being buried, cremated and memorialised according to their customs. Handbooks appeared for clergy, medical workers and undertakers.[28] Only in the 1990s did books appear on a larger scale in The Netherlands presenting a range of burial and mourning customs from various minorities present in the society, sometimes accompanied with striking photographs.[29] Years before that the variety of funeral rites was a regularly recurring subject for documentaries in newspapers, weekly magazines and on TV.

When after the Bijlmer disaster a public memorial service had to be organised in Amsterdam in less than a week, a collage was created. Following democratic principles as many groups as possible were represented

---

[28] See SPRUIT & SORGEDRAGER, *De dood onder ogen* (1986) (published well before the disaster); FORTUIN, VAN KILSDONK et al: *Afscheid nemen van onze doden* (1988). For historians the publications of Ph. Ariès are particularly of importance. Cf. ARIÈS: *L'Homme devant la mort* (1987); IDEM: *Western attitudes* (1977).

[29] For more recent publications, see for instance TIEMERSMA (ed.): *De vele gezichten van de dood* (1996); BOT: *Een laatste groet* (1998) and PESSIRERON: *Rouwen in zeven 'Nederlandse' culturen* (1999).

in the programme, so that those directly affected would all feel represented. In addition to the fundamental principle of equal representation, we can identify another rule of thumb: discretion. Colourful Netherlands showed its religiosity in subdued colours. Whatever expressivity had found its way into collective ceremonies, or would find its way into the separate gatherings, in the collective memorial the separate groups mixed into the whole. While the various non-Christian believers would be represented by their religious leaders, there was no priest or Protestant clergyman among the speakers. And although the various churches in the Bijlmer played an active role in sheltering the homeless and offering counselling, they did not appear as speakers in the collective service. This discreet reticence on the part of ecclesiastical authorities certainly played a role in the general positive evaluation of the Amsterdam memorial rituals. At the same time there was no dominance of African elements, although there were many black participants in both the silent procession and the service. It may be concluded that no single ethnic or religious group appropriated this disaster at the expense of others.

Yet it was precisely this colourful expression by which the participants and television viewing audience in The Netherlands were pleasantly surprised. First, there was the ritual enrichment through expressions that until then had hardly been connected with mourning: drums, dance, the colour red, the varied musicality and textuality, the plurality of language. Second was the informality, so entirely different from the national commemorations for the dead of the Second World War. Everyone mourned in their own manner. Participants mixed with one another. Everyone laid their flowers for themselves. The black balloons were released at random times. During the mass memorial service children slept on their parents' laps, ate candy out of bags, sucked their thumb and look around. Third there was the sense of mass, positive mass, of solidarity, not only with the dead but also with the living. For a longer or shorter moment 'they' became 'we'. Fourth, the event was pleasing theatre. In both the silent procession and the service there was much to feed the senses. There was an alternation of looking, listening and being carried along by the many voices and multicultural expressions of condolence. However harrowing the cause was, collective mourning can apparently do something for the soul and the senses.

This was the first occasion in a long time that The Netherlands collectively participated in national mourning, on the street, during the

memorial service, and at home through the television.[30] In the preceding
years there had been no occasion for it. The SLM disaster of 1989, the
previously discussed crash of an aeroplane at Zanderij airport, near Paramaribo in Surinam, had been the occasion for a massive gathering in
Amsterdam, but white Netherlanders had hardly been touched by it. The
SLM memorial remained to a great extent 'theirs'. The Bijlmer disaster
was 'ours'.

While, quite independent of the Bijlmer, all sorts of experimental
forms surrounding death could be found in Dutch society in that period,
such alternative funerals remained limited to a rather small trailblazing
group. Such events could be seen now and then on television news
reports, however, and in general there was a tendency to deal with death
in more inventive and personal ways. More than one source pointed to
the gradual changes in death notices in the newspapers, as well as developments in the fields of counselling for the dying and funeral ritual.[31]

As of that point, however, these developments did not appear to have
involved the ethnic groups present in The Netherlands. Immigrants who
had settled here for economic or political reasons initially did not have
the status of conveyors of culture, and were not immediately seen as
potentially enriching for Dutch society. For example, it was precisely
from the Bijlmer that voices had been raised in the years before the disaster that while all sorts of cultural institutions did fulfil a trailblazing role
in bringing non-Western musicians to The Netherlands for several performances around the country, they paid little if any attention to the
wealth of musical expression on their own doorstep, in communities of

---

[30] The term 'national mourning' is not used here in its official sense. The previous
time that official national mourning was proclaimed in The Netherlands was for the
death of Queen Wilhelmina in 1962. National mourning was not officially a factor with
previous large-scale disasters such as the Great Flood of 1953.

[31] For the developments in death notices, see among others FRANKE: *De dood in het
leven van alledag* (1985). In the first part of this book the author discusses two centuries
of death notices, through about 1985. We must also mention here the phenomenon
whereby, in the case of national disasters, beginning with the Bijlmer disaster, both
regional and national newspapers are glutted with condolence advertisements from all
sorts of organisations and businesses wishing to express their sympathy. It is often hard
to imagine any direct connection between these businesses and the victims. In the aftermath of the fireworks disaster in Enschede (2000), after several days this deluge forced
the local newspaper, *de Tubantia*, to take only death notices from those directly affected.
Critical observations had been made concerning this phenomenon of a flood of condolence notices already in the case of the Bijlmer disaster.

foreigners such as the Bijlmer. The collective Bijlmer memorial made the fact that all sorts of such musical traditions were being kept alive in The Netherlands visible for a much larger group. That their mourning rituals too could be an enrichment, and not only a complication for public health and social policy, also became clear to many after 1992.

The multicultural mourning ritual of the Bijlmer disaster was not the only factor in this. Well before this an uneasiness about the Western manner of dealing with death was being expressed in all sorts of ways. Since the founding of their discipline cultural anthropologists had considered the handling of death in other cultures as one of their most important foci. While scholars in academic circles viewed the mourning rituals of others as a fascinating object of study, this had hardly any impact on their own usages. Even in circles of personally interested intellectuals and esoteric practitioners, among whom alternative ideas about dying, death and reincarnation did find an entry, the primary interest was in the concepts and not in applying other practices themselves.

Through Dutch connections with Indonesia and Surinam and the presence of individuals from these parts of the colonial empire in The Netherlands,[32] there were gradual accommodations here and there that went some way to meeting their cultural requirements regarding burial or cremation. When the first Hindus and Muslims in our country had to provide for their dead, it was seen primarily as a question of policy. The adaptations and easing of restrictions they asked for were seen as an obligation, something the Dutch were required to grant as a matter of political correctness, rather than as cultural enrichment or a blending of cultural practices.

Through ever increasing cross-cultural mobility, tourism and the international publishing market, and in general through the West's own cultural discomfort and the loss of idea of self-evident Western superiority, at the same time however there also gradually arose in other parts of Dutch society a practical, personal interest in the manner in which others dealt with that unpleasant fact of death. It was in that context that the books of Elisabeth Kübler-Ross and the Tibetan Sogyal Rinpoche could become worldwide best sellers.[33]

[32] Indonesia was a possession of The Netherlands until 1949, Surinam until 1975.
[33] KÜBLER-ROSS: *Death* (1975); IDEM: *On death and dying* (1993); RINPOCHE: *The Tibetan book* (1998).

When in the Bijlmer rituals a glimpse was to be caught here and there of other manners of coping with death, The Netherlands was ready for it. While the really 'other' was kept discretely obscured in the public rituals, something of it still showed through. At that moment it appeared that a large part of Dutch society were farther along than the television commentators, for whom Grimes's dictum was still valid: " 'We' are at the center, 'they' are on the circumference."[34] Although people of non-Dutch background were involved in later disasters too, chiefly in Enschede, and although the country felt sympathy on a mass scale for the earthquakes in Turkey, and showed interest in the memorial services in the mosques, the mixed character of the Bijlmer memorial has remained unique. For a moment, the fact that multiculturality could mean mutual enrichment, even in the case of death, became visible and tangible.

3.2. SEARCHING FOR WORDS: THE 'RELIGIOUS, LITURGICAL' PART OF THE MEMORIAL SERVICE AFTER THE HERCULES DISASTER (AEROPLANE CRASH, EINDHOVEN, 1996) (P. POST)

The national memorial service after the Hercules disaster

On Monday, July 15, 1996, a Belgian Hercules C-130 military transport plane brought members of the brass band of the Royal Dutch Air Force back after a performance in Modena, northern Italy, to the air base at Eindhoven, in the southern Netherlands. During the landing the aeroplane crashed and burst into flames. It has since become clear that immediately before, during and just after the accident a large number of things went wrong: an inexperienced crew, swarms of birds, air controllers who did not immediately notify the fire service that in addition to the four-man crew there were another 37 people aboard, an emergency exit that could not be opened, a fire service that arrived too late and made no attempt to enter the plane. Four Belgian crew members and 28 members of the brass band died in the crash and blaze. Another two would die subsequently. Ultimately there were four survivors.

In the midst of the familiar memorial repertoire that has been (and will be) repeatedly noted in this book (condolence registers, minutes of silence, flags at half mast, business closures and postponed events, tolling bells, expressions of condolence from governmental institutions and the

---

[34] GRIMES: *Reading, writing and ritualizing* (1993) 78.

Royal House, funerals, military memorial ritual in barracks, memorial services in the locality, construction of a memorial monument, initiatives to organise annual commemorations, etc.), in the case of this disaster there was an official memorial service especially for public consumption which also had an important place in the structure of collective and less large-scale rites. Because of the military context of the disaster this was an exceptional memorial service. The service – although the organisers spoke more generally of a 'ceremony' – was prepared and directed with extreme care. Those involved would later reveal how complex and delicate the structuring of the final scenario was, how variants of all sorts were considered and discussed. Within the rather austere ceremony there was an effort to give as many as possible of the involved countries, services, military units, churches and life philosophies and international, national, regional and local authorities, as well as the next of kin, a fitting, balanced place and role in the ritual.

The national memorial service was held on the morning of July 17 in a storage hanger especially adapted for the occasion, on the terrain of the military air base at Eindhoven. The ceremony, termed a solemn observance, was broadcast live on television and lasted one hour and four minutes.

There are a number of reasons that the service deserves separate examination. First, there is the military setting already mentioned, through which the service was linked with a very important type of profane/secular ritual, that of the military services, court and nation. This is the type of ritual which in our discussion of the concept of rituality above (1.2.2) has been characterised as political ritual, the genre that Bell designates as civil ritual, where power, hierarchy and identity are or primary importance.[35] Later in this study, in the discussion of the phenomenon of the silent procession and the more general sketch of ritual dynamics in our culture as a context for disaster ritual, this will be taken up again.[36] Further, the strongly composed nature of the ritual is interesting, the way it is constructed and the relationship among the actors and participants, between distance and involvement. The service also provides reason for further reflection about 'adequacy', and the relation of the fundamental ritual dimensions of word, act, actors, time and space.[37]

---

[35] BELL: *Ritual* (1997) 94ff.

[36] See 3.5 below; see also Chapt. 2, above.

[37] For a summary of the perspective of adequate and inductive ritual, see LUKKEN: *Rituelen in overvloed* (1999) Chapt. 6, 213-232 and IDEM: 'De liturgie rond een overledene' (2000).

More specifically we will devote attention to what commentators called 'a three-part, almost religious ceremony', 'the almost religious part' or 'the religious, liturgical part' of the service: the contributions of the Humanist advisor and the Roman Catholic and Protestant chaplains in the middle of the ceremony.

As the structure of this case, we have opted for first giving a short and general descriptive and evocative sketch of the service. We will next focus in on the semi-religious section, in which we will reproduce the three addresses, with their texts and prayers, in their entirety. Then will follow a series of observations arising from this religious-liturgical component, but also with regard to the service as a whole.

Structure of the ceremony

The service took place late in the morning in a hanger on the military air base at Eindhoven. The large space had been substantially altered for the purpose. A new floor covering of grey carpet tiles had been laid, and the walls were hung with dark blue curtains (made available by the commercial airline Martinair, which had previously used them at the memorial service for the Faro disaster (aeroplane crash, Portugal, 1992)). The 32 coffins were arranged at the front, with 32 candles, and separated from the rest of the space with ropes. Flowers and the national flag lay on the coffins, and more candles stood in front of them (including one from the residents involved in the Bijlmer disaster). There were also floral pieces and potted shrubs in larger and smaller sizes. The over 600 seats were arranged in rows in massive blocks with wide aisles running lengthwise, and smaller aisles crosswise. A military band sat separately at one side, at an angle to the blocks of chairs. Dark colours predominated, and there were nurses on hand for every block of seats who provided water and other assistance as needed. The seating was carefully assigned. Front and centre were seats for various dignitaries, representatives of the Dutch Royal House (Prince Willem-Alexander in the uniform of the Army), representatives of the national governments of The Netherlands, Belgium and Italy, representatives of the various divisions of the armed forces, and of national, regional and local authorities. The lectern was central, both in the organisation of the service and the space, constructed of two platforms three steps high placed together, with Belgian and Dutch flags at half mast on each side. A master of ceremonies (Colonel Winkelmolen) briefly introduced each component of the ritual, indicated who the speakers were and who they represented, and indicated what acts were required (standing, military attention).

The order of service was as follows:

— instrumental music (by a combined military band from the Army and Air Force);
— opening, with the entrance of the Crown Prince and representatives of the government;
— instrumental music: 'Abide with Me';
— announcement by the master of ceremonies of three addresses;
— three addresses from the governments of The Netherlands and Belgium: Prime Minister Kok and Minister of Defense Voorhoeve of The Netherlands and Minister of Defence Poncelet of Belgium; after the end of the speeches the speakers bowed briefly to the left and right of the lectern in respect to the coffins arranged there;
— the 'religious, liturgical section', led by representatives of the spiritual care in the armed forces: Humanistic advisor Van der Kolk (Air Force), Roman Catholic chaplain Meurkens (Army) and Protestant chaplain Paulsen (Army);
— request by the master of ceremonies for the audience to rise;
— announcement by the master of ceremonies of the reading of the names, minute of silence, and Last Post;
— reading of the names of the dead by Chaplain Meurkens;
— minute of silence;
— sounding of the Last Post;
— announcement by the master of ceremonies of the national anthems of Belgium and The Netherlands, and an order to uniformed personnel to stand to attention;
— national anthems of The Netherlands and Belgium (instrumental)
— music (instrumental);
— invitation to Dutch Crown Prince Willem-Alexander to lead the procession past the coffins;
— procession paying final respects, with musical background;
— recession.

The 'religious, liturgical' section

The central part of the service was what has been termed the 'religious' or 'liturgical' section, the input from the three religious advisors. It was a service within the service, so to speak, in which the Protestant chaplain led his own service, a nearly classic liturgy with *votum* and opening, two Scripture readings, the Lord's Prayer and closing prayer. This 'religious' section, which took up seventeen minutes, can be seen as the hinge that closed the 'service of the Word' with the political addresses and bridged into the second part of the ritual, in which words were replaced by acts and non-verbal expression received a place. The texts are reproduced literally;[38]

Without any introduction, statement or explanation, Mr. Van der Kolk, a Humanist advisor, read a poem:[39]

> Stone is strong, but iron breaks it.
> Iron is strong, but fire melts it.
> Fire is strong, but water extinguishes it.
> Water is strong, but sun evaporates it.
> The sun is strong, but cloud hides it.
> The cloud is strong, but wind drives it onward,
> The wind is strong, but man can withstand it.
> Man is strong, but death strikes him down.
> Death is strong, but love is stronger than death.
> Love never passes away.

The Rev. N. Meurkens, Roman Catholic chaplain, took more time and read an text written out in its entirety:

> Abide with us, for it is toward evening, and the day is far spent. Dear friends, this gathering on this intensely sad morning seems unreal, illusory. What is going on here? An unutterable suffering has come over us all, the fibre of our being has been touched at its very deepest. Last Monday, July 15, along toward evening, life fell still for them. Fate caught up our loved ones and took them away in the space of a breath. Suddenly the effervescent melody of life, the fanfare of all our being, evaporated from them. They were messengers of flowing music, they brought forth homage and praise to all that lives and breathes with dance and drum, with strings and flute, with beating tymbals and sounding cymbals. They were bringers of joy in the often difficult journey of discovery in this terrestrial life, creating

---

[38] The translations were made from unaltered transcripts of recordings, and reflect the oral character of the presentations. There were a series of wordplays in Dutch in Meurkens's speech which it has not been possible to fully reflect in English. In Paulsen's presentation, where he used the Dutch *Groot Nieuws* translation, the comparable *Good News Bible* has been used for the English.

[39] As of this writing, the authors have not been able to determine the source of the poem.

space and relaxation in the tension of our society, of military organisation, offering perspective through their melodious playing, thereby granting sense to, and giving us a fancy for the disciplined contacts we all have with one another.

So senseless, speaking in human terms, so beyond our grasp, so incomprehensible. Why should this have happened to them, falling from the highs of life into the depths of death?

Stillness and silence speak volumes. Our grief is intense, we are beaten people, not just those who are left behind, but also those who stand beside those who have been wounded, and for whom the way to the future will not be easy. This is the down side of life, to be snatched away, so vital, often in the unfolding bloom of their life, as the psalmist wrote centuries ago, "Their days are like grass, they flourish like a flower of the field, then the wind passes over it and it is gone."

We hardly have any words for it, this brutal reality is hard as a rock in the midst of the delicate fragility of all of our lives. I see them yet before my eyes, when they were called up and sent out to the former Yugoslavia, as professional musicians to stand next to our men who were sent out there, showing compassion for them in an inimitable, sensitive manner, so precisely their own. Through their music they were wonderful travelling companions for their colleagues in often radical, existential crisis situations.

Our beloved colleagues of the band, and our four colleagues from the Belgian Air Force are no longer among us; they have flown away to distances beyond our conception. At the same time they are now more than ever among us and remain anchored in our memory, because they have rendered a creative service to so many in such a wonderful way. From pianissimo to fortissimo, they formed the often swinging stave of the Royal Army, and were always able to creatively and vitally make music of even the hardest notes they encountered in that institution.

They have become riders on a road that can only be trodden lightfootedly. There are so many light things in life: springtime, the blackbird, Mozart, love, a girlfriend's eye, dance, yes, this brass band. In this hour they are intensely with us in our hearts. They remain close to us in grief and tears, in the deep realisation that they are now in peace and in the undying light playing before God's countenance.

In the name of my sisters and brothers in faith, I bear witness that God is our life, our future, our eternal light. We testify to our deep sympathy with you, dear friends, and will remember your loved ones and our colleagues in the solidarity of the living and dead in the annual requiem service in 's Hertogenbosch, celebrated by the Military Vicar for the Dutch Armed Forces.

May you rest in peace, delightful music makers, beloved musical mates! It is as Kahlil Gibran wrote,

"You have sung for me in my aloneness, and I of your longing have built
a tower in the sky...
If in the twilight of memory we should meet once more, we shall speak
again together, and you shall sing to me a deeper song."
Dear friends, hopefully we will find consolation and comfort one another
in this unfathomable vision of the future:
"I saw a new heaven and a new earth... and He shall wipe all tears from
our eyes, and there shall be no more death, neither sorrow, nor crying, neither shall there be any more pain, for the former things have passed away."

The Rev. Paulsen, Protestant chaplain, lead a small liturgy, as it were.
Most of it he had written down, but here and there sections were impro-
vised. He always had a Bible in hand, from which he read several passages.

Once again our branch is suddenly roughly confronted with the transience
of human existence, with the fragility of our being human. It was such a
short time ago that we lost Colonel Engelen, and now once again it appears
here how persons can totally unexpectedly come to stand before the eternal and exchange the worldly for the everlasting.
Monday evening I had gone to bed very early at Camp Heumersoord. My
intention was to walk with a group of National Guard reservists in the Four
Day Walk at Nijmegen.[40] Just before midnight I was awakened and given the
terrible news that 32 people had died, of whom 28 were from our barracks.
My first reaction was: there are no words for this, here I fall silent, but that
silence did not last long. Very quickly many thoughts forced themselves
upon me: how could this have happened? Why did this happen to us? And
you, the families, will surely have thought, why my son, my daughter, my
wife, my husband, partner, friend or girlfriend? These are questions for
which I have no answer.
Although I cannot influence the depth of your pain, grief or anger about
this terrible event, I would still read some words of comfort from the Bible,
God's word, for you. You will find the first reading, the twenty-third Psalm,
in the Old Testament, the collection by David. I have chosen the Good
News Bible with the translation in the vernacular:

The Lord is my shepherd;
I have everything I need.
He lets me rest in fields of green grass
and leads me to quiet pools of fresh water.

---

[40] The Four Day Walk at Nijmegen is a long-distance hiking event spread across four
days, which draws international participation. Traditionally many military personnel from
The Netherlands and other countries join in the event.

He gives me new strength
He guides me in the right paths, as he has promised.
Even if I go through the deepest darkness,
I will not be afraid, Lord, for you are with me.
Your shepherd's rod and staff protect me.
You prepare a banquet for me,
where all my enemies can see me;
you welcome me as an honoured guest
and fill my cup to the brim.
I know that your goodness and love
will be with me all my life
And your house will be my home as long as I live.

Then, improvising, without written notes:

My thoughts go out especially to the fourth verse: "Even though I go through the deepest darkness, I will not be afraid, Lord, because you are with me". What the Minister of Defense also said this morning, that you have need of much strength, I agree with that, and I would in fact ask the Christians of The Netherlands and Belgium to pray for strength for you, who must bear this terrible suffering. That God's reality and truth may be in your life, to experience strength in this terrible event. That is also my prayer that it may be a reality for you.

Returning to his notes:

I would still want to read from the New Testament, the second and later part of the New Testament, from the letter of Paul to the Christians at Thessalonica, I Thes. 4, verses 13 through 18, what I hope will be words of comfort for all of you:
"Our brothers and sisters, we want you to know the truth about those who have died, so that you will not be sad, as those are who have no hope. We believe that Jesus died and rose again, and so we believe that God will take back with Jesus those who have died believing in him.
What we are teaching you now is the Lord's teaching: we who are alive on the day the Lord comes will not go ahead of those who have died. There will be a shout of command, and the archangel's voice, the sound of God's trumpet, and the Lord himself will come down from heaven. Those who have died believing in Christ will rise to life first; then we who are living in that time will be gathered up along with them in the clouds to meet the Lord in the air. And so we will always be with the Lord. So then, encourage one another with these words."
Finally, I would pray the prayer that the Lord Jesus himself taught us, the prayer from Matthew 6:

"Our Father in heaven, hallowed be your name.
Your kingdom come, your will be done on earth as it is in heaven.
Give us today our daily bread, and forgive us our debts, as we forgive our
debtors.
Do not put us to the test,
and deliver us from the devil.
Because yours is the kingdom and the power and the glory for even and ever.
Amen."

Personal experiences

The accounts of personal experience collected from those involved reveal
a coherent picture. In a general sense the next of kin valued the service.
People also appreciated that all immediate relatives later received a video
recording of the service (with 'In memoriam' on the sleeve). It is true that
most did not consciously evaluate the service at the time; most were still
too numb. People experienced the ritual primarily as a purely military
occasion, a military farewell to which, as not members of the military,
they were outsiders. In hindsight many were annoyed that 'the brass hats'
were allotted such a central place, literally and figuratively, in the ritual.
As an example, many cited the fact that regular people had to be in their
seats well before the commencement of the service, while Crown Prince
Willem-Alexander and his entourage made a separate entrance. They
linked with this the critical question of just who this whole ritual was
really for: the authorities in the armed forces and the national government,
or the victims and their families?

In retrospect there were also questions about the hour chosen. In hindsight, those involved, family and organisers alike, agreed the afternoon
might have been better. The idea at the time was that by holding the ceremony in the morning the families had the afternoon available for memorials in their own circle, at home or elsewhere. But having to confront
the ranks of coffins, closed and anonymous, proved difficult for many.
A viewing for the families only in the morning, where they could have
been by coffin of their loved one, would have been more suitable, followed
by the official collective viewing for the ceremony, and then, for instance,
the service in the afternoon.

The religious portion led by those from the armed forces responsible for
pastoral care was highly valued. The poem read by Van der Kolk made a deep
impression. The meditation by Meurkens was also appreciated by many,
not so much for its content as for the manner in which it was presented, in

which many sensed genuine grief and sympathy ("He spoke holding back tears, you could see that"). There was considerable criticism of the Protestant chaplain, who made too much of a sermon out of it ("That Paulsen confused the lectern with a pulpit"). From information from those who were directly involved with the preparation, it appears that this component was rigorously planned, but that in the end Paulsen did his own thing. The intention was that this section would be a unit: an opening with a prayer, a moment of reflection and meditation through Psalm 150, in which the various musical instruments in the psalm would be connected with the band, and then to close, a reading from Scripture (Psalm 23 was chosen) and the Lord's Prayer. As we saw, the chaplain (a Baptist) violated this structure.

People further spoke of their appreciation for the television crew. They praised their restraint, without intrusive mobile cameras but with cameras set in one place, under a black hood; they also complimented the clothing of the crew, who were all in neat black suits. Later, in viewing the tape, one realised how they had never zoomed in on the audience, on weeping individuals. When there were emotional moments the camera cut to the flowers and candles near the coffins.

Evaluative impressions regarding the ritual

Our evaluative notes can be closely joined with these experiences of those involved. The first thing that strikes one about the service in a general sense is its character. The ritual is very ceremonial in nature, contains definite references to national repertoires such as those of May 4 and 5, with which The Netherlands annually commemorates its war dead and the end of the Second World War, as well as the rigid ritual of the army, dictated by protocol. The attire (many military uniforms), the master of ceremonies and the design of the space underscored the ceremonial atmosphere in which hierarchy, order and protocol held sway. Aside from the division of roles in the ritual (who did what), it was primarily the division of the space which emphasized this aspect. Everything was divided up into separate rectangular blocks, everything had its own proper place in the order of priority, reflecting its identity. Especially the layout of the chairs was telling: ranks forming massive blocks. One might try to imagine other spatial arrangements, with arcs or ellipses, through which – as in the design of modern liturgical arrangements in church spaces – more solidarity and openness might have been expressed. Only the placement of the band which had been assembled for the occasion deviated from this: it was grouped around the director's podium. We have just seen how in the experience of the next of kin all this raised the question of for whose benefit this ritual was primarily intended.

Although it involved a new ritual designed for the occasion, there nevertheless is a sense of a familiar, prescribed scenario that unfolds as a ceremony in 'the traditional way'. Still, this is only apparent, for at many points people are unsure of the ceremony, do not know what to do or where to go. This was particularly visible at the beginning of the procession past the coffins.

The ritual is strongly defined by a tension between distance and engagement. In the language, the addresses, involvement and closeness is evoked in all sorts of phrases; nevertheless, the ritual acts themselves are dominated by the distance of ceremonial and protocol. Those immediately involved, next of kin, family, friends, colleagues from the barracks have no active role or input whatever. Indeed, there are hardly any opportunities for active involvement in the ritual. At the most there is the standing during the reading of the names, the minute of silence, the Last Post and the national anthems, and particularly walking in procession past the coffins. But those present are primarily a seated audience, observers of the whole; they sit, watch and listen, sometimes weep aloud, cry out a couple of times. They were given care if emotions became too much; they were offered a glass of water, or led away behind the scenes. The remarkably formal and emotionless announcements by the master of ceremonies reinforced this experience of distance, although in the file of collected personal experiences no one mentions this point. The strikingly inconspicuous presence of the media, the television up front with cameras shrouded in black and the commentator's voice, geometrically increase this sense of distance.

As a whole, the memorial service is recognisable as such. It is a collage from classic memorial services: addresses by authorities, instrumental music, the reading out of names, a minute of silence, national anthems, a procession. In comparison with other official Dutch memorial services (Bijlmer, Dakota disaster, Enschede, Volendam) it is striking how this occasion was dominated by the word, through the addresses. The 'second language', open, metaphorical language of narrative and poetry, the play of language that is preeminently suited for giving expression to emotion, is almost entirely absent.[41] In this regard, the religious section discussed

---

[41] For language and ritual, see LUKKEN: *Rituelen in overvloed* (1999) 29 and GOVAART: 'Spreken en horen' (2001).

above, and the contribution of the Humanistic advisor to it, stands out. After the service, those directly involved were almost unanimous in their evaluation of this; the poem read by Van der Kolk had far and away the most impact. This impact also certainly had something to do with the direct manner in which the Humanistic advisor presented it: entirely in accord with the rules of ritual play, without announcement, without explanation before or after. Afterwards the anonymous poem – sometimes entitled 'Transience' and sometimes 'Love' – was widely photocopied and hung up in the barracks. It later also became a sort of emblem associated with the Hercules disaster, and was repeated in numerous other memorials for larger and smaller disasters. In May, 2000, the Hercules Disaster Foundation offered the poem to all those involved in the fireworks disaster at Enschede, and it was printed within a black border in the book *De ramp van Enschede*.[42] In addition to this poem, bits of 'second language' were to be found in the words of Meurkens and Paulsen through the Psalms (23 and 150) and the passage from Kahlil Gibran's *The Prophet*.

In summary, it is striking just how strongly dominant the word is within the first part of the ceremony, the genre of the address read from paper, with bits of 'second language' in the semi-religious section as oases. Looking at the relation between word and act, there is a clear transition: after the addresses, in the second part of the ceremony act is given more place, and at the close there is for the first time a real collective act in processing (for our purposes we do not designate standing in silence as spectators as a collective act). We will return to this act shortly.

When we further consider the texts of the speeches, it would appear that in the search for suitable words people often end up in stereotypical phraseology and even cliches. Without calling into question the sincerity of the speakers, it is notable how often someone begins with saying that words are insufficient, that one stands silent in the face of such a terrible event, only to then devote many, many words to the disaster. In addition to stereotypical and also archaic phraseology and word choice (although it does not come through in the translation, the archaic Dutch *aller* for 'all' appeared frequently), we also see the frequent and conscious search for original and surprising expression, words and phrases specifically tailored to this unique situation. It is only rarely that this succeeds;

---

[42] DE LUGT: *De ramp van Enschede* (2000) 106.

rather, it comes across as artificial and forced. We see that very emphatically in Meurkens's contribution, which continually rings changes on the obvious theme of the military band and music: "Suddenly the effervescent melody of life, the fanfare of all our being, evaporated from them"; "From pianissimo to fortissimo, they formed the often swinging stave of the Royal Army, and were always able to creatively and vitally make music of even the hardest notes they encountered in that institution"; "delightful music makers, beloved musical mates!"

Without here further analysing the texts themselves, it can be said that for the Roman Catholic and Protestant chaplains the element of identity, specifically of group identity, played a large role. In their speeches the branch of the armed forces and the barracks are obvious, but even more so, their ecclesiastical identity. Meurkens explicitly mentions the Roman Catholic requiem service celebrated by Military Vicar Punt in Den Bosch, and Paulsen celebrates a small-scale Protestant Service of the Word with the Bible (in the vernacular) in hand.

In addition to the elements of poetry and collective act we have mentioned, there was one specific ritual element that lifted the whole up above a mere matter of protocol: the reading of the names (first and last) of the victims by Chaplain Meurkens after the introductory formula "They have departed from us and we remember them". The ritual of speaking out names is part of a long ritual tradition, every bit as much as the ritual silence and the procession ('défilé') past the coffins.[43] One's name is directly linked with one's identity, and the public naming of a name is a strong expression of that person's presence, despite their absence. The naming of names is no empty or innocuous ritual act. It was (and still is) powerful protest in the context of South American dictatorships where people read out the names of dead or disappeared comrades and then respond with 'Presente!' Schuman describes this rite as an extraordinarily expressive memorial ritual:

The custom stems from the socialist tradition in Latin America. A roll call, as it were, is held at the burial of a *compañero*; the dead answer through the mouths of the living: 'Present!' Their lives may have come to an end; their ideals are taken up and carried forward by others. This is an act of remembrance, par excellence. In it a person or event, though sometimes chronologically far in the past, is in word and gesture brought very close by, made present. We could also say that in remembering, the past is effected

---

[43] For names, see: STOCK: *Poetische Dogmatik* (1995) and IDEM: 'Namen' (2001).

in a literal sense, because it now takes on meaning for the present, and that in turn has a direct effect on the future. This one person who is remembered, this concrete event which we pause to remember: in this way they come to life again and begin to accomplish something in the lives of others.[44]

In Eindhoven the situation was of course different; there was no acclamation, but always a short silence filled with sobbing, sometimes a cry or scream. Naming the dead by name becomes a powerful, emotional litany that through the cadence of the successive names can create a sort of trance among those present. It is a ritual that demands extreme care: one cannot forget or skip a single name. At the Belgian memorial rites after the Dutroux affair names were sometimes accidentally or deliberately left out, provoking fierce emotional outbursts. That happened, for example, during the famous White March in Brussels in 1996, where during the ritual it appeared that the name of Loubna Benaïssa was missing from the sign with the names of dead and missing children. It remained a painful incident despite the fact that the name was quickly added in felt pen. Pronouncing the name correctly is also essential, because here more than any other time engagement can suddenly turn into detachment, and a mispronounced name is experienced as an assault on the identity of the person involved.

In the course of the 1990s names took on an increasingly prominent place in memorial ritual. Names were read at memorial services, they were projected onto large screens (as at Enschede), they are printed on panels present at the rites (Brussels) and ultimately are displayed on monuments. In the case of the Hercules disaster the names return twice in the monument designed by Hans van Eerd, a sculptor from Oirschot, which was dedicated just before the first annual commemoration in 1997. The monument which, thanks principally to the efforts of the municipality of Eindhoven, graces precisely the spot of the crash on the air base itself, consists of a large circle with a replica cast in bronze of the simple wooden cross that Chaplain Schiebaan set up at the site immediately after the crash, together with a provisional monument of lights and flowers. Around the cross stands a stone socle for each victim. Two large paths lead to and from it, with at the beginning and end a plaque with the names of the victims.

A sharp dichotomy can be observed from ritual accents briefly discussed above. The ritual process, the allocation of roles, and the design and ordering of the space announces a triple division: first there are the

---

[44] SCHUMAN: 'Gedenken' (2001) 181.

coffins, with flowers, flag, wreaths and candles, and opposite them the actors and participants, who are divided into two groups: dominant, front and centre, and present in the ritual process of word and act, are the authorities, representatives of the institutions involved, for the most part in uniform, and behind them the next of kin, families and friends, at a distance and as spectators. It was striking that the television commentary always spoke of "next of kin, authorities and invited guests", while in the acts (for instance the procession) the order was exactly the reverse.

Later, for instance in the memorial services in Enschede and Volendam, people gave special attention to the place and role of the directly involved survivors when they structured the ritual. The wishes of that group were heard with regard to the place in the ritual which they desired (sometimes they consciously opted for an anonymous place, a spot off to the side); they also expressly received a voice in the ritual.

A final note involves the close of the ritual: the procession. This is a sort of transitional ritual. Really one might say that the memorial ceremony had formally ended with the two national anthems. With the procession people marked this closing and left the space. In a solemn procession past the coffins, a last honour is paid to the dead. It is a typical example of civic ritual, familiar from feudal court culture and from Communist parade culture.[45] We know the ritual in this form in The Netherlands from the 16th century onward, into the forms of emerging ritual in the 20th and 21st century. The rite has chiefly a military connotation. There is a rigid military form to a parade or defile. For the latter formations of troops march past a high officer or commander on solemn occasions, for instance in a parade or at the close of military manoeuvres. The element of viewing or inspection is emphasized through the context of marching past. A parade proper is a viewing (of troops or weapons) accompanying a celebration or commemoration. The parade consists of an inspection in which the parade commander moves along the troops from right to left 'reviewing' them, and a defile in which the troops march by the inspector in sequence. This strict form of defile has subsequently become a very generalised form of honour and remembrance, especially in national, profane/secular ritual. As we have said, in Eindhoven people appeared to be somewhat perplexed about the rite. Precisely how did one walk past – fast or slow? Can one stop at any point? Where does one

---

[45] Cf. COHEN: 'De militaire parade' (1996) and NAUTA: 'De militaire parade' (2001).

direct one's attention? Does one bow or nod one's head in respect? Once the defile has begun, does one stand or remain seated? The long procession of next of kin who participated in the procession after the authorities dealt with the ritual more spontaneously and informally. They had brought along flowers that they laid by the coffins, they paused in groups, embraced one another, stopped before a coffin. Here, rather than the defile and parade of army and nation, the reference is rather to filing past to pay last respects at the coffin of the deceased in much funeral and cremation ritual – a true ritual of farewell.

3.3. Rituals and coping with trauma: the silent procession and memorial service after the cafe fire in Volendam (2001) (H. Zondag)

In this third exploration, through the case study we will be examining the significance of ritual in coping with the suffering caused by a disaster. To do so, we will be scrutinising in depth the silent procession and service of remembrance after a cafe fire on January 1, 2001, in Volendam. Fourteen young people lost their lives in this fire. Because the coping with suffering has not yet been explicitly discussed in this book, in the first section we will introduce the concept of 'coping'. We will discuss three dimensions of coping (confrontation, social and mythological), and sketch the significance of rituals in the handling of suffering. The silent procession and memorial service held in Volendam on January 12, 2001, will be described in the second section. Finally, the third section is devoted to an analysis of this procession and service, using the previously introduced dimensions of coping.

Prior to beginning, as context for the whole section, we should again repeat what was said before regarding the special status that Volendam has in The Netherlands. It is a Roman Catholic enclave about 20 kilometres north of Amsterdam. It was originally a fishing village on the coast of the Zuiderzee, now reclaimed as the polders of Flevoland and the fresh-water IJsselmeer. The town is a very close community. It has two parishes, with a total of slightly over 20,000 residents.

Coping

Disasters radically affect the lives of people, inflicting both physical and mental damage. They fill people with a sense of impotence, vulnerability and brokenness. In a number of cases those who have been involved in a disaster from close up become traumatised.[46] Overcoming this pain is generally termed 'coping'. Coping can be described as a stabilising factor that helps people in psychosocial adaptation in periods of stress. It includes cognitive and behavioural efforts to limit or eliminate stressful circumstances and the tension connected with them.[47]

Hamburg and Adams formulate four criteria for the effective coping with a disaster or other serious event.[48] In the first place the 'distress' or turmoil must remain within limits. In popular terms, one must not break down under it. Second, a person must retain their feeling of worth, that their self-esteem must remain intact or be restored. The third criteria listed by these authors is the restoration of relations with other people who are important for the individual. The fourth criterion is the prospect of restoration or improvement of physical and mental functions. As sequelae of a failed coping process one can list social isolation, abuse of alcohol and drugs, a psychiatric case history, and inflexible, rigid patterns of behaviour.

In the light of these criteria, one must not think that coping means that people no longer have pain. This is too hedonistic a view on trauma coping. It suggests that people can leave behind forever the negative consequences of an unpleasant experience. That is incorrect. After a serious negative occurrence the pain continues to exist; successful coping means that people can live with the pain, that the suffering does not have the final word in their life. Pain continues to exist, and becomes an integral part of the person's life. What coping does mean is that lives are not broken under it.[49]

In order to clarify the concept of coping, it will be useful to distinguish three dimensions: a confrontational, a social, and a mythological dimension.

---

[46] FRANCES: *Diagnostic and statistical* (2000); KLEBER: *Het trauma voorbij* (1999); KLEBER, BROM & DEFARES: *Coping with trauma* (1992); KLEBER, MITTENDORFF & VAN DER HART: 'Posttraumatische stress' (1997).

[47] HOLAHAN, MOOS & SCHAEFFER: 'Coping, stress resistance' (1996); LAZARUS & FOLKMAN: *Stress, appraisal and coping* (1984); MOOS & SCHAEFFER: 'Coping resources and processes' (1993). For an overview of definitions of the concept of coping see for instance: PARGAMENT: *Psychology of religion* (1997).

[48] HAMBURG & ADAMS: *Coping and adaptation* (1974).

[49] KLEBER: *Het trauma voorbij* (1999); KLEBER, MITTENDORFF & VAN DER HART: 'Posttraumatische stress' (1997); VOSSEN: 'Religieuze zingeving' (1992); ZONDAG: 'De herinnering' (1999).

The confrontational dimension

A recently married woman loses her husband in an aeroplane crash. In the first period after his death she is constantly reminded of this loss. She sees the empty chair, the coat hook where his jacket still hangs, and she now does the shopping for the weekend all by herself. She is continually confronted with his absence, which creates grief, pain and anxiety for her. She tries to divert her mind; she turns on the television or visits a friend, upon which the pain decreases. After the pain and anxiety ebb, she can again allow the memories of her husband to return, at which the whole cycle repeats itself. Here one sees a pattern particularly characteristic of coping with suffering, that of denial and confrontation.[50] This cycle repeats itself until the memories and the emotions which go with them no longer overwhelm the person involved, and she no longer fends them off.

Such a process takes considerable time, and coping with serious suffering may take years. This is because people generally do not question their notions and certainties about themselves and the world. For them, such convictions are simply self-evident. If someone leaves and says 'good-bye', they assume that others will respond to the farewell – and generally that is the case. Only when someone hears a silence after their words and asks themselves what is going on, are the expectations shaken. These notions and expectations are termed 'schemata'.[51] These schemata are acquired in the course of life and seldom are reflected upon, put into words or systematised. Thus these schemata are accepted as self-evident. They are necessary for a good adaptation to the world, to process and deal with information.

Over the course of life these schemata expand. This development consists of two processes, 'assimilation' and 'accommodation'.[52] Assimilation involves receiving information about the world within an existing schema. People accept new facts in such a way that they fit within their notions and expectations. They approach the world in terms of a schema that is already present. Accommodation is the adaptation of a schema so that it can deal with new information. It involves the revision of expectations and notions so that one can integrate new experiences and altered circumstances.

After an event that causes considerable suffering, schemata no longer function, and this malfunction explains why it often takes so long before

---

[50] HOROWITZ: 'Psychological response' (1979); IDEM: *Stress response syndromes* (1986).
[51] NEISSER: *Cognition and reality* (1976).
[52] PIAGET: *Structuralism* (1971).

people can cope with suffering. The woman who lost her husband in a disaster expected to be with her husband for many years to come and bear children. The accident cancelled out these notions about the future and disrupted all the expectations which she deemed self-evident. Now she is a widow and must rebuild her existence alone. How she is to do that is something which is not yet obvious; she must construct new expectations. Thus the woman's old notions are no longer adequate, but she does not yet have new and adequate perspectives. If we formulate this technically, we can say that the existing schema no longer functions, the process of assimilation has been disrupted, and that the woman is faced with the task of accommodation, of constructing a new schema. For the woman that could be that she now views herself as a single person for the present, but will enter a new relation in the future. The coping with suffering is the construction of new, adequate schemata, or in other words, coping is accommodation.

The confrontation with suffering is important for accommodation. A confrontation presents a person with accomplished facts and 'forces' them, as it were, to construct new and adequate schemata.

An important component in confrontation, and thus in coping suffering, is the acquisition of meaning.[53] One of the ways in which to answer the question about the meaning of suffering is to search for a cause. In this case the meaning is conceived in a 'causal' sense. People want clarification of the circumstances which created the suffering. The woman will want to know how the accident in which her husband died came to happen. In many cases, however, people do not search for causes, but for the meaning of the suffering for their lives.[54] One might term this a meaning in a 'consequent' sense. After the loss of her husband the woman will ask herself "What is it that is really important in my life?"

Questions that have to do with the meaning of suffering confront one with that suffering and thus contribute to its coping. The confrontation with pain through assigning meaning to it is one element of the process of accommodation. Assigning significance to misfortune involves giving a place to that misfortune. In this it appears to be less important what meaning is assigned to it – in either a causal or consequent sense – than that the sufferer succeeds in giving it meaning. What is important is that someone can do something with the calamity that has disrupted their life,

---

[53] KLEBER, BROM & DEFARES: *Coping with trauma* (1992).
[54] BAUMEISTER: *Meanings of life* (1991); TAYLOR: 'Adjustment to threatening' (1983).

and that the painful event not continue to rattle around in their life like a loose stone.

The social dimension

People do not cope with suffering within a social vacuum, but in relations with other people. The acknowledgement of sorrow contributes to the process of coping with it. That acknowledgement confirms the personhood of the sufferer, which has been destabilised precisely by the suffering, since pain erodes such certainties in life. Thus acknowledgement contributes to the restoration and normalisation of existence. Inversely, the absence of acknowledgement impedes coping with suffering. American veterans returning from Vietnam received hardly any acknowledgement of their military experience. Generally they were give the cold shoulder, which complicated their dealing adequately the trauma inflicted by their war experience.[55]

Social support from others comes in all sizes and shapes.[56] 'Cognitive' support is particularly important. Examples of cognitive support include the provision of advice and information. This information is important to set new goals and build up new expectations. Put in other words, information helps in constructing new schemata. In addition to cognitive support, material support is important, for instance in the form of finances. Material support can also take the form of concrete activities, such as assistance in moving house. Friendship – doing things together with others, for instance going out to the cinema or going out to dinner – and emotional support in the narrower sense of the word – someone putting a hand on your shoulder when you are feeling down – also appear to stimulate a positive handling of suffering. For the rest, there can be occasions when the support of others will also have negative consequences. Too much presence and influence from others can sometimes hinder people from building up a new life.[57]

The mythological dimension

People living with pain have the feeling that their life has reached an impasse. Myths can offer a helping hand in rising above this problem.[58]

---

[55] SILVER: 'Posttraumatic stress' (1985).
[56] FLANNERY: 'Social support' (1990).
[57] PARKES: *Bereavement* (1986).
[58] VAN DER HART: 'Het gebruik van mythen' (1981).

From the perspective of coping with suffering, myths are narratives about the cause and course of evil. In addition, myths indicate what has to happen in order to pick life up again. One can tell the story of the stilling of the storm to someone in need: the disciples were afraid that they would be lost in the storm, and Jesus bids them to have faith and trust. From this account those involved can learn to believe that in the end good will come, whatever may happen. In this way people are not captive to the events of the moment, which contributes to realising a good outcome. The Bible story provides a model of how to meet present problems. Moreover, these myths afford frames of reference in which someone can give meaning to that which happens in their life.

One can place the story of their own suffering in a more comprehensive story.[59] For instance, a person in whose life things are going wrong can see these as part of the decline of society. The micro-narrative of one's personal life thus becomes interwoven with a macro-narrative about society. Gergen and Gergen term this intertwining 'nested narratives'. Someone can consider the narrative of their own religious experience, or episodes of it, as a part of a more comprehensive religious narrative. The Jewish American journalist Leon Wieseltier provides a fine example of this when he tells how in reading of medieval Hebrew texts in a quiet room, he felt his own life story linked with Jewish tradition.[60]

It is important to note that the confrontational, social and mythological dimensions can be closely linked. Myths can contribute to assigning meaning because they confront people with suffering; in this way the mythological and confrontational dimensions are intertwined. When someone talks with another about his or her suffering, in the encounter with the other there is also a confrontation with the suffering, and thus the confrontational and the social dimensions are linked. Finally, myths are often told by others, at which point the social and mythological dimensions coincide.

Coping and rituals

Empirical research indicates that rituals contribute to the coping with suffering. Anyone consulting the PsycINFO data bank, an extensive international reference source for social sciences research, using the subject

[59] GERGEN & GERGEN: 'Narratives of the self' (1988).
[60] M. KRIELAARS, in the *NRC-Handelsblad*, June 16, 2001.

headings 'rituals' and 'coping', gets dozens of hits. It is impractical to discuss them all. We will mentions some of the facts which surface in order to give an impression of the purport and breadth of rituals with regard to the coping with suffering.[61]

Rituals are called upon for coping with a great variety of problems, among them loss and grief, sexual abuse, Parkinson's disease, pain, divorce, war traumas, psychosocial problems, important transitions in life, disasters and AIDS. Rituals produce effects not only for 'normal' adults, but children, the mentally handicapped and psychiatric patients can also benefit from them. They are salutary for those in need of help, and for those providing help. Finally, rituals demonstrate their effectiveness in a multiplicity of cultures.

The qualities of ritual can also be seen in the positive correlation between rituality and mental health. Harold Koenig compiled several bibliographies in which he discusses hundreds of research projects on rituality and mental health.[62] From Koenig's work it appears that people for whom rituality is a part of their life, suffer less from depression and anxiety. Suicide is also less prevalent among this population. Furthermore, participation in ritual correlates positively with a sense of well-being and the capacity to resolve problems.

On the other hand, one must not overestimate the significance of rituals for mental health. For some people they have a very positive effect, but for many people they mean nothing. Sometimes there is even a negative relation between ritual activity and well-being. Koenig explains this as follows: many people with problems who seek refuge in rituals stop their ritual activity once they have overcome their problems.

Rituals also contribute to the coping with loss after a disaster. That is the unanimous judgement of everyone who has published on this question, albeit that there is considerably less written on this matter than on rituals and the coping with loss in general. For Zinner and Williams, rituals are a manner of generating meaning in which the dead are allotted a place.[63] Rituals supply narratives as a manner of creating order. For instance, they contribute to the assimilation of negative memories. In

---

[61] In doing so, we will limit ourselves to the fact that rituals contribute to the processing of suffering. We will not consider how they accomplish this. For that, see for instance: JOHNSON et al.: 'The therapeutic use of ritual' (1995); SCHEFF: 'The distancing of emotion' (1977); IDEM: *Catharsis in healing* (1979).

[62] KOENIG: *Religion, health and aging* (1988); IDEM: *Research on religion* (1995).

[63] ZINNER & WILLIAMS: *When a community weeps* (1999).

short, rituals are beneficial for the survivors of a disaster. It does not matter what form that disaster takes – the explosion of a space shuttle, the
sinking of a ferry boat, an earthquake or a politically motivated bombing.[64] Rituals are not only beneficial for the direct relatives of victims, but
also useful for those providing assistance. Ritual activity contributes to
their capacity to endure the tension that working in disaster situations
brings with it.[65]

Zinner formulated 'the social rights of survivor groups'.[66] These are
rights that survivors of disasters and the next of kin of victims must be
able to claim. One of them is the right to participate in transitional rituals, precisely for the purpose of coping with suffering.[67] Zinner believes
that those who are responsible for the care of people affected by disasters
must create space for such ritual activities. This example illustrates how
deeply people's lives are affected by the consequences of omitting ritual
activities after a disaster. Zinner and Williams instance the earthquake in
Kobe, Japan, in 1995, where countless bodies were never recovered. That
meant many were never able to bid farewell to their dead according to
ritual prescriptions, which negatively influenced coping with their loss.[68]

Sitterle and Gurwitch cite the actions of the social workers and authorities after the Oklahoma City bombing as an example of an adequate
approach.[69] In the April, 1995, bombing of the Federal office building
there 168 people died. Three weeks after the attack social workers offered
the next of kin, friends and acquaintances of the victims an opportunity
to visit the site of the disaster. Most of the next of kin had never been there,
and knew the site, a ruin, only from television or photographs in newspapers. A whole day was set aside for the visit, and psychologists, volunteers
from the Red Cross, clergy and police accompanied the visitors. The Gov-
ernor of Oklahoma spoke individually with all the next of kin. In order to
guarantee privacy, curiosity seekers and the press were kept at a distance.

---

[64] For the destruction of the space shuttle, see ZINNER: 'The Challenger disaster'
(1999); the sinking of a ferry boat, NURMI: 'The Estonia disaster' (1999); an earthquake,
WILLIAMS, BAKER & WILLIAMS: 'The great Hanshin-Awaji Earthquake' (1999); political
attacks, SITTERLE & GURWITCH: 'The terrorist bombing' (1999).

[65] NURMI: 'The Estonia disaster' (1999); ØRNER: 'Interventions strategies' (1995).

[66] ZINNER: 'Group survivorship' (1995).

[67] SITTERLE & GURWITCH: 'The terrorist bombing' (1999); ZINNER: 'The Challenger
disaster' (1999); ZINNER & WILLIAMS: *When a community weeps* (1999).

[68] ZINNER & WILLIAMS: *When a community weeps* (1999).

[69] SITTERLE & GURWITCH: 'The terrorist bombing' (1999).

A route that the mourners could follow was laid out at the site of the disaster. They could make photographs, pray, place flowers, and on request receive a piece from the ruins. This ritual confronted the next of kin with the deaths of their loved ones and thus contributed to coping with the loss.

The silent procession and memorial service in Volendam

We will first briefly sketch the background for the silent procession and memorial service, then describe them. In doing so we will devote attention to the considerations advanced for holding a silent procession and service of remembrance, reservations with regard to the ritual, and responses afterward.

Fire in a cafe

Fourteen dead and more than 200 injured were the consequences of a short but fierce fire during New Year's Eve festivities in the cafe De Hemel in Volendam, patronised primarily by young persons. The youngest fatality was 13 years old, and many of the injured young people will bear the scars for life. The fire broke out shortly after the New Year had been welcomed in. Christmas decorations which had not been impregnated with flame retardants hanging from the ceiling caught fire after someone threw a firecracker. There were hundreds of young people in the premises at the time. The owner was held responsible for the fire; he had systematically ignored fire safety regulations. The municipality of Edam-Volendam also held responsible those among its employees who should have more strictly monitored compliance with the regulations.[70]

Mourning and sympathy

Volendammers (and other Netherlanders) express their grief and condolences in their own unique manner. There are ways of mourning that are peculiar to the town itself. For instance, for the whole of Roman Catholic Volendam it is the custom that the church bell is tolled for a quarter hour at 4:00 p.m. after each death, and to fly the flag on the church tower at half mast. Sheets are hung in the windows on the street side of

---

[70] The towns of Edam and Volendam together form the municipality of Edam-Volendam.

a house where a deceased person is laid out. The neighbours on each side cover half of any window that faces the home of the deceased. Furthermore, the family of the deceased cover their windows.

In the week after the disaster the two Roman Catholic churches, the St. Mary's and St. Vincent's, held a well-attended vespers service each day. Condolence registers were opened on the internet. In the first two weeks after the fire one of them recorded more than 100,000 visitors, of whom over 14,000 left behind a message. Sometimes spontaneous condolence registers were started on an internet site, such as that of the football club FC Volendam. As the second half of the football season resumed, a minute of silence was observed at the beginning of every fixture. The Don Bosco College, the only secondary school in Volendam, where the victims were students or graduates, opened a special space. One of the classrooms was fitted out as a sort of chapel with photographs of the deceased victims, candles, and a bulletin board for posting notes. Notebooks were also left, in which the pupils could write whatever they had to say. In addition St. Mary's parish in Volendam opened a space as a memorial to the victims. Among the things to be seen there were the hundreds of cards sent by people from all over The Netherlands to 'the residents of Volendam'. Later the flowers which had been left at the cafe and the materials from Don Bosco College were also brought to the space at St. Mary's. In the first period after the fire there was a special prayer service every Wednesday evening in St. Vincent's. After the service people could visit the graves of the dead victims, who were buried next to one another. Candles were specially lighted by the graves for these visits.

The annual pilgrimage to the famous Marian shrine of Lourdes in France, in June, 2001, was also devoted to the disaster. That year the pilgrimage was for the intention of "calling on the help of our heavenly Mother for the victims of the disaster, as well as for their parents and all involved, and to pray for healing and recovery". In May, 2002, Father Berkhout accomanied survivors, their family members, and next of kin of the fatalities on a pilgrimage to Lourdes.

A silent procession and a memorial service

On January 3 the decision was made to hold a silent procession and service of remembrance. This was planned for Friday, January 12. The procession and memorial service were together to be termed the Procession and Gathering of Solidarity. Cees de Wit, master of ceremonies at the memorial service and lector of the St. Vincent parish, put the several motives for the procession and memorial into words: "For me, it was most important that people have the opportunity to express their feelings. And that the institutions see that there must be adequate relief for the parents and the children who were involved in the disaster, not just now but in the future."[71] Those who joined the procession frequently identified the expression of feelings as their motive. A girl of seventeen who had two friends hospitalised, one in serious condition, said, "You do it for yourself, for your own feelings, it is a bit of coping with it, it's been pressing on you the whole week, it's like a tidal wave bearing down on you." Others expressed their motives in terms of fellowship and community: "It is important that everybody comes together here one more time, otherwise they are just buried and it's all over. After the funerals everybody goes their own way, here everybody is together." Some participants were characterised by a negative motivation: what could they expect if they did not join in? "You feel obliged to do it. As a young person here in Volendam it would just not do not to join in; the following Monday all you'd hear would be "Where were you?"", a young Volendammer acknowledged. And not all did feel obliged, as appears from this reaction: "I find it's all exaggerated. Don't get me wrong, that's just how it is for me at the moment. Because you grieve for your own." Finally, there were participants who saw it as a way of drawing a line under the event: "For me, this procession is a way of closing a period of mourning. Except for those directly involved, I think that is also going to be true for many others. Life does still go on." And in the view of another: "I see it as one large funeral, and after that you can turn the page."

Precisely the idea that the procession and the memorial service would mark the close of a period made some reluctant. They emphasized that there was nothing to close off. "There are still people in hospital, and no one knows what will happen with them. I would rather have waited until there was certainty that they were coming back. They could also have

---

[71] Processing emotions thus had a central place in the motivation for holding a silent procession and memorial service. The coping process played a conspicuous role in the decisions that people took after the Volendam disaster. Discussions regarding holding the Volendam spring carnival and the demolition of the De Hemel cafe illustrate this. The answer to the question "What function will the carnival celebration and the demolition have for coping with the fire?" was the criterion in the decision to cancel the carnival and postpone the demolition of the cafe.

benefited from that, because they could have drawn support from that," explained the headmaster of Don Bosco College. Curate Mantje of St. Vincent's parish shared this view: "We will all still be sharing a lot of hopes and fears, nothing is at the point of closure, there is nothing of which we can say, "we are all standing here and looking back together"." At the time the procession and service of remembrance took place there were still 55 people in the intensive care departments of various hospitals. Four of them would still die. Father Berkhout of St. Vincent's expressed the disappointment about the deaths after the procession and memorial service in saying, "After the procession I had the feeling that we had opened a new chapter. But that was not to be; there were still bereavements."

Course of the silent procession

The silent procession began at the Europaplein and went via the Haven, past the cafe De Hemel, to the stadium of the Football Club Volendam. It was a distance that normally could be walked in about ten minutes. The memorial service took place in the stadium. It was comprised of silence, addresses and readings, and appearances by Volendam artists. The wounded who could not yet walk joined the procession at the stadium. The owner of the cafe where the fire had raged was not present. People in Volendam were divided over this. Some found it sensible – "if he wasn't there, nothing could happen" – while others thought that he should have participated, to 'show his concern'.

Many of the young people who participated in the procession met first in homes. That is normal for Volendam's young people before they go out. "We did that on New Year's Eve too, there were about twenty of us then, now there are less." Then followed the departure for Europaplein, where people took their places. The head of the procession was formed by 200 young people from the Pius X Youth Centre. They had all lost friends in the fire. The boys walked on the outside, carrying gas lanterns on poles that rose above the crowd. Girls walked in the middle, carrying white roses. There had been a deliberate decision not to carry torches, as has been the custom with many silent processions, in order to avoid all associations with fire. Dignitaries formed the second unit of the procession. Among them were the City Council of Edam/Volendam, Prime Minister Kok, the Vice Premiers, Crown Prince Willem-Alexander, the Royal Commissioner for the Province of North Holland, the Secretary of State for Internal Affairs, the Chairman of the Upper House of Parliament, and Archbishop Simonis and representatives of the Diocese of Haarlem, to which Volendam belongs. Then came the whole team and staff of Football Club Volendam. All wore black leather jackets and carried white roses. Finally came all other participants. Among them were the next of kin of the young people who had died as of that time, and families of many of the injured. At their own request their participation was kept as anonymous as possible. Someone who knows the Volendam community explained, "They wanted to grieve in the privacy of the Volendam community." The silent procession included many rescue workers who had assisted in Volendam the night of the disaster: policeman and firemen in uniform, volunteers from the Red Cross, ambulance personnel and other members of medical assistance teams. There were also many people who were not from Volendam and were not directly involved in the fire who participated in the procession. Among them were about fifty people from Enschede, victims of the firework disaster of May, 2000, and members of the fan clubs for Sparta and Ajax supporters.[72]

The procession moved through a place where at nearly every house the Dutch flag hung at half mast, and candles burned in some windows. The arms of the windmills stood in 'mourning position', stores turned off the lighting in display windows, and the cafes, restaurants and bars were shut. Requests from TV reporters to say something for the camera were declined; it was, after all, a silent procession, and people wanted to keep it that way. The request not to applaud after speeches, readings and performances at the memorial service was in keeping with that. In order to guarantee as high a degree of silence as possible the authorities had imposed a ban on aeroplane flights over the area for the duration of the procession and service. The scraping of shoes on the bricks and asphalt, the rustle of clothing as people walked, and the tolling of church bells accentuated the silence.

Passing the cafe the pace of the procession slowed to a shuffle. Most looked straight ahead expressionlessly or averted their eyes. For many it was the first time since the disaster that they had passed the cafe De Hemel. The building had been boarded up with planks. Notes had been taped up on them with texts such as 'Things will never be the same again' and '2000-2001. I'll never forget your last half hour. Strength, everybody.' Opposite the cafe a platform had been constructed, on which many flowers lay: bouquets, floral pieces – among them, those from the government

---

[72] Sparta and Ajax are popular Dutch football clubs. There is a particularly close relationship between the Amsterdam club Ajax and Volendam.

and royal family – wreathes, and also separate white roses. Here and there among them were stuffed toys. On the platform stood two rows of young people from the Pius X Youth Centre. The first row received the flowers, primarily white roses, from the marchers, and passed them to the second row, who laid then down carefully. The florists in Volendam had bought 5000 white roses, which they sold for two-and-a-half guilders (a bit over one Euro) apiece. The proceeds went to the victims of the fire. The three flags of higher governmental levels hung at half mast on the platform: the national flag in the middle, the left the city flag of Edam-Volendam, and right the flag of the Province of North Holland. After passing the cafe the pace of the procession increased. When they arrived at the Volendam Football Club stadium for the memorial service, there were still thousands of people waiting in the Europaplein to begin the procession.

The memorial service

The lector of St. Vincent's church, acting as master of ceremonies, opened the service. He stood on a platform on one of the long sides of the grandstand. The back of the platform was closed off with a dark red curtain. On it stood a wooden lectern on arched wood base. No one would make use of the glass of water which had been placed there. The choirs which would perform sat on either side of the platform. Invitees took their places in the seats of honour. Victims who required extra care were accommodated in the business boxes. Next of kin were scattered anonymously through the crowd in the grandstand or on the field, as they 'did not want to be labelled'. In his words of welcome De Wit emphasized the young people in the hospitals. (They could follow the procession and memorial service on television.) Speaking slowly, he continued:

> "It was twelve days ago that a disaster struck our town. It is dark now, darkness covers Volendam, the same darkness that we experience in our homes and families. Will it ever become light, now that so many continue to be confronted by the disastrous consequences of the New Year's night just passed? We are gathered here in the open air; the temperature is below freezing and it is cold. It is also cold inside; our thinking and doing is frozen, we are petrified, we can hardly move on. The moon and stars are in the sky tonight. They are witnesses to infinity and eternity. They give light. Light in the darkness, however small and weak, gives comfort and strength for the future. Your presence this evening also gives light, is a sign of hope, hope that is rooted in deep faith. We have no words for what has happened to

Volendam, it leaves us in silence, the silence of death. What cannot be said in these difficult days is understood through our silence and gestures. In silence we are with those who cannot be here with us this evening. Let us make a gesture. Fold your hands, or hold the hands of those next to you, put your arms around each other's shoulders, all signs of solidarity, for a minute. I invite you to observe a minute of silence for all those who have been touched by this disaster."

A minute of silence followed.

Representatives of the three layers of government

The first speaker was Burgomaster IJsselmuiden of the city of Edam-Volendam. He had been burgomaster since 1995, and would resign in 2001, as a result of a report on the New Year's fire that was devastating to the community authorities. It appeared from the report that the regulations with regard to fire prevention had been ignored for years.

Burgomaster IJsselmuiden dwelt on the young age of the victims. "Young people who stood at the threshold of life were snatched from our community in one blow. They lost the lives on which they had scarcely begun, lives with so many expectations, so much to hope for, so much to discover." He emphasized the importance of mutual support, and pointed to the close bonds that Volendammers have with one another. These "bonds provide strength, strength that we will need in the years to come."

After the address by the mayor the Petruskoor (St. Peter's Choir) from Volendam sang the Kyrie Eleison with an adapted text that made reference to the fire in the cafe.

The second speaker, Prime Minister Kok, also emphasized the importance of support and solidarity. In his speech the Prime Minister profiled himself as an involved outsider who empathised with the Volendammers. "That is why we, people from outside the Volendam community, are also here this evening: to be silent together, to grieve together, to support and find comfort in one another. A hand on the shoulder gives strength to better handle feelings of powerlessness." The Prime Minister linked this with promises of aftercare and investigation into the cause of the disaster. "For that reason high-quality, long-term aftercare, the best possible medical and psychological support for the victims, is also so important, and you can count on receiving it. And of course serious questions force themselves upon us. What could or should have been done to have prevented this? There will have to be answers given, and the analysis and investigation will be thorough." At the end of his address Premier Kok referred to human vulnerability. "The tragedy of that recent New Year's Eve makes us realise once again how vulnerable human life is, how fragile the thin layer of ice on which we skate, each one of us and all of us together."

Subsequently the Little Singers of Volendam, a children's choir, dressed in traditional Volendam costumes, sang the 23rd Psalm, *The Lord is My Shepherd*. The third speaker, Van Kemenade, the Royal Commissioner for the Province of North Holland, also represented a layer of administration. After his address the Volendam Opera Chorus, like the previous choir clad in traditional Volendam costume, sang Mozart's *Ave Verum*.

Six youth

Next six youth people, all involved with the community centres and neighbourhood clubhouse network in Volendam, came to the stage. They would address the audience and read poems. The first to speak was Marjorie Koning:

> "I am angry, no, I am furious that we could not have prevented this disaster. I am furious that, with all our modern knowledge, the safety of people, of youth, is subordinated to money, a complex of interests and laziness. I do not understand why the victims are innocent children, who will never more fulfil their dreams and desires. I cannot comprehend a media that so mercilessly recorded our despair and emotions that night. Show some respect; is staying back ten metres too much to ask? I am furious with people in the tram, in waiting rooms and on internet who think they have the right to make judgements about our situation and make crude jokes about stars in the heavens.[73] But I also have immense admiration for the heros who, already inebriated themselves, still responded so quickly from the Joppekop, the Kakatoe, 't Gat,[74] all the surrounding cafes and homes, the firemen, ambulance personnel and the first aid workers who did all that was possible that terrible night. And police, your organisation was indispensable, and in the aftermath a bit of sympathy with despairing parents who in panic were seeking their children. Admiration for every Volendammer, who despite traumas, the loss of loved ones, are still able to keep their heads

---

[73] In Dutch the name of the cafe, 'De hemel', means 'Heaven', and jokes were current about the fireworks that started the fire being 'stars in heaven'. A similar though more positive wordplay on the name of the cafe occurs in Vincent Tuyp's speech.

[74] The Joppekop, Kakatoe and 't Gat are all cafes in Volendam.

up and try to go on living, however difficult that is, with all the suffering they have shouldered. I thank The Netherlands and the whole world for their moving expressions of support in the daily newspapers, on internet, and in all the flowers that now lie on the Dijk. Family, friends and school-mates, the most difficult is still to come, help for those stricken by this in all possible ways, not just today or in two weeks, but in two years, respecting them and helping to rehabilitate them, because that is the difficult task that lies before us."

Against the protocol, the audience responded with thunderous applause. That was also the case for the other speakers and performers who followed, all of whom came from the Volendam community.

The second young person was Nick de Koning. He introduced his contribution with the words, "This is a short poem for my best friend, who was murdered by the disaster."

> Suddenly he's no longer there,
> one of my best mates.
> I miss his voice
> talking as only he could.
> He was a great guy
> as lots of people know;
> but now he's gone,
> and that hurts so.
> Missing him hurts,
> almost too much to stand
> but I know he's in God's hand.
> Ruud, a good friend,
> That's what you were,
> but now you're at God's side.

The third, Arthur Veerman, began by saying, "A friend told me, "You can't talk about things for which we have no words, but you also can't be silent." That's why I wrote this poem, inspired by a poem of Esther Jansma, also called 'New Year'.'[75]

> New Year's,
> you still taste only smoke
> the darkness sticks in your hair
> boys in sleeveless shirts rub tearing eyes

---

[75] Esther Jansma is a Dutch poet.

ambulances flash around the corner
their sirens breaking the silence
then everyone goes down to the harbour.
Among singed party dresses of the night
and the sharp screams of breaking glasses,
you run after them.
You feel yourself becoming heavier,
yet you go on.
In other places there is laughter
and glasses being filled,
your legs give way
you wish that the small private gathering
from before the champaign and fireworks
had turned out differently.
There is no way back.
With so much pain, you think you can feel no more,
because you feel nothing
and you turn around
and look up
and see that the sun is shining
with the taste of smoke still always in your mouth."

The fourth to appear was Vincent Tuyp. He is the son of the bassist of the well-known Volendam pop group BZN. Tuyp introduced his text by saying, "This text is about how I experienced New Year's Day."

"What is to be said about so much sorrow? How can you express so much suffering? Do you know? I don't. I woke up on January 1 with the unreal feeling of two hours before. It really wasn't waking up, for I hadn't shut my eyes. In the corner of my eye was the sleep of a dried tear. Suddenly I remember again the first hour of the new year: felicitations, laughter, dancing in a circle. It seemed as if no sorrow existed. The telephone rang with best wishes for the new year. But not this time, it was not true. Struck dumb, staggered, riveted to the spot. Heaven was alight, but there were no longer skyrockets to be seen. Never have I seen so many people running from their houses as on that night. Back home the first news came in, hoping that it would not be confirmed. But nothing could be less true; one thing was certain, Volendam would have no happy new year. What is to be said about so much sorrow? How can you express so much suffering? Do you know? I don't."

After that Wieneke de Boer read a poem. Essential elements of this poem are lost in print. De Boer worked with many well placed silences, which contributed significantly to the effect of the poem.

Everything's fine, and I laugh at the rain
I take step
after step
after step
on the way to the sea.
Then something stops me
the rain does not cool my face
and the light is too hot to laugh at.
I must sit down
I can now go no further
I sit on the road and look at the ground
I sit
I sit
I sit

until long after today I will sit here before I can go on.

The final contribution from the youth was that of Niels Bergsma. He made a comparison between the lot of the town of Volendam and that of their football team FC Volendam.

"We sit here in the stadium of the football club FC Volendam. A year ago FC was beaten by all the other teams in the first division and the club stood dismally at the bottom of the league table. A year has gone by and we are now third in the tables. We even won a period title. By the willpower and perseverance of the players and technical staff and through the support of the fan club, the team has climbed back up. At this moment the whole town is playing against a much tougher opponent, against the disaster. Its first strikke has hit home, and presently the score is 1-0 in favour of the disaster. But just like the football club, the town will also come back. We can score the equaliser by standing behind the wounded like a gigantic fan club. We have to continue supporting them in their difficult battle. With willpower, perseverance and the help of their technical staff they have to climb back up to the top again. If in the course of time we can again return to life like it was before the disaster, if we can all again laugh, throw a party and drink a glass of beer on the Dijk, if the bond we have with one another becomes stronger than before the disaster, then the referee can blow the final whistle. Final score: Volendam 2, disaster 1. Disaster, Volendam is stronger than you are! Let's play this game!"

Father Berkhout

The final speaker was Father Berkhout, pastor of St. Vincent's parish. He addressed the crowd, and then led a prayer:

"Twelve midnight, New Year's Eve, the bells of Volendam rang out to welcome the new year. But just a short time later this joyous sound was drowned out by the screams of young people in panic and the throes of death. Lightning fast word spread through Volendam "The Wir War is on fire." Our hearts trembled. In desperation parents ran to the Dijk in search of their children. When evening fell on that first day we came together in homes to grieve, dazed and resigned. And how we hurt. It was so painful we had no words for it. Whole families waiting at hospitals in anxious expectation. In the week that followed long funeral corteges wound through our town ten times. Ten times a young person, ten times a father and mother broken by sorrow, ten times all the young people of our town, joined together in an immense grief. This week I visited hospitals in Brussels, Louvain, Liège, Aachen and Beverwijk; I had already been to the AMC.[76] Fifty young people entirely swathed in bandages and under sedation. Your heart breaks; you cannot believe what you are seeing. And all of them, they all come from one town. Parents balancing between hope and despair; the situation can change from hour to hour. Some in our town have asked, "Father, why is God doing this to us?" Dear friends, God is not doing this to us, really not, He does not desire the death of young people. In a number of the funeral services we have listened to the story of the boy from Nain. A widow was bringing her only son to the grave. And it is written there, "Jesus had pity on this mother." But that pity also knows anger, his heart is moved as he sees this. Young people should not die; they have their whole life before them yet. He commands the bier to stop, and says, "Young man, arise!" and restores him to his mother. That is what God wills. God does not want the death of young people.

The solidarity is strong in these days, we support the families where death has cruelly struck. We are there for the victims and their fathers and mothers in the hospitals. Where will we go on from here, as normal life soon resumes, as the young people return to your midst, injured and scarred? How will they find their place in our community again? And where will we find the resiliency and inspiration to continue to care for them?

In these days I have been reminded of my Volendam grandmother, born on the Zuideinde. As a boy I greatly enjoyed coming to visit her, and I can again see her before me, just as she was, just as your grandparents were, sitting at her table, in her dress of crepe de Chine, with her silver rosary within reach. While I sat near her she told about the old days, her Volendam. She relived the time in 1916 when the dike broke and the whole village found itself under water. She returned to the time of great poverty, the togetherness of the big families, the warmth and security. She spoke of Volendam's

---

[76] The AMC (Amsterdam Medical Centre) is a university hospital in Amsterdam.

love for the Zuiderzee, and how the same sea demanded great sacrifices,[77] how the bell tolled again and again in mourning over our village, how people found comfort, fortitude and strength in faith. And she told about the fishing fleet, how it was blessed by the pastor as it left this harbour. She always rounded off her memories with this lesson. "Child", she would say, "whatever happens to you, always trust in God, never let go of your faith." And what she said was true, because she believed it so herself.

In these days we see that the old faith not only kept previous generations going, but it would appear that we can also draw strength from it. This faith of our forefathers will give us the strength to endure this test, because God will not abandon us. It is the legacy of older generations which is passed on to us today, through our young people who have died, through those who now lie in the hospitals.

There are an awful lot of young people here, here in the stadium, and I want to say something to you. Look, soon the young people who are now in the hospitals swathed in bandages, I have seen them, almost all of them, they will be coming back to our community again. And they are hurt, injured, perhaps scarred. And in these days I have seen how you have stood by each other, supported each other, how you have been a source of strength for each other. You were friends in good times; be friends in difficult times soon too, the bad times as these come. Don't be that just for a week, just for a year, but they will be part of your generation as long as you live. And if you don't know where you will find the strength, think of the old Volendammers, where they found their strength.

We are one with the young people in the hospitals, you are watching me now. I greet you, I wish you strength. Fight, hey, because we can't do without you. And we hope that you will be back soon! And I want to ask all the people here in the stadium to applaud for you, that you receive the power needed for the times that are going to come."

Loud applause followed, after which Father Berkhout prayed the Lord's Prayer and the Hail Mary.

Jantje Smit, a boy singer who began his musical career with the Volendam Opera Choir, closed the memorial service with Gounod's *Ave Maria*. As he came onto the platform some applauded and whistled as though at a regular concert. After the performance by Jantje Smit the master of ceremonies closed the service by thanking everyone for coming and their involvement with Volendam.

---

[77] In those years Volendam was still on the open sea, on the Zuiderzee coast. With enclosure of this body of water with the IJsselmeer Dam in 1932, Volendam came to lie on a lake, the IJsselmeer.

Interest

Interest in the silent procession and service of remembrance was great. Estimates placed the number who joined the procession at between 20,000 and 25,000. Four Dutch television stations broadcast the procession and the memorial service which followed live. When the Dutch channels RTL4 and Net5 broadcast direct reports from Volendam during their news programmes, 3.4 million people watched.[78] The NOS sold images on to television stations in 20 countries.[79] According to the Kijk- en Luisteronderzoek[80] the broadcasts were highly regarded; the procession received an approval rating of 7.6, and the memorial gathering scored 8.2. It is rare that any broadcast will earn a rating of over 8.

Responses

The procession and memorial service called up memories of the night of the disaster and the days which followed. "It all ran through your mind again at that moment" and "it awakens memories" were typical responses. That was the case not only for Volendammers but also for emergency workers who came from outside the area. A member of an emergency response team who was in Volendam that night said, "That is where I was. That's where it all happened. The tent stood there, the fire department there, there the police. That's where the parents were milling around searching for their children. It all flew through your mind again at that moment." In addition, many people felt a sense of connection through the procession and memorial service. "There is fear and grief, and you think that you are facing it alone. But when you walk with a group like that you get a feeling of strength. Together your will get through it." For people this communality was a counterweight to powerlessness. "You are powerless. Everyone is touched by it, directly or indirectly, and if you stand here with 15,000 people, then at least you have something in common." It lifts the feeling of powerlessness with regard to the injured a bit. One of the participants said that he was there on behalf of someone who

[78] On January 1, 2000, the population of The Netherlands was 15,864,000 (Central Bureau of Statistics (*Statistisch Jaarboek*) 2000).

[79] The NOS (Nederlandse Omroep Stichting = Dutch Broadcasting Foundation) is an umbrella radio and television organisation.

[80] This organisation performs ongoing research on viewer and listener numbers and responses to radio and television programmes.

was hospitalised. "It is the only thing that I can do for him." Another felt that "you can give them a bit of encouragement this way". For some participants, protest aspects were most prominent. "In this way it becomes clear to the dignitaries that we are going to need help for many years to come." Others, on the contrary, were sceptical about this. With regard to the speech of the Prime Minister, someone commented, "Fine words, sure, but I've heard it all before." He felt more at home with the speech by Marjorie Koning. "Tremendous, it was straight from the heart." The same man said several months later that the precession and service of remembrance had meant a lot to him. "I was absolutely out of it for two weeks, it was so difficult to come to the realisation of what had really happened. The Procession of Solidarity, the gathering in the stadium and the Match also gave me extra strength."[81] Finally, there were people who experienced the procession and memorial service as a sort of turning point. "That you say 'case closed', for this week at least, and you can take a big step toward the future." That something changed for some can be seen in the response of someone several days later. "It seemed as if the atmosphere in the town had changed somewhat the next day. Not that the mourning is over, but people were talking again all of a sudden. We can go on together: that feeling."

Before the events some had been afraid that 'outsiders' were going to define the atmosphere of the procession and memorial service. It made no difference that the Prime Minister and Crown Prince Willem-Alexander were there, but "this is about Volendammers." After the close of the procession and memorial service many Volendammers therefore were relieved that this didn't happen, that "the procession and service of remembrance were by and for Volendammers."

Analysis

The central focus in the analysis will be how the suffering caused by the cafe fire was dealt with. We will analyse the silent procession and the memorial service on the basis of the three dimensions previously identified: the confrontational, social and mythological dimensions.

---

[81] By the 'Match' the man is referring to a football fixture between FC Volendam and a team of former players from the national team. This match was played on February 27, nearly two months after the fire, the proceeds going to benefit the victims.

The confrontational dimension

The silent procession and the service of remembrance confronted everyone once again with what had happened there. They were an emphatic
reminder that there had been a fire in which many had died and been
injured, which had caused great suffering. The disaster repeated itself,
as it were, now in mental reality. Seen psychologically, remembering is
mental repetition, and this repetition is important for coping with a
disaster.

The remembrance of the disaster through the silent procession and
memorial service took on various shapes. First of all, it took shape simply by the holding of the silent procession and memorial service. Independent of their individual design, such events bring the disaster and its
consequences to public attention once again.

Participating in the silent procession was itself a manner in which people remembered. That began before the procession, as people assembled.
In their thoughts the young people travelled back to the evening before
the fire, when they assembled to go to the cafes. This confronted them
with the empty places that the disaster left behind. "There were more of
us then," said one of them. During the procession also participants were
constantly reminded of the events on New Year's Eve. This can be seen
in responses like, "It all ran through your mind again at that moment."
For many participants it appears that passing the cafe De Hemel was
their first confrontation with the site of the disaster. Many of them soft-
ened the confrontation by averting their eyes as they passed the site. They
seemed to be seeking a sort of balance between confrontation and avoid-
ance, and finding it in not looking at the site of the disaster as they
passed. In this way one can come into physical proximity with the scene
of the disaster, but do not have to be confronted – at least fully – by it.

A third situation in which people are reminded of the disaster and its
consequences is the memorial. A number of aspects are addressed in the
speeches and readings: what happened on the night of the disaster itself,
emotions such as grief, despondency and rage, the chasm the disaster
created in the lives of many, finding meaning, powerlessness and vulnerability. In the theoretical development surrounding coping with suffering, one is constantly reminded of the relevance of these aspects.[82]

[82] KLEBER: *Het trauma voorbij* (1999); KLEBER, MITTENDORFF & VAN DER HART:
'Posttraumatische stress' (1997).

What happened during the fire was particularly raised directly in the poems of several of the young people. These poems are especially evocative because of the use of images that make the disaster tangibly present: tearing eyes, sirens, singed party dresses, shrill screams, breaking glass, the taste of smoke. These images from the poem by Arthur Veerman are an eye-witness account of an inferno.

The disaster fills people with grief, which comes to the fore in the memorial service in many keys. This perhaps happens most concisely in the poem by Nick de Koning, when he writes of missing someone's voice and manner of talking. The memorial service is a manner of expressing mourning and loss, and the addresses and readings are a vehicle for giving form to the painful emotions that the disaster causes.

In their words the speakers refer to the gaps that the disaster has left in the lives of many. The expectations that people have for the young, and that young people have for themselves, were destroyed in a flash. "They lost the lives on which they had scarcely begun," said Burgomaster IJsselmuiden. Here he put into words the conviction – generally implicit – that the projected lives of many had been shattered.

Several speakers directly or indirectly addressed the cause of the fire. In this they ask about the meaning of the fire, and particularly the meaning in the causal sense. Marjorie Koning does this in the form of an accusation. She speaks of her rage about those who place profit above safety. It would appear from the responses ('straight from the heart' and the applause) that she voiced the rage that many felt. The question of the cause was raised indirectly in the Prime Minister's address. He promised an investigation into how and why the fire happened. When people speak of the causes of the calamity, they not only accuse, but also exonerate. Father Berkhout does that; he exonerates God. It is not God's will that the young die "God is not doing this to us," he argues, and he supports his defense with the story of the son of the widow at Nain.

The speeches and readings bring to our attention the sense of powerlessness that overwhelms people. This helplessness is best expressed in a poem by one of the young people, Wieneke de Boer, in her repeated "I sit, I sit, I sit," all the while "looking at the ground." She is no longer able to act, and is in a cul-de-sac. This powerlessness is also expressed in the repeated comments on the failure of language. People have no words to express what has happened; they are left only with silence. Vincent Tuyp asks what one can say, how one can get it off one's chest. He does not know. The silence to which people are as it were forced creates a dilemma, as Arthur Veerman indicates: you can not talk about it, but you cannot remain silent about it. He finds a resolution for the dilemma in writing the poem. In the opening to the memorial service Cees de Wit refers to the silence to which the unutterable leads. At the same time he seizes on silence as a means to realise what has taken place. Precisely in silence do people express what they cannot say. Silence is a manner of comprehending what people would seek to say. In this De Wit demonstrates that powerlessness does not have to have the final word, however helpless people are. Finally, powerlessness can be seen in the totally unexpected character of the disaster. One cannot defend oneself against it in any manner whatsoever. Vincent Tuyp expresses this strikingly when the contrasts the felicitations, laughing and dancing with the telephone call that is not wishes for a happy New Year, but about the fire in the cafe De Hemel.

A final aspect to which people referred during the service of remembrance is human vulnerability. This vulnerability is raised chiefly by the images used by Father Berkhout, when he describes his visit to the young people in the hospitals: swathed in bandages, injured, hurt, scarred, sedated. Premier Kok explicitly mentions human vulnerability. According to the Prime Minister, the fire persuades people of their vulnerability, and in this context he compares life with skating on thin ice.

During the procession, and particularly when passing the site of the fire, the confrontation is physical in nature; at the memorial service the confrontation is verbal in nature. It appears that we can distinguish two variants in this verbal confrontation: the 'plastic' and the 'abstract'. In the plastic confrontation people speak about the disaster and its consequences in concrete images. The sensory images in which people describe the disaster remind one of eye-witness reports. It was primarily the youth of Volendam who made use of such images. Abstract confrontation is less direct and immediate than plastic confrontation. The speakers do not avoid discussing the disaster, and in that sense this is a confrontation with what happened, but the descriptions have a general and sometimes almost reflective character. Particularly the representatives of the three levels of government operated on this level.

The social dimension

For those involved in a disaster, the involvement of others is of crucial importance for coping with such an event. Their support and acknowledgement mean much for victims. The organisers of the silent procession and service of remembrance in Volendam appear to have been conscious of this, as is demonstrated by the title they gave the ritual, the Procession and Gathering of Solidarity.

The simple presence of a large number of people generates acknowledgement. A silent procession and memorial service offer possibilities for mobilising large numbers of people. Many of those directly involved experience this mass solidarity as a comfort. Their suffering is not thoughtlessly pushed aside, but people feel it is worth the trouble to come out for the procession and service, or at least follow it on television. One might term this a non-specific effect of the ritual. On the basis of ritual sympathisers assemble around the victims, and that sympathy has great value for those involved.[83] Through the massive turnout it becomes clear that the victims do not stand alone. That sense is reflected in the words of Marjorie Koning, who thanked "The Netherlands and the whole world."

Numbers reflect the 'quantity' of the participation. In addition, the 'quality' of the participants seems to be of importance. There must be a sufficient number of 'weighty' participants. That also generates acknowledgement. It is for that reason that the presence of representatives of the national government and Royal House is valued.[84] At the same time, the response to the Prime Minister's address, "Fine words, sure, but I've heard it all before", indicates that there are also reservations about their presence.

The prominent place victims – be they those immediately involved or next of kin – were allotted during the silent procession and memorial service is also felt to be a form of acknowledgement. They have lost friends and family and identify most easily with the dead and wounded, all youth. In the procession the young people formed the vanguard, received the flowers opposite the site of the disaster, and played a crucial role in the service. These prominent places were further accentuated by the violation of the protocol in the applause for their contributions. Precisely in connection with acknowledgement it is remarkable that Marjorie Koning

---

[83] The silent procession after the fireworks disaster in Enschede (May, 2000), in which about 100,000 people participated, called forth many responses in the spirit of "it was so beautiful that so many people came to Enschede to weep with us" and "that so many are showing sympathy with me does me good."

[84] The reaction of a Volendammer to the appearance of football stars like Marco van Basten and Ruud Gullit at the benefit match for the victims of the fire, on February 27, 2001, is also telling: "I can't believe that they are doing this for us."

garnered considerable praise for her address in which she criticised the behaviour of the media. In their sometimes intrusive conduct on the night of the disaster they gave no indication of respecting the suffering of the Volendammers, and showing respect is a form of acknowledgment.

Support and acknowledgement are touched upon in the speeches in various ways. They are, for instance, dealt with in general; the speakers exhibit an awareness that support is important after a disaster and indicate that it is a condition for conquering the problem. In addition there are speakers who promise support for Volendam. These are chiefly speakers who come from outside Volendam, for instance Prime Minister Kok. He profiled himself as a representative of 'outsiders' who want to support Volendammers when he said that "we, people from outside your community" were there to help Volendam. He promised assistance in the form of aftercare for the physical and psychological effects of the fire.

There are regular references in the speeches and readings – for instance, by Father Berkhout and Niels Bergsma – to the tradition of solidarity with one another in the history of the Volendam community. The 'application' of this tradition is clear: from this tradition people can gain the hope that this time too people will succeed in being there for one another. Speakers also tell stories that offer perspectives for the future.

During the memorial service people were exhorted to give support to the victims. An ethical aspect of the ritual manifests itself in this. The ritual is used to encourage humane action. Father Berkhout calls on those present to give support to the victims as long as they live. In this, he also does something striking. He not only calls for support in a general sense; he moves beyond that to an act of support. He calls on his audience to applaud for those who are still in hospital, in order to encourage them. This draws attention to the fact that people are not only supporting the silent procession and memorial service, but that these rituals also provide an opportunity to give support. In addition to a passive aspect (being supported), these rituals have an active aspect (giving support). "You can give them a bit of encouragement that way" was the reaction of one of the participants. People are given the chance to act in a situation that is full of feelings of powerlessness, and in doing so assure that powerlessness is not the only feeling present.

The mythological dimension

The mythological dimension involves the myths or stories that were told during the speeches. Stories are important for coping with suffering; in stories people reach out in order to conquer negative situations. Here we will discuss two such stories, those told by Niels Bergsma and Father Berkhout. Niels Bergsma compared the disaster with the vicissitudes of Volendam's football club. His story takes place in the present and the main characters are football players, figures with whom the young can easily identify. In addition, an important role is reserved for the fans and the technical staff at the football club. Bergsma locates his story in the same stadium where the memorial service was at that moment taking place. He introduces a negative situation that must be overcome: the football club's low ranking on the league tables. The means for overcoming the negative situation are help, support, willpower and perseverance. Particularly willpower and perseverance seem important, as Niels Bergsma lists this pair twice in his speech. Thanks to these means the football club succeeds in climbing up from last place and even wining a period title. This title gives them the prospect of promotion – that is to say, a considerable improvement in the situation. What is true for FC Volendam is also true for the victims of the fire. When Volendam stands behind them as they stood behind their football club, people can rise above their present travail. Even more, an improvement can even occur. Just as the football club has the prospect of promotion, Volendammers have the prospect of a mutual bond that is stronger than it was before the disaster.

The story told by Father Berkhout takes place in the distant past, in Volendam before the construction of the IJsselmeer Dam. The main figure in his story is his grandmother, whose home he visited as a child, and whose visual presence he evokes through the use of details such as her dress of crepe de Chine and her silver rosary. She would be a woman such as older Volendammers themselves possibly still remember from their youth. Perhaps their grandparents told the same stories that Father Berkhout heard from his grandmother. The threatening elements in this story are poverty and water – the water of the sea, in which the fishermen drowned and that, after the dike broke in 1916, flooded the village, but water that in a fire meant deliverance. Faith in God, in whom people found comfort, fortitude and strength, and warmth and security are the instruments for countering the bane of water and poverty. The means that worked in the past will also work in the present; today too that faith will "give us strength to endure this test."

The stories of Father Berkhout and Niels Bergsma are in agreement at a number of points. Both make use of comparisons, both refer to social elements, both reveal how people can rise above the present crisis. One can typify both stories as a drama.[85] Dramas are stories in which a negative situation suddenly arises, and in which a turn for the good comes after a number of conditions are fulfilled.

But there are also significant differences between the two stories. These involve not only the main characters, time and place, but particularly the means for overcoming the affliction. Niels Bergsma sees the solution in perseverance and willpower. He suggests people can take their fate in their own hands and win out by their own power. His story is a modern myth, tailored to people who live in a 'modern' society, where people call on autonomy and self-determination. Father Berkhout seeks deliverance from powers that transcend the human horizon: from God. His coping strategy has a religious character. It is not, however, that this operates of its own accord; people have to do something substantial too. They must place their trust in God. We would characterise this form of religious coping as 'surrender'.[86]

Both stories refer to the importance of social means; in that their narrators are in agreement. But again there are also differences. Niels Bergsma speaks about 'help'; he appears to speak somewhat in the language of the professional approach in a welfare state. Father Berkhout points toward 'warmth and community'. These are more terms from a society that is characterised by informal close mutual ties. By this, however, we do not intend to suggest that there is no role reserved for strong mutual engagement in Niels Bergsma's story. Quite the contrary. What is important for us is to show that in the stories – and in the solidarity – people find accents from different worlds of experience. The two stories each assume a different audience. Niels Bergsma's story is directed toward young Volendammers. Father Berkhout appears to focus on the older generation. For both speakers the story is a manner of showing how order can be restored. It is precisely through their different accents that they connect with the different experiences of those who attended the memorial service. In this way each is offered a story, adapted to their own manner of living, that indicates how to cope with suffering.

[85] GERGEN & GERGEN: 'Narratives of the self' (1983); GERGEN & GERGEN: 'Narrative form and the construction' (1986); GERGEN & GERGEN: 'Narrative and the self as relationship' (1988).
[86] PARGAMENT: *Psychology of religion* (1997).

3.4. MONUMENTS (A. NUGTEREN)

Introductory remarks

While here and there in the preceding discussions we have already mentioned memorials that commemorate the victims of a disaster, we are now going to devote a separate section to monuments.[87]

Just as the growth of collective rituality surrounding disasters seems to be an indication of, among other things, an inclination (either despite or because of far-reaching secularisation) to form positive mass, it is striking that commemorative culture in the collective domain exhibits a flowering rather than a decline. In the book with the pregnant title *Wij herdenken, dus wij bestaan* [We commemorate, thus we exist] various factors for this are listed: live television reporting, the wave of nostalgia, attention in the mass media for recent history, imitation, prosperity, free time, commemoration as a pastime for well-off senior citizens, the cult of anniversaries preceding the beginning of the new millennium, the shrunken future horizon of postmodernism, reverence for ancestors, the increasing need for ritual and myth, etc.[88]

The design of monuments is almost always a source of controversy. "Commemoration is an ancient, universal phenomenon which has survived secularisation",[89] but its visual vocabulary appears to be time-linked. The generation of monuments from soon after the Second World War was not free from old-fashioned national heroism, but for a long time there has been an ongoing search for a new means of expression. After September 11 people immediately began to discuss how Ground Zero in New York could fittingly be marked.

In addition to inflation of the phenomenon of commemoration, we also see an increasing inclination to give commemorations a contemporary relevance. Often authorities will seize upon commemorations of past wars to involve the population, and particularly youth, by making references to current armed conflicts and their victims: Bosnia, Rwanda,

---

[87] The words *monument* and *memorial* will be used interchangeably here. There is a spontaneous distinction which can however be made: "The word 'monument' implies death and the past. A 'memorial' is more active and is intended as an aid to 'memory'." Interview with Jan Kloppenborg in VAN TEESELING: *Het oog van de storm* (2001) 95.

[88] PERRY: *Wij herdenken, dus wij bestaan* (1999) 11-12.

[89] *Ibidem*: 21.

Sudan, Kosovo.[90] For instance, Perry writes of the annual Dutch commemoration of the victims and the end of the Second World War:

> The commemoration becomes a supermarket where everyone must be able
> to come seeking whatever they fancy: older people and younger people,
> those who look back and those who look ahead, activists, doomsters, natives
> and immigrants, those who hope to sell something and those who want to
> buy, pop musicians and their fans.[91]

An example of what can be considered a successful war monument is the
Vietnam Veterans Memorial in Washington, D.C.: two long, black granite walls with on them the names of all the 58,000 American men and
women who died in the Vietnam War. The initial design expressed grief
rather than national glory, fame or bravery. Yet in its final execution in
1982 there were several elements added: an American flag, an 'heroic'
sculpture of three soldiers, and the inscription 'God Bless America'. This
monument became a place where people could express their personal
grief, and it quickly appeared that visitors brought personal objects to leave
behind at the monument: a pair of old cowboy boots, a series of personal
letters, photos from teenage years, plastic roses, teddy bears, baseball caps,
etc.[92] This place has sometimes been called 'the only real living war
monument' in the Western world. For many the desire of 'Never again!'
is there united with personal mourning.

Especially in Europe war monuments appear to be objects of rituality.
Particularly the First World War, the 'Great War', left behind impressive
and still cherished ritual landscapes with monuments and accompanying
ritual repertoires (war grave pilgrimages, etc.).[93] It appears that in the
20th century The Netherlands has been extremely sober when it comes
to its commemorative monuments. Sculptures of national heros are hardly
ritual centres; the same is true for commemorative sites for disasters such
as the Great Flood of 1953.

Things have changed since the beginning of the 1990s. In addition to
monuments for victims of senseless street violence, we have annual rituals surrounding the monuments which were set up after disasters. The
annual Bijlmer commemoration appears to be the most heavily attended

[90] *Ibidem*: 80-81.
[91] *Ibidem*: 80.
[92] *Ibidem*: 81-84.
[93] WALTER: 'War grave pilgrimage' (1993).

of these gatherings, and draws the most media attention. At a more individual level we often see that some spontaneous monuments, for instance those which are created after a traffic accident in which a child died, are always provided with fresh flowers, potted plants and personal memorabilia.[94] Here an important parallel with the disaster monuments appears to be operating: the site of the fatality seems to have a different value from the place where the victim is buried.

Collective commemorative rituals focus primarily on the place where the event happened at the time. If it is decided to place a lasting monument, then people prefer that it be immediately at the site of the disaster. Why? What explains the preference for the site of the event as the *locus sacer*, rather than the grave? In Volendam, the section of the cemetery in which the fourteen young people are buried has indeed become a commemorative site.[95] Does this have to do with the communal burial site created there, while the victims of the other disasters discussed above generally received separate burials, determined by where they had come from? After disasters in The Netherlands the bodies are generally sent to various places for burial. Some were even flown to other countries, such as the person's land of origin, Surinam, the Dutch Antilles and Turkey. Therefore here we will only discuss the collective monuments and not the individual grave monuments or the diverse commemorative tables or exhibitions set up at the initiative of friends, colleagues, schools and churches.

The memorials

In the Bijlmer we saw the spontaneous creation of a memorial: 'the tree that witnessed everything'. Like the streetlamp poles that are decorated with flowers, notes, photos, stuffed toys and paraffin wax candles for children who were victims of automobile accidents and young persons killed in street violence, so the tree in front of the Bijlmer apartments was a marker of the spot where everything had taken place. The apartment buildings themselves were barricaded and eventually demolished. The

---

[94] This can vary greatly. There are such sites which are rather quickly abandoned, but one can also find memorial sites which are maintained for years. See also POST: *Ritueel landschap* (1995) 42-46, as well as the illustrations there on pp. 18, 21 and 22; see also FRIJHOFF: *Heiligen, idolen, iconen* (1998).

[95] In fact, it is a typical corner of the new portion of the cemetery behind St. Vincent's Church. What distinguishes this place from its surroundings is the niche deliberately created there, with two benches and several small trees.

tree remained as the central point in front of the buildings, and began to function as a ritual focus. This occurred spontaneously: first the tree itself, then the foot and the lower branches of the tree became a place for the deposit of ritualia, and finally the wood fence turned into a sort of votive table or altar on which flowers, plants, notes, photos, paraffin candles and stuffed toys were placed. Although the whole area can be considered as a memorial park, the tree has remained its ritual centre for both ordinary visits and the annual memorial procession. In 1998 the permanent monument was ready: a landscaped park designed under the direction of the landscape architect Georges Descombes, in consultation with those concerned. Residents, next of kin and others involved had made a mosaic carpet. On a commemorative wall stand the names of the fatalities, with one place left open for all the unidentified dead. Around it a park was constructed with a flower garden and a 'footprint' of the buildings which were wiped out. Actual objects found in the rubble were sometimes incorporated into the paving stones with the mosaics. Amongst the mosaic tesserae, marbles, shards of mirrors, shells and beads are expressive personal fragments: crucifixes, toy cars, hair pins, buttons, keys, toy figures, coins, hearts and house numbers. Personal motifs were also formed: the word 'love', a name, a sunflower, and there is even a tile with a toy aeroplane, a cross and a heart enclosing a teardrop.

The site began to function as a monument, but also as a platform for protest, meetings, comfort and identity.[96] It was as Burgomaster Van Thijn had predicted in 1993, at the first commemoration: "The Bijlmer disaster is part of our collective memory." In the collective memory the tree began to also function as a pillory. As the investigation into the causes of the disaster dragged on, there were increasingly often notes of protest hung on the tree among the notes of support and sympathy. All nature of institutions thought responsible were pilloried there.

Gradually there were other voices raised to say that this place should be not only a commemorative monument for the victims of the disaster, but

---

[96] Since 1999 the management and maintenance of the monument has been in the hands of the Stichting Beheer Het Groeiend Monument [Stewardship of the Growing Monument Foundation], with Helen Burleson-Esajas as chairwoman. At the presentation of the plans she said, among other things, "The monument is for everyone. We will not define from above what all can happen there. But we think that it must become a real meeting place, and must be bubbling with life. It must be a place where prejudices and differences can be bridged, and where people can come to get energy." Quoted in VAN BOXTEL: 'Het monument is van iedereen' (1999).

also a meeting place for the many nationalities and cultures that make up the Bijlmer community, and a point of reference where a much greater protest, a much wider complaint could be seen and heard, if possible in the presence of the press.[97] Here we can see a process happening over a short period that also on a wide scale can be seen with war monuments: not only the actual victims of the First and Second World War, whose names are often inscribed on the monuments, are commemorated in such places, but all the victims of those wars, or of other wars and recent outbursts of violence. Respect for the specific victims then coincides with the dream of 'Never again!' In a society full of risks, aeroplane and train crashes and factory explosions can never be entirely excluded, but yet at disaster monuments the hope is proclaimed, the promise exacted, "this may never happen again!" With that, in addition to its commemorative function, the monument takes on a function of complaint, protest and hope. The monument assumes a role in referring to issues beyond itself, and attracts activities to it that are no longer directly connected with the events it commemorates. One could speak here of collective soul-searching.

As of this writing, other monuments that have been created in the last decade after disasters have not yet been appropriated for this function. Only the disasters in the Bijlmer and in Enschede are still commemorated with an annual public silent procession. The commemorations for the other disasters are less collective and massive in nature. On Texel, in Haarlem, in Eindhoven and in Laren there are also memorials for victims of aeroplane accidents. In Bovenkarspel, in a specially planted grove of trees, is a monument for the legionella victims. In Enschede and Volendam temporary monuments are in use, which will perhaps still grow up into official commemorative sites: in Enschede the fence around the levelled neighbourhood,[98] and various individual memorials around the city, in Volendam a separate corner of the cemetery. To what extent such disaster monuments will also begin to fulfil wider functions remains to be seen.

The memorial grove at Bovenkarspel belongs to a totally different category. Not only was a garden planted there with a number of young trees

---

[97] In the article by VAN BOXTEL previously mentioned (see note 96) one can note how the relationship between the survivors and the press is ambiguous: there is a desire to be left in peace, and a need for acknowledgement. See also the personal stories in the book by VAN TEESELING: *Het oog van de storm* (2001).

[98] The fence stood until the autumn of 2001; all the drawings and inscriptions on the fence are recorded in a photo book (the 'photo monument').

that commemorate the fatalities in the legionella outbreak, and all kinds
of bushes that represent the others involved, but there was also a monument placed in the form of a granite book with a memorial text and a
poem by the Dutch poet Ida Gerhardt, 'De gestorvene'. Survivors leave
all sorts of objects, such as letters, stuffed toys and items of clothing, in
the monument as memorials to their loved ones. Just as a form of universal symbolism is connected with the tree in the Bijlmer, as the tree
which survived the fire sea and became a focus for reflection on death
and life, so in Bovenkarspel people chose a park with trees to symbolise
the questions of life and death.[99] Here the issue is not whether the plan
was a good one and whether the grove can be said to be successful as a
memorial site aesthetically and in a ritual sense. Rather, it is whether
after a disaster which claimed fatalities from all parts of The Netherlands
– and over a considerable period, at that – a collective site can indeed be
created, which except for the local people involved can also become a ritual centre for the other victims. A second ritual 'awkwardness' here lies
in the concept of a grove itself: at the time it was created there were 28
fatalities, but in the meantime that number has risen to 31. For safety's
sake the text in the granite book speaks of "at least 30 unique people".
What is seldom mentioned in other monuments, namely the number of
non-fatal but seriously ill victims, is here expressed as follows: "Over 200
people became seriously ill."[100]

The planting of trees on special occasions is a universal phenomenon,
and also has a long tradition in The Netherlands. The best known are what
are termed the 'Orange trees', planted to mark events in the lives of members of the Dutch royal family, the House of Orange, such as the corona-
tions of Queen Wilhelmina in 1898 and Queen Juliana in 1948, the marriage of Princess Juliana and Prince Bernhard in 1937, the fiftieth birthday
of Queen Beatrix in 1988, and the silver wedding jubilee of the royal pair
in 1991. There have also been many trees planted to mark national events,
such as the Liberation Trees. But there are few trees linked with death.

---

[99] One can also think of the Cancer Woods that has been planted at the initiative of
the Queen Wilhelmina Fund (the Dutch Cancer Society) (see note 23).

[100] We have already referred above to the statistical distortion that takes place when
we speak only of the fatalities. Particularly after Volendam people have devoted considerable attention to the victims whose lives will be marked to the end by their burn
wounds, but among the survivors of the disasters at Faro and Enschede there are also
many who are scarred by burns.

Many trees have been planted on private property connected with a birth, or possibly a marriage, and are from this fact seen as 'trees of life', but it is often only in cemeteries that trees are planted to commemorate a mourned loved one. Especially when a tree is literally fed, as it were, from the old life that lies buried in the ground, such a tree can be seen as a symbol of continued life, and sometimes becomes explicitly linked with Christian faith in the resurrection. At the same time there is sometimes a pagan connection between the grave, the soul of the deceased and the young tree. The choice of a grove of trees in Bovenkarspel is however not linked in this way with this primeval symbolism, because the bodies are not buried there.

For some time we saw another spontaneous monument in Enschede: the plywood hoarding that was constructed around the disaster site directly after the event. Very quickly texts in felt pen, flowers, paraffin candles, photographs, stuffed toys and other memorial gifts began to appear, but later groups of school children also went to work making drawings that could play a role in their process of coping with the disaster. This wall was often photographed and used as a background for interviews. Disaster tourists also seem to want to make their presence known through graffiti of condolence. In the reconstruction of the disaster area, a permanent monument is being taken into account that will commemorate not only the fatalities but all the victims involved. In the meantime the hoarding has been photographed and recorded for the future in its entirety in what is termed a 'photo monument'. The hoarding has since been removed, as necessitated by the reconstruction work.

The memorials created elsewhere after disasters have a less public character. For instance, the monument in the military base at Eindhoven is in an area not open to the public. The temporary memorial that arose there at the time – a cross of birch trunks, with a row of paraffin candles, plants and flowers – made way for a permanent monument: a gravel path that begins with a small plaque with the names of the fatalities, and which runs around a memorial circle in which the original birch cross stands, with a small stone bearing only the date, July 15, 1996. Around the edge of the circle stand, at equal distances, 34 stone blocks, one for each fatality, with on top of each block a candle protected by glass. At the annual commemoration seven torches, which symbolise the survivors, are placed by the cross.[101]

---

[101] At the commemoration on July 15, 2001, three circles of chairs were set up around the memorial circle. On the chairs immediately behind the blocks of stone with the candles sat one of the immediate next of kin, who lit the candle as part of the ceremony. The seven torches were lit by the seven survivors.

In the basilica at Laren a vase commemorates the victims of the aeroplane crash at Faro. There are 50 names on it, rather than 57. The relatives of the other seven found a star sufficient.[102] That the memorial stands here is more or less a matter of chance; at the time of the first commemoration service it was this church which opened its doors during the Christmas season. A year after that a vase, made by the Portuguese ceramist Rodrigues Diaz, was placed in a niche. On the neck are two butterflies, the body of one of which is still caterpillar-like, in order to emphasize the idea of transition, but also with an allusion to the Greek word *psyche*, or soul, which also can mean butterfly. While this vase has a permanent place, a glass sheet with the names of the victims is brought out and placed at the front of the church only for the annual service of remembrance.

Two monuments resulted from the Dakota crash over the Waddenzee: one on the air base at De Cocksdorp on the coastal island of Texel, and the other in Haarlem. The memorial ceremony at the time was held at sea around a yellow buoy that indeed ritually marked the site of the drama, but when thought was given to a lasting monument another location was chosen: the garden of the Provincial government building in Haarlem, where it was dedicated precisely a year after the disaster. The monument was made by a local sculptor and consists of a basalt plinth with a glass sheet on it, onto which the names of the 32 victims have been sandblasted. The sheet is combined with a bronze sculpture that is constructed of wings that appear to fly away. The second monument was placed on the airport grounds near De Cocksdorp. It consists of a Dakota cast in bronze, flying above a silhouette of the island executed in stainless steel.

Overview

When surveying the series of memorials, it strikes one that monuments for disasters have different functions. The survivors could say with Jos Perry, "We commemorate, thus we exist." The public commemoration of the victims of disasters is a way of maintaining the visibility of a

---

[102] In The Netherlands statistics speak of 56 fatalities. A young man in Faro who was closely involved in the rescue action became severely depressed, and a week later ran off the road in his automobile and was killed, is regarded by all the immediately involved as the 57th victim.

disastrous event which happened in the recent past. It is also a complaint against the institutions involved, which failed and did not prevent the disaster. It is a meeting place where grief binds people together. It is a point of reference that acknowledges the risks in society. It is a stimulus for collective soul-searching. It is a ritual focus where the spirits of the dead can come to rest.

What also strikes one immediately is that in the ritual marking of the site of the disaster there is a division between the place where the disaster took place and the place where the bodies are buried. When victims are killed instantaneously a ritual marking of the place could also have to do with a sometimes implicit, sometimes explicit belief in "something that hangs around there," restless souls that are still a vague presence at the scene of a sudden death. In the case of traffic accidents and street violence – and not only in Southern European countries – this vague concept of a numinous, charged place might also play a role in the ritual marking of the location where "the soul was suddenly snatched from this life". In the Bijlmer we saw this idea expressed several times in the exorcism and reconciliation rituals performed by immigrant groups in front of the fenced-off disaster site.

The remembrance of the dead is however not just something which operates in the domain of religion or philosophies of life. It also has a clear social function. Remembrance is a social phenomenon. A monument is seen as a public acknowledgement of what happened to the victims. In his sociology of religion Durkheim explains it as follows.[103] Through the rite the group breathes new life into the feeling of solidarity, what is termed the 'we-feeling', at regular intervals. In the case of rituals surrounding disasters, a larger group of sympathizers demonstrate their sympathy for the smaller group of those directly involved. At the same time the larger group collectively acknowledge that this could have happened to them too. This collective acknowledgement of human vulnerability also creates positive mass. At the same time, in addition to the lament, there is a protest, complaint, rebellion being expressed. Commemorations that keep a disaster alive are a continuing complaint. A tangible monument is an adequate aid in all this; it defines the direction (sometimes literally, as in the case of a silent procession) and it marks the place. The memorial is a tangible reference, but is only a part of the collective

[103] Articulated in this context by JANSSEN: 'Stille omgang' (2000) 65-79, among others; see also PERRY: *Wij herdenken* (1999) Chapt. 1 and 2.

memory: *monumentum aere perennius*, it is in the mind of a people that a memorial exists that is more lasting than stone.

The monuments we have discussed above can be divided into three categories: 1) spontaneous, temporary monuments; 2) official monuments produced by an artist at the initiative of those directly involved and the authorities; 3) the individual grave. In the disasters studied here, only in Volendam is there a collective burial site; in none of the other situations do the public memorial site and the individual graves coincide.

The visual vocabulary of the spontaneous, temporary monuments is an expression of the masses immediately involved, but here too the spontaneity appears subject to the context. Thus the tree in the Bijlmer can be connected with the worldwide symbolism of trees, precisely suitable for the colourful, multicultural Bijlmer. In Eindhoven, on the contrary, the spontaneous monument was in the form of a birch cross and paraffin candles. Possibly a cross of birch branches, which after all sometimes yet begin to put out shoots, is a fitting symbol for those involved; but as a cross it strikes one as somewhat less spontaneous and open to fresh associations in this day and age. The hoarding in Enschede as a sounding board for sympathy and protest fits in the urban agglomeration of construction material, felt pens and graffiti with, now and then, a high 'I was here' content.

The visual language of the official monuments is very diverse. In the Bijlmer a mosaic and landscape were shaped around the tree, retaining the spontaneous centre and supplementing it with a memorial wall with texts that accompany the mosaic. Beyond that, the names of the victims were listed,[104] as well as, in smaller letters, the names of those who conceived and made the memorial. The two monuments arising from the Dakota disaster are clearly thought-through and placed in locations arrived at as the result of a logical process. What we see appear with many memorials is the ritual listing of names, first in the memorial service, then as a part of the physical monument. They are absent from the granite book in Bovenkarspel; this can be explained by the special nature of the legionella disaster, in which the number of fatalities was rising with rather long intervals between the deaths. In Enschede the names were read aloud during the service of remembrance, and at various places in the city personal memorials appeared, with a name on them. In addition to names we see birds (Haarlem), aeroplanes (Texel, Vught) and a music

---

[104] Among the names of the dead an empty space has been left to commemorate the anonymous, undocumented or unidentified victims.

staff (Vught). The references are clear. However, the aeroplane which crashed into the Bijlmer is not to be found in any form whatsoever in the memorials there; the same is true for the vase in Laren. Thus both spontaneous, artistically designed interpretations and traditional figurations have been used. This is also true for the individual graves which, except in Volendam, are generally shielded from the public eye.[105] What the developments have been in grave culture in the mother countries of the immigrant victims of the disasters in the Bijlmer and Enschede, is invisible for us.

In all cases, that there should be a monument was felt to be more or less self-evident. What will develop from the plans in Enschede and Volendam is still in the future, but the need for a collective memorial site is apparently intertwined with our era. In all cases the creation of a fitting monument is a delicate question. Initiatives from various directions coalesce and long discussions take place regarding the form, location and content. Names seem to be an almost invariable ingredient, but a list of names can also be experienced as unsuitable, for instance in cases where the number of dead could still rise, or where next of kin prefer that the name of their loved ones not be mentioned. There is also interaction necessary among the interested parties, local authorities and possibly the airport, airline, land owner or, on the other hand, the 'guilty' institution. In general it appears that those directly involved prefer to keep the control of the monument, and with that the annual commemoration, in their own hands as much as possible. Often the trust relation with authorities, investigative committees, 'guilty parties' and funders is so disrupted that such a process moves forward only with great difficulty.

It is striking that people often prefer to call upon an artist who comes from the region. Perry says of this,

> With an abstract monument he perhaps gains the approval of experts, but he runs the risk of not addressing the wider audience. Added to that, every monument right down to this day is by definition a congealed concept, a

---

[105] Upon seeing a photograph of the special corner of the Volendam cemetery, one gets the impression that there is something peculiar to these graves: all have a portrait photograph of the young person on the stone. Further investigation on the spot indicates, however, that almost all the other gravestones in the new portion of the cemetery also have photographs on them. It is true, though, that in the niche by these graves there are comparatively more 'youthful' paraphernalia to be seen, such as stone bears, a little horse, a bird and a hedgehog.

frozen expression, and therefore doomed to quickly – and in our time more quickly than before – become outdated.[106]

Apart from the question of the form, it appears that in The Netherlands both Calvinistic and republican traditions sometimes still exercise an inhibitory effect.

The role of monuments in the annual commemorations is clear. But not every survivor appears to be emotionally capable of participating in collective memorials. For them, sometimes choosing to visit and care for the grave is a more intimate and fitting act than participation in an annual memorial surrounded by cameras. Also, culture can determine that the mourning process comes to an end after the first year. Monuments however have a significance that influences much larger circles than that of the immediately involved. Monuments keep the memories and the demands alive. Monuments are therefore often at the same time a finger raised in warning, a call to vigilance and continued protest. In this sense, in addition to their anamnestic function, they evidently retain a certain social/critical function, even over the passage of time.

3.5. The Compassionate or Silent Procession (P. Post)

Plan and approach

From both memory and experience, it would appear that in a relatively short time in The Netherlands the phenomenon of the silent procession has developed into one of the most prominent public rituals after a disaster. With the disasters in Enschede and Volendam the question was not *if* a silent procession would be organised, but only when, where and how. Moreover, in a relatively short span of years in the 1990s, the silent procession appears to have become a rather general ritual.[107] It can be more broadly employed than just for collective disasters. In the public mind in The Netherlands the phenomenon of the silent procession is chiefly connected with the White March in Brussels (October, 1996) and with the many cases of senseless street violence in the 1990s. In other countries this strikingly Dutch phenomenon is spontaneously connected with the funeral of Princess Diana or with American 'march culture'. As

[106] Perry: *Wij herdenken* (1999) 98.
[107] See, in general, Post: 'La marche silencieuse' (2001); Idem: 'Silent procession' (2002).

we will soon see, both parallels miss the mark: at Diana's 'procession' everyone stood silent along the route, and American marches are anything but silent.

Surveying the repertoire of rituals after disasters (see Chapter 2), it becomes clear that the silent procession is not an isolated ritual, but it has become linked with the collective service of remembrance, and also with other localised memorial rituals at the scene of the disaster. Again, Enschede and Volendam offer examples. In these cases the silent procession was a march past a floral monument to a memorial service, in the Volkspark and the football stadium, respectively.

Silent processions particularly attract attention for their massive character. In Gorinchem, after the fatal shooting of two girls in a disco, on January 16, 1999, about 25,000 people joined the procession, in Enschede after the fireworks disaster (2000) more than 100,000, and in Volendam, after the cafe fire (2001) between 20,000 and 25,000.

For the media the silent procession is often the point on which a critical consideration of public memorial rituals focuses. In their reflections critics, cultural analysts and essayists readily point to the mass of people who walk one behind another, to the powerless character of the procession, to there being only the suggestion of community, and to the media that 'create' the procession.[108]

In this section we will further explore the phenomenon of the silent procession as a ritual. First, as a stepping off point, the procession in Enschede on Friday, May 19, 2000, will be described. Thereafter the development of the argument begins with an impression of the current situation with regard to reflections about and research on the phenomenon of the silent procession, first more generally in the media, then in academic investigations. From there, the ritual will be further positioned, and we will digress briefly to characterise and typify it. Finally, in a contextual analysis we will develop seven ritual references which in our eyes are relevant and definitive.

---

[108] For an impression of their critique, see the introduction in Chapt. 1. A list of newspaper articles on silent processions can be found in: POST, NUGTEREN & ZONDAG: *Rituelen na rampen* (2002).

The Compassionate Procession in Enschede

After the fireworks explosion on Saturday, May 13, 2000, in full page advertisements the City Council of Enschede invited people (i.e., the residents of Enschede) to participate in a procession.

The organisers said that they arrived at their initiative because there was a great felt need for collective mourning.[109] On Friday, at 5:00 p.m., everything in and around Enschede changed into a backdrop for the procession. Shops, restaurants, cafes and cinemas closed, train traffic (partially free) and bus lines were rerouted. According to plan, the procession began at 6:30 p.m. with a group of those directly involved and dignitaries (Crown Prince Willem-Alexander, Prime Minister Kok and Burgomaster Mans). It rained softly. The procession was broadcast live on television, both locally and nationally. Immediately after the start the procession grew to a crowd of more than 100,000. This destroyed the original plan for the event. It was no longer possible for a procession of this size to be wound up with the planned gathering in the Volkspark; indeed, at the close of the gathering there, tens of thousands of people were still under way. Later many were to express their disappointment at this: couldn't they have waited until everyone got there?

Even as later in Volendam, the Compassionate Procession went past a floral memorial and ended, in terms of time and space, in a ceremony (the Gathering of Solidarity), with speeches (among others, by Prime Minister Kok), music (by the Orchestra of the East, under the direction of Jaap van Zweden) and poetry. The address by Burgomaster Mans had the procession as its chief theme:

> In silence we have marched past the places that will always remain seared onto our retina, to which our memories will return again and again in time to come. Our hearts cried out with each step, with each step a thousand questions arose, grief and unbelief were to be read on every face.
>
> People walked with us who know unfathomable depths of grief because they have lost friends and loved ones, people with incoherent fears, people in tears, people with harrowing uncertainty and in total confusion. The terrible knife of the disaster has left us deeply wounded. We walked with citizens of this city from diverse backgrounds, many come among us long

---

[109] For the procession, with a description, photographs and the mayor's address, see DE LUGT: *De ramp van Enschede* (2000) 116-121. Cf. VAN HAASTRECHT, MARLET et al.: *Enschede, de ramp* (2001) 66-68.

ago from other cultures and become part of our society, others here but for a short time, all radically touched by this disaster. We have marched together and are here with each other, but not for an official memorial. That is still to come. For that we must find peace together, and sit down together. We hope that we will at that moment know more about the persons not yet found, about the missing, and the situation of the seriously wounded. There is not much that can be said at this moment, because our shock is too raw and our anger and revulsion too great. Among all of us, residents of Enschede, this shock and bewilderment will not disappear into the background. But there is also something else, which offers comfort to all of us. During a silent procession like this you do not say much, but you experience all the more for that. You experience the silent power of the people, as has been seen and felt in the days just past: the conspicuous, natural solidarity when disasters like this strike. We have seen unprecedented courage to face life, resiliency and great determination, to rise above this disaster, to do what is at hand to be done, to survive and move on together. This was a march of more than precious compassion, an expression of that inner strength of our solidarity. Let us encourage one another to hold fast to that strength in the difficult times that are still to come, as the big questions have to be answered and all the problems that are bearing down on us demand solutions.

We still have a silent procession ahead of us through a mine field of problems and cares. I am not going to thank you for your presence – that was natural and good, it was real, and straight from the heart. We are now going to continue our march together.[110]

Impressions of reflection and study

By means of a small diptych we will now offer an image of reflections on the phenomenon of the silent procession to date. We will make a distinction between more intuitive journalists and reflections expressed in essays, and more academic approaches.

In Chapter 1 we already gave several impressions of the first category.[111] We saw how the silent procession has become *the* paradigm for ritual after disaster. When speaking of it as such, people repeatedly point to the at least ambiguous character of the ritual, or frankly its veiling function. Without a basis in research, in various media journalists, cultural analysts, commentators and particularly social scientists indicate the problems they see

---

[110] DE LUGT: *De ramp van Enschede* (2000) 120.
[111] See Chapt. 1, 6-9.

with this new ritual. Further analysis of this file (leaving short columns and cartoons out of consideration) leads to the following five observations:

(a) First, it can be said that the discussions all show strong similarities. They take a critical stance in regard to the ritual as related to various events, sometimes disasters but generally cases of senseless street violence; they want to 'unmask' the ritual, as it were ("The silent procession is the lazy man's way to emotional composure"). They point to the dominance of the expression of collective emotions, the emotional high of group experience, and the short life and superficiality of this high and emotion. They note how there is never real protest involved. The suggested solidarity is adjudged to be wafer thin and false; for real depth and engagement or rootage in society there is the test of repetition, and few processions pass this test. It is a ritual that disguises impotence and obscures real analysis and responsibility. One constant in the critical evaluation is especially the element of decontextualisation. The procession leads to silence; everything connected with the disaster is set outside the society. Through this the ritual becomes hollow and empty; participation becomes risk-free and pointless. Again and again critics focus on the role of the media that make a circus of the event, on the role of the victims who are elevated to martyrs, and the mechanical and compulsive nature of the ritual. A disaster or a fatality, struck down in a suddenly and 'undeserved' manner in the public domain, appears to be automatically the cause for a silent procession.

In summary, there are really three questions or parameters by which people critically test the ritual: the question of the authenticity of the ritual, of genuine *communitas*, and of point and sense. The ultimate judgement is generally, as we have said, very critical: "too big, too much sentiment, too much ritual, too much a media event".[112]

(b) A frequently recurring theme in the discussions of the ritual of the silent procession is what in this study we term ritual interference. In this case what is involved is the reciprocal relation with Christian, ecclesiastical rites. Parts of the Roman Catholic repertoire such as processions and pilgrimages are often cited specifically.[113] Various authors point to the semi-religious elements in the processions and connect these with changes in the field of ritual: ecclesiastical rites are receding and these functions are being taken over by new public rites. The 'new ritual' of

[112] Quoted from the psychologist Koops in *Trouw*, May 18, 1999; cf. JANSSEN: 'Stille omgang' (2000) 72.
[113] Cf. ALBERS: 'Stille tochten' (2000).

silent procession is termed a free-floating ritual, detached from church and liturgy; the burgomaster is seen as the new clergyman; the presence of recognisable ritual acts, such as those with candles and paraffin lights, is underscored. In itself this is an interesting observation, but in the journalistic discussions however it often immediately takes on the character of a critique of religion. As we will see further on, the perspective is valuable, although on further consideration the degree of interference will be found to differ sharply from case to case. For instance this was strong and eye-catching in the case of the silent procession in Gorinchem, where the Burgomaster and a Protestant clergyman were co-leaders, and again clear in a way peculiar to the place in Catholic Volendam, but less so, or not at all the case in other processions such as the one in Enschede just sketched.

With regard to the reference to ecclesiastical/liturgical connections, separate mention should be made of a more general connection between the rise and popularity of silent processions and the general religious and spiritual revival. The silent procession then functions as a signal of a growing craving for spirituality, in the company of other very diverse signals such as the demand for contemplation and meditation centres, the attraction of Taizé among young people, and full bookings for weekends at monasteries and abbeys.

(c) Only in a few cases is there a more systematic and well-reasoned consideration.[114] A newspaper essay by Van Rensen stands out for its accurate positioning of the ritual, in which diverse connections are made with other adjacent ritual such as the massive mourning at the death of Princess Diana, the 'Dutroux affair' and the rituals of the Dutch national remembrance day observances on May 4. The author also poses the question of 'ritual calibre', and discusses the peculiar symbolism of the procession. Van Renssen also has an eye for the spatial dimensions and division of roles in the ritual. Ultimately his judgement too is critical: the procession is an expression of sympathy and rage, yet above all else it is mute, being silent together. The ritual places everything just outside of society.

(d) It is important to indicate how the journalistic reflections here mentioned are strongly defined by the specific context of 'senseless violence'. As we will show, various elements are at work here. There is the important fact that the ritual of the silent procession came to public

---

[114] Cf. BROER, et al.: 'Blind geweld, selectieve verontwaardiging', *Vrij Nederland* Jan. 23, 1999; VAN RENSSEN: 'Achter de stille tocht', in *de Volkskrant* Feb. 26, 2000.

notice in the 1990s, thanks to a series of processions following atten-
tion-grabbing cases of street violence, especially those after the death of
Meindert Tjoelker in 1996 in Leeuwarden (the death of Joes Kloppenburg on August 17, 1996 in Amsterdam was not followed by a procession at the time), through the processions in Vlaardingen (Daniel van
Cothem, January 14) and Roermond (Amin Quich, February 15) at the
beginning of 2000. With the recognisable perpetrator/victim perspective
there is a clear difference from a disaster, in which people rather think
and speak in terms of fate. Also, it is sympathy rather than rage and
protest that is involved in processions after disasters.

(e) The contexts which we have just distinguished, of senseless violence on the one side and disaster on the other, and the dominance of the
former in the critical discussions in the media which we have cited, explain
– so we can finally conclude – the absence of more positive or neutral
responses to the silent processions. This also has something to do with the
genre of the critical essay. For positive responses one must look to the
genre of the address, such as that by Burgomaster Mans after the silent
procession in Enschede quoted above, and in the traditional Christmas
address by Queen Beatrix, on Christmas Day 2000. There she termed the
silent procession a new, adequate ritual for compassion in solidarity.[115]

When we look at academic research, the yield is very modest. So far
as we can determine, contemporary silent processions have never been the
subject for a separate study. Directly and indirectly, the following studies
can be listed:

(a) A collection of papers from a symposium on senseless violence
addressed the rituals.[116] The contributions by Janssen and Van den
Hoogen which were discussed above must be particularly noted there.[117]

(b) Next, a series of sociological, empirical surveys coming out of the
White March (Brussels, 1996, 300,000 people), a response to the
'Dutroux affair,' are important. These specifically involve the question of
motivation: what brought out so many people? Reports on this Belgian
research appeared, among other places, in a special issue of the *Sociologische Gids* edited by Hellemans, a sociologist specialising in religion.[118]

---

[115] See footnote 18, Chapt. 2.

[116] D'HONDT (ed.): *Zinloos geweld herdacht* (2000).

[117] JANSSEN: 'Stille omgang' (2000); VAN DEN HOOGEN: 'Is de zonde nog te redden?'
(2000); cf. Chapt. 1.1.

[118] HELLEMANS (ed): 'Wit van het volk' (1998).

In particular, this important investigation reveals how specific the context of the White March was, and how the March can and may be linked with Dutch silent processions only with distinctions and many qualifications. The White March was first and foremost situated in the context of public distrust of governing authorities. It was thus not a real silent procession, but on the contrary a march against silence, as was made explicit in the title of the second White March on February 15, 1998 (in which 'only' 30,000 people participated): a march 'for the truth and against the law of silence'. The researchers emphasize the specifically Belgian political background of the procession, which was distorted by the Dutch media. The central factors named in the ritual explosion through the march are the enormous attention from the media, the intense emotionality and what is termed 'victim charisma'. Empirical research by Walgrave and Rihoux among 864 participants in processions of this sort enabled the researchers to sharpen the image.[119] It appears to be primarily a modern form of popular rebellion, an emotional movement and mobilisation in the sense of a moral crusade against the degeneration of the political and social situation in Belgium. In addition to the role of the media,[120] an important facilitating factor was the role of the spokespersons, of leaders. Among the meanings attributed to the marches, we find recognisable lines: the ritual of the collective procession is a form of civil religion; it works primarily to encourage community; and serves to exorcise danger and channel feelings of anxiety, but especially protest, vengeance and impotence.

Because this research indicates and develops precisely what in social and political terms was specifically Belgian about the White March, beyond this point it becomes less interesting for our examination of silent processions, although, as is still to be seen, in a general sense the White March certainly appears to have been an important ritual reference in the crucial period of 1996/1997 in The Netherlands.

(c) A Masters thesis by Bal does focus on the Dutch context of silent processions.[121] Bal's thesis in pastoral psychology takes the great silent procession in Gorinchem, approached as contemporary collective ritual,

---

[119] WALGRAVE & RIHOUX: 'De Belgische witte golf' (1998).

[120] See particularly WALGRAVE & MANSSENS: 'De Witte Mars' (1998).

[121] BAL: *De stille tocht in Gorinchem* (2000); see further MENKEN-BEKIUS, BAL & VAN DIJK-GROENEBOER: 'De kerk en stille tochten tegen geweld' (collection of articles) (2001) 272-301.

as its subject.[122] It is a modest theological project in which the primary emphasis is on developing and applying a theoretical framework. This framework is specifically formed and defined by the pastoral-theological model of ritual analysis and evaluation of the thesis supervisor, Menken-Bekius.[123] That is in itself somewhat surprising, since that model, as presented in her dissertation, is extremely oriented to the individual, while it is here employed for what is a collective ritual par excellence.[124] Nevertheless, Bal's thesis is a Masters level project with numerous valuable contributions for our subject.

The writer chiefly wants to bring to the surface the role of religion and discovery of meaning in the context of collective ritual. The procession is characterised as an intensified process of interpretation on the part of the participants. In the procession that process is further intensified by the confrontation with death and in a strong identification with other participants. The project is based on a series of sources which supplement each other: an extensive file of 255 newspaper articles, video and radio material, and a modest empirical survey, carried out with the aid of ten students (five in-depth interviews with persons directly involved and 111 survey responses from on the street in Gorinchem during the procession). The significant role played by the massive character of the event emerges from the inquiry: the crowd is impressive. Repeatedly the question of the point, the meaning, the effect of the procession comes to the fore; particularly the dimension of protest and complaint against senseless violence is named. It is striking that it appears from this inquiry that the aspect of silence is less prominently experienced than, for instance, the flowers. All told, the size and the flowers score highest.

(d) Finally, more indirectly, we can list a series of diverse studies in which silent processions and adjoining rituals are discussed. There is Post's inaugural lecture on open-air ritual tied to specific sites,[125] a study of

---

[122] As mentioned above, in 1999 two girls in the city of Gorinchem were victims of violence in an entertainment venue; on January 16, 1999, there was a large memorial in the city centre which included a silent procession.

[123] MENKEN-BEKIUS: *Rituelen in het individuele pastoraat* (1998); cf. now also: IDEM: *Werken met rituelen* (2001).

[124] To some extent one can note a change of perspective or difference in level. Collective phenomenon have consequences for groups *and* individuals. These are not exclusive approaches.

[125] POST: *Ritueel landschap* (1995); cf. the cultural geographic study: FOOTE: *Shadowed ground* (1997).

interference between popular religious and ecclesiastical-liturgical ritual[126] and a study of popular Christian ritual.[127] The silent procession is here linked with the tradition of ecclesiastical processions and funeral ritual. It is argued that we are here dealing with 'defective' ritual, in the sense that a silent march, as a procession, is really less linked to a defining ritual framework than a traditional procession is, whether that framework be a liturgy for stations of the Cross[128] or funeral ritual.[129] Also, the suspicion is expressed that as emerging ritual the processions chiefly have a prophylactic dimension: they are our society's means of warding off contingency.

Authors of various responses expressed their indignation at this approach.[130] The analysis was interpreted as arrogant and seen as following the line of the journalistic critique discussed above. The tenor was that justice was not being done to the silent procession as a modern ritual. Although these authors hardly did justice to the broad ritual analysis, and appear to have missed the much more important point of the connections with forms of ritual linked with specific sites such as pilgrimages and processions, we do have here an indirect witness to the remarkable appreciation with which the silent procession is received.

(e) Further, as indirect materials, we can list the studies into the ritual surrounding the death of Princess Diana[131] and the studies of Dutch processional culture by P.J. Margry, from which we will be drawing.[132] The many references to current silent processions in studies of rites and symbols we will leave out of consideration.[133]

---

[126] POST: 'Van paasvuur tot stille tocht' (1999).

[127] POST: *Het wonder van Dokkum* (2000).

[128] BALDOVIN: *The urban character* (1987).

[129] Cf. POST: *Ritueel landschap* (1995).

[130] Cf. for instance *de Bazuin* July 7, 2000, 27; MENKEN-BEKIUS: in *Inzage*, book journal, Sept. 2000, 5; DE BOER: in *Trouw* June 30, 2000, 16: headline: "Stille tochten zijn de bezweringsriten van weleer" (Silent processons are yesterday's exorcisms).

[131] GRIMES: *Deeply into the Bone* (2000) 275-280; POST: *Het wonder van Dokkum* (2000) 124-126; SHEPPY: *Funerals* (2001); SPEELMAN: 'The 'feast' of Diana's death' (2001).

[132] MARGRY: *Amsterdam* (1988); IDEM: 'Gebed en verbod' (1990); IDEM: 'Processie' (1993); IDEM: 'Processie-exercities' (1993); IDEM: 'Bedevaartrevival?' (1994); IDEM: 'Accommodatie' (1995); IDEM: *Goede en slechte tijden* (1995); IDEM: *Teedere quaesties* (2000).

[133] Cf. for instance MENKEN-BEKIUS: *Werken met rituelen* (2001) 13-15.

Further considerations on the rise of the ritual of the silent procession

When we place the current phenomenon of the silent procession in the descriptive and categorising context of ritual repertoires, five closely connected sub-repertoires come into the picture: the already frequently described rituals after disasters, rituals after fatalities arising from what is termed 'senseless violence', rituals after the sudden deaths of prominent persons, national remembrance of the dead, and finally all sorts of memorial and protest rituals.[134] There is clearly a strong mutual interrelationship among these repertoires, and also mutual influences. Although in the discussion of historic references we will shortly be casting the net more widely in terms of time, it still appears that the 1990s (and indeed the second half of that decade) was the key period for these relations. We will here be focusing on the occasion for holding the ritual, and zeroing in primarily on the silent procession and the ritual directly connected to it. We will leave other related ritual and general considerations on the ritual market out of our discussion. Thus, for instance, the wider context of new memorial rituals will only be mentioned briefly in our wider references still to follow, and will be discussed separately in Chapter 5, in relation to contemporary ritual dynamics.

Silent processions and disaster ritual

Referring back to the earlier survey of Dutch and international disasters in Chapter 2, for The Netherlands in the 1990s the Bijlmer disaster of 1992 can be cited as the first occasion where a silent procession was part of the ritual after the disaster, a procession that developed into an annual ritual of remembrance.[135] Every year a silent procession moves from the

[134] See above, section 2.3. Here we proceed from the current phenomenon of the silent procession. The context of these repertoires can be corroborated by the internet, for instance. Various search engines turn up an average of about 3000 'hits' for the term 'silent procession', which involve disasters, assaults of 'senseless violence', memorials and protest. The search engine Google yielded the highest score (3140, on December 3, 2001).

[135] See also the case study in 3.1. Whether the silent processions in Enschede or Volendam will develop into an annual ritual is still to be seen. One year after the firework disaster in Enschede, on Sunday, May 13, there was a procession past a series of designated points around the devastated neighbourhood (including the floral monument), as a part of a very diverse but also small scale remembrance. The precise number of participants cannot be given; the police and media spoke of 'several thousand'. If this disaster procession does develop into an annual tradition, even on a smaller and local scale, then we have here an obvious distinction with regard to processions after episodes of senseless violence.

Taibah mosque to the monument by the 'tree that witnessed everything', where a wreath laying then takes place. There is certainly the impression that the procession generated less public response at that time than has been the case for more recent disasters, and that actually the memorial service in the RAI was the central national disaster ritual on that occasion. The Faro disaster in December, 1992, the Hercules disaster in July, 1996, and the disaster involving the Dakota in September of that year were not followed by a silent procession, but by a memorial service.[136] The more recent disasters at Enschede (2000) and Volendam (2001) were marked with processions. Surveying the period from 1992 to 2001, from the Bijlmer disaster to Enschede and Volendam, one can note a remarkable change. The silent procession has developed into an almost natural and dominant standard ritual in the whole of rites after a disaster. Participation is very massive – more than 100,000 in the case of Enschede. We will here omit further consideration of international disaster ritual, as it is our judgement that it is of much less influence on the ritual of silent procession. A number of other international ritual references can certainly be of interest to us, as we will see.

Silent processions and episodes of street violence

The development we have just sketched has everything to do with a second repertoire to which we will now refer: rituals in the context of episodes of senseless violence. In the period 1996-2000 there were a series of successive cases of senseless violence in The Netherlands, which have appealed to the popular imagination. The victims are often young, and fall in urban areas devoted to recreation and entertainment. Although the ritual attention seems extremely selective if we survey all cases of fatal street violence, after the death of Meindert Tjoelker a pattern did develop: people remembered the victim shortly after the violent death with a silent procession early in the evening, in which the site of the attack was an important point. In the case of Tjoelker, there was also a new ritual that does not later return in this mass form: during the funeral pupils joined hands in a great silent circle, a chain of solidarity.

---

[136] For the Hercules service see section 3.2; the Faro disaster on December 21, 1992, was officially remembered with a service on December 30, 1992, in Martinair's Hanger 32 in Schiphol East.

Thus for this repertoire the following picture takes shape: after the death of Joes Kloppenburg (Amsterdam, August, 1966), no procession; after the death of Tjoelker (Leeuwarden, September, 1997) one of the first large silent processions (about 23,000 participants). Then come a series of silent processions with sharply differing participation and degrees of media attention: April, 1998, in Tiel (5000 participants); December, 1998, in Amsterdam (several hundred participants); January, 1999, in The Hague (300 participants); January, 1999, in Gorinchem (25,000 to 30,000 participants); May, 1999, in Zwaagwesteinde (20,000 participants); August, 1999, in Assen (200 participants); September, 1999, in Zwolle (300 participants); September, 1999, the first National Silent Procession, with 2000 participants; October, 2000, in Utrecht (about 2000 participants); January, 2000, in Vlaardingen (30,000 participants); May, 2000, in Zeeburg (an Amsterdam neighbourhood; several hundred participants); and July, 2000, in Vught (several hundred participants).

This survey is far from complete, but certainly gives one a picture. Through memorials for victims of violence, since 1997 in The Netherlands the ritual of the silent procession has become connected with, and visible as, collective ritual in the public domain.

If one looks further at the bulging files on silent processions in the 1990s, then the next thing that strikes one is that the point of concentration lies in the period 1996/1997. The great White March for Belgium's missing and murdered children took place in Brussels in October, 1996, an event which in Dutch perceptions came across primarily as a silent procession. All sorts of components of that ritual, such as the reading of names and the colour white (for clothing and flowers) also recur later in other mass processions. In terms of ritual form, there is unmistakably a direct link between the White March and what can be considered the first real Dutch silent procession, that in Leeuwarden in September, 1997. But there are other ritual connections.

Silent processions and death of prominent persons

Another major source of influence has been the rites after the sudden deaths of prominent figures. Because of the wide media attention that accrues to famed persons who are murdered or die in accidents, the public memorial rituals which follow also bathe in the media spotlight.

Here we have in mind, for instance, the Palme[137] and Rabin assassinations (February, 1986, and November, 1995, respectively), but especially the explosion of memorial ritual in August and September, 1997, following the death of Princess Diana. In a general sense, in various manners – informally and on smaller scale in Paris and London, but impressively and in a manner peculiar to this event itself in the funeral rites in London – this included the ritual of the silent procession. Quite correctly, by now numerous publications have pointed to the enormous impression that this ritual made worldwide at the time, and the great influence that it exerted on memorial ritual.[138] Thus around 1996/1997 there arose a whole concentration of collective and public memorial ritual that was mutually closely linked: the White March in Brussels, the death of Tjoelker in Leeuwarden and the death of Princess Diana. It can be suggested that it was this concentration, in which processions and silence are prominently present in the memorial ritual, which placed the silent procession on the map as a public, collective ritual, so that subsequently for every disaster, larger or smaller, people began to organise a silent procession as an obvious response.

Thus here the international perspective is emphatically present, and decidedly not only linked with Diana. We can also briefly refer to the massive silent procession that was held on August 16, 1997, on the 20th anniversary of the death of Elvis Presley. About 40,000 fans walked in a silent procession around his home Graceland in Memphis.

Since that time, for The Netherlands, the explosion of rituals after the murder of the politician Pim Fortuyn (May, 2002), including a series of silent processions, can be added to the list.

Silent processions in the context of national remembrance of the dead of World War II

Without listing all the other, wider ritual frameworks that have a long tradition internationally, such as Roman Catholic liturgical silent processions, marches, parades and defilés, as a fourth repertoire running into the silent procession we can point to the silent processions that are still held throughout The Netherlands on May 4, as part of the commemoration of those

---

[137] SCHARFE: 'Totengedenken' (1989).
[138] See note 131.

who died in World War II.[139] Although the initial centralised initiative
after 1946 to organise an official silent procession in each community has
since been abandoned (see below), in hundreds of places around The
Netherlands silent processions, mostly rather small-scale and without
media attention, continue to held as part of the national remembrance
ceremonies. Sometimes these will include strongly localised rituals near a
former prison camp or execution site, but often the community war monument is the end point of the procession. Generally the ritual of the procession is coupled with the national Memorial Day on May 4, although
sometimes there are peculiar memorial dates. The memorial ritual has a
fixed pattern: several dozens or several hundreds of participants walk to the
war memorial in a procession organised by the civil authorities or a local
committee. There a period of silence is observed, an address is delivered,
followed by a ritual involving the national flag, the national anthem and/or
the Last Post, and a defilé with flowers and the laying of a wreath. A difference from the silent processions after disasters is that a collective memorial service generally precedes the silent procession to the monument.

We are here dealing with a rather autonomous, often forgotten ritual,
which since 1946 has taken place annually, and now and then has reso-
nance with contemporary developments in silent processions. We will
return to this in the broader contextual discussion.

Silent processions in memorial and protest ritual

Finally, as the fifth line we can list general public, collective memorial and
protest ritual in the second half of the 1990s.[140] We will shortly characterise and describe the genre of new memorial ritual and the longer tradition of protest ritual as important references. At this point it will be
sufficient to briefly recall and note how here too the silent procession was
employed as ritual.

First, in the context of attacks and remembrance of the dead there is
often connection with the repertoire mentioned. We are here dealing

---

[139] The Dutch 'Nationale Dodenherdenking' on May 4, the national remembrance
of the dead of World War II, is equivalent to the American Memorial Day (May 30,
celebrated on the last Monday of May). The British equivalent is Remembrance Day or
Remembrance Sunday, celebrated on the Sunday closest to November 11.

[140] For memorial ritual in a general sense, see FRIJHOFF: *Heiligen* (1998), and PERRY:
Wij herdenken (1999).

with marches as protest against senseless violence and discrimination, or for human rights and peace, for instance. In the period 1997-1999 there were smaller silent marches held many places in The Netherlands against rising violence and discrimination, organised by schools, neighbourhood centres, churches or municipalities. White flowers were a regularly recurring attribute in these marches.

Likewise a connection with both outrages and memorialising the dead can be assumed in the silent processions with which, beginning in 2000, people demanded attention for the violence in Indonesia, and more particularly in the Moluccan Islands.

Further, with increasing frequency there are new annual memorials for groups of victims of all sorts (AIDS victims, victims of traffic accidents, cancer victims, etc.), but such marches can frequently also mark various other events or be expressions of diverse forms of protest. What is being protested may differ greatly, but it is striking that the silent procession rather generally defines the ritual design. Furthermore, this is clearly an international phenomenon. The many processions held in Spain after still another bloody attack by the Basque terror organisation ETA can be named in this regard.[141] In The Netherlands there has been a wider range of diverse processions: in Amsterdam a silent procession was held to mark the abolition of slavery in Dutch colonies, and civil servants in the Province of South Holland held a silent march to protest the firing of a colleague.[142] In many places Amnesty International organises silent torchlight parades on December 10, Human Rights Day; in 1999 Women for Peace marched through the city centre of Eindhoven for peace in the Balkans; in Hilversum, on Saturday, July 28, 2000, the 250th anniversary of the death of Bach was marked by a proper silent procession.

This is but a random selection of the explosion of silent processions after 1996/1997. One could also say that there has been a certain degree of ritual inflation. As it happens, the file on silent processions also has marches for fatal assaults on animals, such as the baby camel Abdulah in the Circus Bongo, stoned to death by malicious teenagers in Zwolle (June 14, 1999). But silent processions occasioned by the foot and mouth epidemic in the first half of 2001, when a large proportion of the livestock in England and The Netherlands were destroyed, always a combination

---

[141] One of the largest took place in Bilbao on August 7, 2000.
[142] The procession on September 22, 1999, was termed 'an expression of alarm'.

of protest and grief at the massive slaughter ('clearance'), drew few participants.

These dimensions of protest and remembrance are, as we have said,
also to be found as part of the ritual after episodes of street violence. Certainly when a march is detached from any concrete instance, the dimension of protest can come to dominate over the memorial, as was the case
in the first National Silent Procession in The Hague, September, 1999,
which preceded the handing in of a petition against street violence. There
have recently been various signs that, from the feeling of a certain inflation, people feel the need to rethink what a 'real' silent procession is.

In summary, from this description of the repertoire it can be said that,
through mutual connections and influences within the five repertoires
discussed, in The Netherlands the ritual of the silent procession has developed into an established, universally employable public collective memorial and protest ritual. Sometimes the accent clearly lies on remembrance,
sometimes on protest, but most often both are present in the procession.
Generally the processions share dimensions of remembrance, sympathy
and protest. The previously mentioned Christmas address by Queen
Beatrix in 2000 formed a sort of official, national acknowledgement or
'canonisation' of the ritual as an expression of sympathy.

Digression: short ritual characterisation of a silent procession

In terms of ritual form, looking at both internal components and surrounding ritual, and despite the discussion mentioned above regarding
the precise definition of the concept of the silent procession (in particular focusing on the memorial and protest dimensions), a further interim
definition and characterisation can be given:[143] a silent procession is first
of all a memorial ritual. Since 1946 it has belonged to the annual Dutch
national ritual of remembrance of the dead. In the 1990s it became the
collective, public ritual par excellence that took place after poignant,
impressive, sudden undeserved death, individual or collective. More generally, after 1996/1997 the phenomenon of the silent procession has been
connected with all sorts of memorial and protest ritual.

---

[143] As characteristics BAL: *De stille tocht in Gorinchem* (2000) lists, successively (a)
sudden, undeserved death; (b) no natural catastrophe as cause; (c) the large number of
people; (d) a collective and public, and (e) ephemeral nature; (f) accompanied by
particular symbolic acts such as placing flowers, lighting candles, addresses and music.

The current popularity of the silent procession is chiefly linked with a series of dramatic events in the 1990s, both street violence and disasters. As a rule the procession takes place one to two weeks after the event (Gorinchem, Vlaardingen and Enschede: about a week; Volendam: 12 days; there are also processions that are held much later, for instance 40 days after the event, for Recep Uzur, in Zeeburg, May 14, 2000), in the evening around dusk (Gorinchem, 6:30 p.m., Vlaardingen, 8:00 p.m., and Volendam, 7:00 p.m.). Frequently Friday is chosen (Vlaardingen, Enschede and Volendam). Sometimes the day on which the original event occurred is decisive, as Saturday in Gorinchem.[144]

The timing after the original event seems not unimportant. There is much to indicate that, among other things, this type of silent procession serves as a *rite de passage*:[145] with the procession, those involved close the phase of direct confrontation with the disaster or attack, and proceed to the subsequent phase of coping, in which there is room for more distance and further processing of what has happened. Frequently the victims are buried by the time of the procession. The specific situation in Volendam therefore explains the discussion there over the scheduling of the procession. Many were still in critical condition in hospitals in The Netherlands and adjoining countries, and many were not yet ready for a rite of passage in which a certain phase could be closed.

Initiative and organisation are diverse. They can be in the hands of family, friends or acquaintances, but also of the municipality (Vlaardingen, Enschede). Well prior to the procession a route of about two kilometres is planned (there are longer processions, such as Enschede, and shorter, such as Volendam). A silent procession is related to a specific location: it passes the site of the attack/disaster, and/or a monument or floral tribute.[146] As the starting and ending points for the route suitable gathering places such as a square or park are generally chosen. At the beginning there can also be multiple collection and starting points for various groups. As well as the relation to specific places, the procession also has a collective and public nature. It takes place in public space; in

[144] Not only had the fatal violence taken place on the night of Saturday/Sunday, but the funeral of one of the victims took place on the Saturday of the silent procession.

[145] For a recent treatment of the genre of the *rite de passage*, see GRIMES: *Deeply into the bone* (2000).

[146] For ritual connected with a specific location: POST: *Het wonder van Dokkum* (2000) Chapt. 5: 89-114, particularly 107-111; cf. also DEPONDT: 'Monumenten', in *de Volkskrant* Oct. 17, 1997.

principle everyone can participate. Yet it is generally rigorously organised and from the moment it steps off has a predetermined succession of participants. Generally the procession is a one-off event; on rare occasions the procession develops into an annual tradition, as it has in the Bijlmer. The procession is closed with a sober or more elaborate ceremony, which can include a wreath laying, addresses, music or the delivery of a petition (as in the case of the first National Silent Procession in The Hague).

One of the more or less invariable components is silence (public transit is suspended, stores and restaurants close, and in the case of the Bijlmer there were no low-flying aeroplanes during the procession); sometimes a ritual silence (one minute or longer) is also observed as a part of the ritual, for instance as a bridge between the procession and the service of remembrance which follows it (Volendam); bells toll (sometimes not just locally, but nationally, as in the case of Gorinchem, sometimes for a set time, sometimes during the whole procession, as in Volendam).

Attributes include flowers: particularly white roses or other white flowers have become popular in silent processions. One may suspect that the influence of the White March in Brussels was important here. The white rose was the symbol for the first National Silent Procession in The Hague, and subsequently returned in Volendam.[147] Light or fire in the form or torches, candles, paraffin candles, Chinese or propane lanterns are also important attributes. There are actually no variants of this ritual; the shape is reasonably fixed. At the most one can point to the ritual which according to our research appeared only once: the mass silent circle which was made by the students in Leeuwarden joining hands during the funeral of Meindert Tjoelker (September, 1997).

The media play an important role in relation to silent processions. A procession is publicised through the media and the participation is to a large extent dependent on media notice. Larger processions such as those in the Bijlmer, Gorinchem, Enschede, Vlaardingen and Volendam were all broadcast live on multiple networks, nationally and locally simultaneously. This media attention has evoked various responses. There appears to be a paradox here: on the one side there is the irritation that was expressed so strongly in the memorial service in Volendam; on the other

---

[147] The florists in Volendam had bought in 5000 white roses which were sold for the benefit of the victim support fund. For the rest, the white rose has become popular apart from disasters and processions; together with the red rose it is the favourite flower for Valentines's Day. See section 3.3 in this book.

side there is the acknowledgement of the dramatic events through media attention.

Seven ritual references

As a further contextual ritual analysis of the contemporary silent procession, seven ritual references can now be elaborated. These are the contexts which in our opinion are relevant and definitive. The contextual perspective here is now wider, both in terms of the phenomenology of ritual and in time. The order of the references is not random. First we stay close to the ritual phenomenon, and then draw larger circles of influence and connection. These will be, successively, the ritual cluster of 1996/1997, the Dutch national Remembrance Day, processional culture, funeral ritual, marches, silence, and new forms of memorial ritual.

The ritual cluster of 1996/1997

As we have already suggested above, there is a good deal to indicate that memorial ritual which arose in the period between October, 1996, and September, 1997, had a large and immediate influence on the rise and establishment of the ritual of silent processions in The Netherlands. Particularly involved were the White March in Brussels, the ritual after the death of Meindert Tjoelker in Leeuwarden, and the explosion of ritual after the death of Princess Diana. We also saw that in the case of the White March, and likewise in the case of Diana's death, it was not so much the actual ritual repertoire that was important, as particular appropriations and images of it. A collective act which broke through the everyday order and which expressed both solidarity and protest became the response to a sudden, undeserved death. This reference will not be further developed here; in the discussion of the five immediate ritual contexts we have just elaborated upon it.

Dutch National Remembrance Day

In discussions of the phenomenon of the silent procession, remarkably little reference has been made to the connection which exists with the tradition of the Dutch national memorial observance for the dead of the Second World War.[148] This is where the term 'silent procession' has its

---

[148] BARNARD: 'De Nationale Herdenking' (2001).

formal origins. A silent procession is part of the ritual for the annual
remembrance of the Second World War in The Netherlands, which in
turn is a part of the national celebrations and thanksgiving days that
arose all across Europe from the end of the 19th century in the context
of more or less explicit nationalism and the civic ritual connected with
it. After 1945 Prime Minister Schermerhorn and Queen Wilhelmina
called for memorials for the dead to be held everywhere in the country,
and for silent processions to be organised as a part of the observance.
Initially this initiative had a strong tendency to uniformity, and national
guidelines for the memorial ritual were promulgated. Over the course of
the years many of the local memorial processions disappeared. Yet, as we
have said, many continue to exist.

Some of the processions have more than a local character. One example is the Overveen silent procession in the community of Bloemendaal.
This procession has been the subject of an anthropological case study by
Marina de Vries.[149] More than 6000 resistance fighters who were executed by German firing squads in the dunes are commemorated annually in the Overveen observance. It is an austere ritual. There is a silent
procession, bells are tolled, there is a flag ritual, speeches, the Lord's Prayer
is said, the national anthem sung, and flowers and wreathes are placed.

The first national Remembrance Day, with silent processions across
The Netherlands, was held on May 4, 1946. Later there was a centrali-
sation of the ritual in the observances on the Dam in Amsterdam, at the
National War Monument. After 1961 the Remembrance ritual was
increasingly freed from the Second World War, and it took on a more
general character. In the 1970s and 1980s there was discussion of dispens-
ing with the national Remembrance Day, which ultimately continued to
exist but took on a broader purpose. In addition to its focus on the Second World War and being an expression of national unity and solidarity, it now also focused on values such as freedom and peace, and protest
against injustice and discrimination. That can be seen in the various May
4 processions.

As a deeply-rooted collective, public ritual with a local focus, the
Dutch Remembrance Day is an important, although primarily indirect
and subconscious ritual reference for the silent processions after the mid-
1990s. The 'original' silent processions in turn carry with them other

[149] DE VRIES: 'Twee minuten' (1991).

references, such as for instance the links with processional and pilgrimage ritual. Those involved in Overveen, for example, see the procession as a pilgrimage to the cemetery as a sacred spot. Elsewhere in Europe this pilgrimage reference in location-specific memorial rituals for the First World War is still much stronger, and to this day the term used is 'war grave pilgrimage'.[150]

A final point of interest is that, in reaction to the rise of all sorts of silent processions, recently the organisers of the Remembrance Day processions have begun to avoid the term 'silent procession' for the war commemoration on May 4, and speak rather of a 'memorial procession'.

Procession culture

With this the third, and now more general ritual context comes into the picture, that of the liturgical procession in general and that of Dutch procession culture and the *stille omgang* (silent round) in particular.

Within the tradition of Christian ritual, ritual going and returning, *procedere*, can certainly be considered the most fundamental basic form of ritual.[151] This ritual takes all kinds of forms: small processions and circumambulations as components of the liturgy inside and outside church buildings, massive processions as pilgrimages, and particularly too the long tradition of stations of the Cross in cities since the fourth century. With regard to contemporary silent processions the tradition of ritual processions in urban settings deserves particular notice.[152]

In the Dutch situation there is a concrete reference to the processional culture as it was shaped in post-Reformation times, and particularly in the 19th century. Through the well-documented research into Dutch processional culture by Peter Jan Margry we have now a good picture of the specific character of this ritual reference. In periods in which Roman Catholic public ecclesiastical ritual acts were repressed by Reformed or neutral authorities, in the Dutch situation a certain sacral/ritual structure was maintained by carrying out particular rites in a non-ostentatious manner. Thus certain processions survived in the 17th and 18th century by 'making rounds'. Here 'round' refers to the old processional route

---

[150] WALTER: 'War grave pilgrimage' (1993).
[151] In general: FELBECKER: *Die Prozession* (1995).
[152] BALDOVIN: *The urban character* (1987); POST: *Ritueel landschap* (1995).

through a city. Through an unobtrusive round, often informal or even individual, contact was maintained with the old medieval processional tradition, and it was kept alive. The modest form fit with the generally retiring stance that characterised 19th century Dutch Catholicism. Silence was here an important element. Indeed, for their silent, retiring character Catholics were referred to as 'silent burghers'. These rounds developed into an entirely unique variant of processional ritual. Margry suspects that the origin of this variant, which came to be called the 'silent round', lay in Den Bosch. The cholera epidemic of 1866 provoked a separate prophylactic ritual directed to Mary as the patron saint of the city. A public devotional procession, such as would have been held before the Reformation, was legally forbidden, but an accommodated alternative was possible. Men walked the route silently, and this silent procession grew up into a massive annual ritual with 15,000 male participants in 1889. Thus, as the silent round, the silent procession became a part of Roman Catholic devotional life in the public urban domain, and developed from an individual ritual act into a successful mass ritual. In Amsterdam, famously, the round grew into one of the largest annual public rituals, but many cities still have their silent round. The rise of these processions was closely connected with the limitations of the ban on processions: in many respects it was a reaction to that law, and the procession or round thus also took on the nature of a protest. In his study Margry shows how these silent processions were no static ritual, but in each city responded to a certain localised context. Across the board however the protest dimension is to be found, as well as a tendency to increasingly dress the procession up and give it more splendour.

In summary, then, we have here an important and typically Dutch historic ritual reference for the present silent processions. In view of this, the silent procession in Volendam, twelve days after the fire, yields still more piquant details. The procession, with gas lanterns leading the column, showed remarkable similarities with the processions that previously moved along the dike to St. Vincent's Church, for instance at the close of the annual pilgrimage to the Marian pilgrimage site at Kevelaer, not far over the Dutch border. A large painting by Nico Jungmann that was acquired by the Zuiderzee Museum in Enkhuizen shows this evening procession around 1900 in all its understated glory (see Plate 13).[153]

---

[153] See POST: *Ritueel landschap* (1995) note 3, illus. 1.

Funeral ritual

A fourth ritual reference is likewise a type of procession, namely the procession which has for ages been part of the funeral ritual. In fact, in a formal sense funeral ritual has two generally silent processions: the first moves from the home of the deceased to the church, and the second, at the end of the church service, to the cemetery. By now the coherence among the several parts of funeral ritual has been disrupted by causes of various natures (they are separated in time and place, and generally are not done on foot). Yet, indirectly in the present silent processions there is still more or less of a realisation of this context of funeral ritual. That came to the fore in the disaster in Volendam, for instance, when in the funerals this pair of silent processions from home to church and church to the cemetery at St. Vincent's was made on foot.

There is also another, smaller reference to the silent procession in ritual involving the dead, namely that of the general ecclesiastical remembrance of the dead on All Saints Day. In several places in The Netherlands it remains the custom to move in a silent procession from the parish church to the cemetery on All Souls Eve (Blaricum and Salland; until into the 1960s this was more widespread).[154] Elsewhere in the Catholic regions of Europe this practice is more widely known.

Marches

Often the long tradition of marches on all sorts of occasions and of all different natures is recognised to be a ritual context. These include legendary marches with strongly political dimensions, such as those of Gandhi and Mussolini. This tradition runs right up through the present; a recent example would be the huge march on Mexico City by the Zapatistas in March, 2001, to stand up for the rights of the indigenous Indians. Particularly in the second half of the 1990s, a period which we have earlier proposed to be crucial, in the United States there were a series of massive marches as public events with specific political themes. These marches have the nature of a moral appeal, and are indeed termed 'moral crusades'. The themes have included family values and marital fidelity. In 1995 there was the Million Man March, in 1996 the Promise

---

[154] This tradition, in Blaricum, was worked up into a case study by Post: POST: 'Religious popular culture' (1998).

Keepers March, and in 1997 the Million Woman March. But there have also been other marches, such as the Gay Pride parades in numerous places. Still more generally, lying behind these were the massive demonstrations of the 1960s, 1970s and 1980s. Especially the rites of the peace movement in these decades deserve mention: marches, silent processions and wakes were part of their standard repertoire. These marches, for instance against nuclear weapons in The Netherlands, could at that time bring out up to 500,000 people. Throughout this period, at various places around the world, there were also marches and silent processions that were repeated monthly or bi-monthly, for instance those against eh military junta in Argentina, beginning in 1976. This tradition of demonstrative protest marches clearly returns in the silent procession as a generally applicable protest ritual, examples of which we have listed earlier.

Silence

One fundamental element of the ritual of the silent procession is the silence.[155] This aspect deserves a separate brief discussion. The ritual of procession, of *procedere*, receives an enormous extra charge and ritual added value through the silence. That has to do with the contrast effect of silence in our noisy culture. Rituality, spirituality, reflection and commemoration are rather generally, and in increasing measure connected with the contrast of silence. One may here think of meditation centres ('stiltecentra/silence centres'), hundreds of which have been established, involving relative silence.[156] One can also think of the attraction exercised by monasteries and abbeys; for The Netherlands there is already an actual 'silence atlas' on the market.[157] For the rest, silence in a ritual setting is strongly linked to culture. For instance, in the ancient and late classical world silent prayer was controversial, being regarded as dangerous. One prayed out loud; ritual acts taking place in silence were seen as magical and suspect.[158] In the monastic tradition silence has a long history as a strong form of asceticism in many religious traditions, but the *favete linguis* is also a powerful protest or an expression of the virtue of *modestia*.

---

[155] PEETERS: 'Stilte' (2001); MATTHEEUWS: 'De stilte zingt U toe' (2001) with literature in note 1.
[156] POST & SCHMID: 'Centrum van stilte' (2001).
[157] BREUKEL: *Stilte atlas* (2000).
[158] VAN DER HORST: 'Silent prayer' (1994).

The widespread ritual of observing a minute or more of silence in a ceremony of remembrance has already been mentioned repeatedly.

The great value that people attach to silence as the general setting for memorial ritual has likewise been mentioned. All 'life' is suspended: no traffic, no public transit, shops, restaurants and bars shut their doors. Breaking the expected silence can lead to considerable annoyance, as was seen at the memorial for the Bijlmer disaster and, later, the dedication of the Dachau monument in the Amsterdamse Bos on Sunday, December 2, 1996: in both cases aeroplane noise from nearby Schiphol Airport provoked strong expressions of indignation and anger.

It was already indicated previously that silence also has something ambiguous about it: as well as powerful and expressive ritual expression, it is also connected with refusal to speak out, with not plainly calling things by their name. In the image we have of it, we often for instance forget that the White Marches in Belgium were at that time processions against silence.

New forms of memorial ritual

All the varied forms of new memorial ritual form a final important reference. These are a particular segment of newly emerging rituals. The silent processions can be connected with a remarkable rise in public and collective memorial rituals by and for diverse groups. Sometimes the link with silence and a procession is direct; usually, however, it involves a general, related ritual. New memorial ritual is a multifaceted whole of memorials for victims in group format, which also arose in the critical period of the 1990s already mentioned. In addition to the previously noticed annual commemorations of disasters at a memorial monument (the Bijlmer disaster, the Dakota and Hercules crashes, and the Faro disaster commemorated in Laren[159]), there are annual memorials for victims of road traffic accidents (generally in a church in different city each year, since 1996), Aids Memorial Day (international), the Cancer Memorial observance since 1999, the memorial in the 'cancer woods' in Lelystad since 2000, the Day of the Missing since 2000 in Utrecht, for all missing persons, the memorial for all missing children at the monument for missing children at Schiphol (dedicated February, 2000), the memorial

---

[159] The commemoration of the Faro disaster takes place annually in Sint Jans basilica in Laren, North Holland, in December. In an action sponsored by the Antony Ruys Foundation, the 57 dead and 106 wounded are remembered with 57 candles.

for murdered children since 2000 in Tilburg, and finally Transplant Day
(biannually since 2000) to remember anonymous organ donors.

The first National Silent Procession (The Hague, 1999) fits in this
context of rising new annual memorials, as does also the memorial conducted at the monument for victims of street violence officially dedicated
in February, 2001, in Vlaardingen.

The similarities running through this new memorial ritual repertoire
are striking. In each case they involve an annual memorial for a certain
group of victims, generally at a monument that has been set up for this
group. The rise of this repertoire has everything to do with the ritual
dynamic which we will discuss later.[160] Here we will simply point to the
fact that on the one side there is a sort of communal ritual setting in the
case of both the emerging silent processions and this memorial ritual, but
on the other side that these memorial rituals are a reaction to the rise of
the silent processions as memorial rituals accompanying certain obvious
events such as disasters. In the memorial rituals people seek to give attention to 'silent victims' for whom no national silent processions are organised. For instance, after the massive attention given to victims of the disasters in Enschede and Volendam, next of kin of traffic fatalities
complained that victims of road accidents (more than 1100 a year in
The Netherlands) received almost no public ritual acknowledgement.
Here, as we have noted previously, recognition again is seen to play a central role in rituals such as silent processions and memorial observances.

Several closing remarks

In a separate chapter we will place disaster ritual, and also the silent
processions, into the wider context of ritual dynamics. Here, by way of
closing this thematic discussion of the phenomenon of silent processions,
we will add several notes:

Scenario or script

As is certainly the case with more rituals, for the silent procession there
is a sort of ritual scenario or script. A script or scenario, as it were,
prescribing ritual responses and actions on certain occasions, is on file in
our collective memory, ready for use. After a disaster or a fatal assault this

---

[160] See Chapt. 5.

script surfaces spontaneously: people know what they must do, or after certain considerations must have others do. This mechanism has been discussed before in studies of religious popular culture[161] or modern rites of passage[162]. In this connection Grimes points to the dangerous side of such pre-existing scripts: to wit, the ritual script is often linked to concrete previous ritual performances and with a hackneyed mental image for which they form the basis. Often this image is determined by appealing and increasingly idealised rituals, which are often also atypical. The script can thus lead to 'ritual idealism', in the face of which the average reality always shades off into greyness, resulting in disappointment and disillusionment. For instance, the funeral ritual after the death of Princess Diana, fairy-tale marriages of royal houses, and 'model' processions such as those in Brussels, Leeuwarden and Enschede are elevated to scripts and ideals; in comparison to these examples, most funeral rites, marriages and silent processions pale into insignificance and tawdriness. Not every silent procession receives, or holds, media attention. It is particularly the attendance that counts in a silent procession. As we have seen, its mass character is an important point. But attendance can vary considerably from procession to procession; many processions have only a few hundred participants, or not even that many. People are then disappointed because they had in mind the script of the ideal, massive silent procession.

The silent procession as a general and basic ritual

As we saw, in terms of its design the silent procession is a very general and basic ritual. One may suspect that this does not have so much to do with a predilection for sobriety and ritual simplicity and directness, as with a relative lacuna in ritual design and a tendency to homogenisation and globalisation, to which we will return when we discuss ritual dynamics in Chapter 5. Especially when dealing with the public domain there is a certain ritual/symbolic vacuum. In our culture people are assiduously seeking a suitable new ritual language and form. Often this search results in short-lived and sometimes bizarre experiments, but more frequently in very general, basic forms. The procession, silence, flowers, light and fire are then constantly recurring elements. That generality and basic nature is both the strength and the weakness of the ritual. It is instantly recognisable and can

---

[161] POST: *Het wonder van Dokkum* (2000) 64-67.
[162] Cf. GRIMES: *Deeply into the bone* (2000).

be used in almost all circumstances, but at the same time people find that basic character too general and too homogenous. They are seeking something with its own face, looking for elements that will make the ritual something that is inalienably individual, a rite that fits with this particular dramatic event. We therefore see the tendency to individualise the silent procession. That happens by introducing entirely unique elements, a special poem, a special attribute or a characteristic slogan. By now processions have their own names: the Procession of Solidarity, the Procession of Sympathy, the Procession of Tolerance. *The* silent procession no longer exists; one silent procession is not the same as the next one. Still...

This same context threatens the collectivity of the processions. The experience of being one of a mass contributes to that very important sense of community and solidarity. But the mass also contributes the making the ritual flat and general in a pejorative sense. Thus in recent processions we see that subdivisions are being introduced, the crowd divided up and thus reduced in scale; the mass is given a face and in so doing an attempt is made to transcend the general and homogenous. It is not by chance that the rituals of certain clearly defined communities, such as cancer patients, road accident victims and AIDS sufferers are developing into annual, and thus traditional rituals, and that such ritual is often less basic and general in design.

As an extremely general and basic ritual, the silent procession is thus in a certain respect a ritual for the lack of anything better, indicative of a vacuum and absence, and thus is increasingly often dressed up and decorated.

Silent processions and the public domain

Another remark involves the important aspect that a silent procession is inseparably connected with the public domain. Through Margry's studies we saw above how in the Dutch situation the relation between ritual and public space has for centuries been a subject of contention. In recent times, viewed from the perspective of general ritual dynamics, we see a sort of ritual reconquest of public space. While ecclesiastical rites have allowed themselves to be pushed back inside the walls of the church, all sorts of old and new rituals have arisen, some of a general religious nature, but usually secular/profane or intercultural, which manifest themselves in public space. On numerous occasions schools of people march through the city, village or neighbourhood: Carnival is often a street party; returning sports heroes are given massive public welcomes. It is noteworthy that even rites closely tied with the family, such as life cycle rituals, now intrude on public space: weddings are announced to all and sundry with notices, complete with pictures of the couple-to-be, on lamp-posts, walls and traffic signs; newborns are welcomed by increasingly obvious storks in front gardens, and even a ritual so strongly linked to domestic sphere as Christmas celebrations around a Christmas tree has begun to creep outdoors with exuberant lighting displays, reindeer sleighs and Santa figures, as has long been the vogue in the United States.

The silent processions unmistakeably share in this tendency to ritual manifestation in public space. A different question is what functions are further at work here. This question need not be answered here, but here and there in discussions classic functions such as purification and exorcism, familiar from ritual studies, are already being suggested.

The silent procession as a type of postmodern ritual

Anticipating the exploration of contemporary developments in the post-modern ritual market in a following chapter, as a final remark it can now be proposed that the silent procession is an illustration of postmodern ritual par excellence. It lives thanks to the falling away of the borders between previously sharply defined repertoires such as Christian/ecclesi-astical, general religious, profane/secular and interreligious or intercultural ritual, it touches on the dominant position of the ritual genre of redis-covered or new, emerging ritual, it reveals all the ritual qualities (and drawbacks) of postmodern ritual, such as the predilection for direct emo-tion and experience, the consumer stance with regard to ritual, the homogenisation, the emphasis on spectacle and event, the complex rela-tionship between the expression of the most personal feelings and the search for the inclusive high of the 'we-feeling', the major emphasis on functionality and effect, and the instrumental dimension of ritual acts. In particular, in the processions we see the problem areas of postmodern ritual: the search for adequate, suitable language and form, the creative and innovative search that often runs out into dream and utopia; the distance with regard to ritual, chiefly through the incapacity to really handle physical, sensory ritual; the complicated role of modern media, with all the consequences of cliched mental images and ritual idealism; and the lack of ritual experts (that is to say, masters at performing ritual acts, and not arm-chair experts, those ubiquitous commentators present in the discussions before and after the ritual).

The peculiar character of the contemporary silent procession stands out well against this background of current ritual tendencies. For instance, these processions have by now almost wiped out the tradition of protest marches. Despite the anti-globalisation demonstrations of recent years, the massive protest marches of old with banners full of slogans, wordy pamphlets and folders with critical analyses of political and social problems appear to have become marginal phenomenon; in their place came processions dominated by silence, direct emotion and personal experience.

4. CASE STUDIES II: INTERNATIONAL

4.1. THE ESTONIA DISASTER (SWEDEN, 1994): THE CHURCH OF SWEDEN AS PUBLIC PROVIDER OF RITUALS (P. PETTERSSON)

Introduction

On the 28th of September 1994 Sweden was hit by the greatest maritime disaster in the history of the country when M/S Estonia sank in the Baltic Sea. Among the 900 people who drowned 580 were Swedes from all over Sweden. This caused not only a shock to the whole Swedish nation but also resulted in the emergence of different crisis reactions. Many forms of religious reactions appeared, and the majority church, *The Church of Sweden*, immediately took on a central role in comforting the close relatives and coping with the feelings of grief among people in general.[1] Although surprised, many observers accepted this central role of a religious institution in a country that is regarded as one of the most secularised in Europe. Religious and ritual needs were obvious and unquestioned.

The Swedish religious scene – the majority church as provider of rituals

As in many other western European countries there is in Sweden a majority church with a national character, the Church of Sweden. It is the dominant religious institution to which nine out of ten Swedes belong, but only one in ten is a regular churchgoer (attends a service at least once a month). The major form of Swedish religiosity can be characterised as private but nonetheless linked to the Church of Sweden.[2] For the majority of people the most important functional role of the church is to provide rituals and life-interpretation in 'liminal' situations, especially in the context of birth and death.[3] In these existentially significant situations the

---

[1] GUSTAFSSON & AHLIN: *Två undersökningar om Estonia och religionen* (1995); PETTERSSON: *Svenska kyrkans folkreligiösa funktion i anslutning till Estonia-katastrofen* (1995).
[2] HAMBERG: 'Kristen på mitt eget sätt' (1989); BÄCKSTRÖM: 'Believing in belonging' (1993); GUSTAFSSON & PETTERSSON: *Folkkyrkor och religiös pluralism* (2000).
[3] BÄCKSTRÖM: 'Från institution till rörelse' (1989); REIMERS: *Dopet som kult och kultur* (1995).

church provides sacred buildings, symbols, rituals, words and interpretations which can be described as various forms of services fulfilling people's needs at crucial times in their lives.[4] These occasional ritualised encounters form a structure of relationships between almost all Swedes and the Church of Sweden, that are life long but inactive most of the time. Since the relationships are normally hidden from view they can be described as implicit religious relationships that are now and then activated during a life time. In a broader sociological perspective this structure of implicit relationships can be regarded as social capital that can function as a societal resource in collective crisis situations.[5] This appeared to be the case in the context of the Estonia disaster.

The following basic statistics give a brief picture of the Swedish religious scene concerning the majority of the population:[6]

- 83% of the Swedish population belong to the Church of Sweden (2000);
- 89% of all funerals take place within the Church of Sweden (2000);
- 73% of all Swedish infants are baptised in the Church of Sweden (2000);
- 43% of all 14 year olds are confirmed in the Church of Sweden (2000);
- 61% of all marriages take place in the Church of Sweden (2000);
- 11% of the population attend at least one Christian service per month (1994);
- 74% of the population believe in some kind of God or supernatural power (1998).

Interaction between individual and public rites

Most significantly the Church of Sweden provides a common frame of reference for almost all Swedish people in the context of death and mourning.[7] Encounters between individuals and the church in this special context form an implicit infrastructure that consists of conscious

---

[4] BÄCKSTRÖM & BROMANDER: *Kyrkobyggnaden och det offentliga rummet* (1995); PETTERSSON: *Kvalitet i livslånga tjänsterelationer* (2000).

[5] DAVIE: *Religion in modern Europe* (2000).

[6] Figures from GUSTAFSSON & AHLIN: *Två undersökningar om Estonia och religionen* (1995); GUSTAFSSON & PETTERSSON: *Folkkyrkor och religiös pluralism* (2000); BROMANDER: 'Då, nu och sedan. Perspektiv på Svenska kyrkans statistik 2000' (2001).

[7] BRÅKENHIELM: 'Den demokratiska staten och medborgarnas religioner' (1992); cf. DAVIES et al.: *Church and religion in rural England* (1991).

and unconscious relationships between individuals and the church buildings, priests, religious symbols and hymns.[8] With this in mind, it is perhaps not surprising that the Church of Sweden turned out to play a significant role even on a public and national level in connection with a major disaster. The church was the safe and comforting place the last time one had to bring up questions concerning death and deal with one's own feelings of anxiety and mourning. The religious reactions in the context of the Estonia disaster illustrates the interaction between the role of religion on individual versus public level in a modern so called secularised society.[9]

Three studies of the Estonia disaster

The empirical material that forms the base for this Swedish case consists of three studies on religious aspects of the Estonia disaster. The first study is a national survey of reactions and attitudes among a representative sample of the Swedish population.[10] The second is a study of the activities organised and performed by the local parishes within the Church of Sweden in the context of the disaster.[11] The third study is a qualitative content analysis of mass media the first week directly after the disaster.[12]

Population survey

In a survey directed to the entire population of Sweden 2002 persons over the age of 15 were interviewed by telephone. They were presented with a number of questions and statements including a number of specified alternative responses to each. The survey took place a month after the disaster had happened. Three areas were focused on in the questions and statements: (a) individual religious activity in connection to the disaster, (b) attitudes concerning the religious dimension in connection with the disaster, (c) opinions as to how the Church of Sweden had managed to handle the disaster.

---

[8] GUSTAFSSON: *Svenska folkets religion* (1969).
[9] BEYER: *Religion and globalization* (1994).
[10] GUSTAFSSON & AHLIN: *Två undersökningar om Estonia och religionen* (1995).
[11] GUSTAFSSON & AHLIN: *Två undersökningar om Estonia och religionen* (1995).
[12] PETTERSSON: *Svenska kyrkans folkreligiösa funktion i anslutning till Estonia-katastrofen* (1995).

The questions concerning individual behaviour focused on four activities characterised as religious and formulated like this: *Have you done any of the following as a result of the shipwreck of M/S Estonia?* Then four possible activities were mentioned. The result was that 21% had lit a candle at home or in a Church building, 9% had gone into a Church building, 8% had participated in a memorial service and 6% had participated in an 'ordinary' service. Altogether 27% of the Swedish population had done at least one of these things.

When it comes to attitudes to the religious dimension in connection with the disaster, a number of statements were formulated with the following results. 85% of the Swedes agree totally or in part with the statement that *The Estonia-disaster shows that people have religious feelings that are not shown under normal circumstances.* 89% agree totally or in part with the statement that *The Estonia disaster shows that people need help in coping with the spiritual dimension in a crisis situation.*

Responses to statements concerning the function of the Church of Sweden showed overwhelmingly positive attitudes. 89% agree totally or partly to the statement that *The Estonia disaster shows that the Church of Sweden can in certain situations also be important for those who are not religious.* 75% say that their general opinion of the Church of Sweden has not been changed as a result of the Estonia disaster. 67% say that the Church of Sweden has managed to act in the disaster situation as one could expect.

The picture is quite clear. The Swedish population regard religious feelings and needs as something 'normal' for people in general in the context of a major disaster. One of four Swedes behaved in a 'religious' way according to four stated actions. People in Sweden generally accepted the presence of a religious dimension in society and the public action of the national Church of Sweden as something natural. Even people who never participate in Sunday services agreed that people have religious needs and that the Church of Sweden, as a national church, has an important role to play in society in responding to these needs. There are no major differences between women-men and older-younger people in these respects. Furthermore the survey shows no differences at all between different geographical areas of Sweden. Thus the results show that the disaster caused similar religious reactions at the same level throughout the whole of Sweden. With so many people from so many different areas of the country dying at the same time, the Estonia disaster became a national disaster with similar religious reactions nationwide.

Study of parish activities

The parishes of the Church of Sweden have a responsibility for geographical areas that cover the whole country. The parish study shows that out of 1036 local parishes in Sweden, 173 or about 17% were directly affected by the disaster (someone from the local parish drowned). About 250 or 25% of the parishes were indirectly affected through relatives living in the parish. That means that 42% of the parishes were directly or indirectly affected. The parish study shows further that in 44% of the parishes from the very evening of the disaster, the church buildings were kept open longer, for private prayer or to light a candle. 60% of all parishes arranged special mourning or memorial services. More than 65,000 individuals took part in these services. More participants than usual were also reported in ordinary Sunday services.

Media content analysis

In a qualitative mass media study the content of five major newspapers published during the first week after the Estonia disaster were analysed. The basic material consists of texts, photos, illustrations etc. In addition to press material observations, interviews, articles from other papers and taped radio and television programmes were also used. Repeated phenomena that touch upon religion and the function of the church was systematised in categories. The following categories touch particularly upon ritual aspects and functions:

– The Church as a provider of rites and other mourning tools;
– Church buildings serve as sacred places;
– Priests as symbolic representatives and ritual actors;
– The lighting of candles as a ritual symbolic action;
– The ritual symbolic function of church bells;
– The significance of prayers.

These categories will be used as headlines for the following deepening discussion concerning ritual needs and practises in context of the Estonia disaster.

Discussion

The Church as provider of rites and mourning tools

In context of the disaster the Church's role and function in relation to the whole population of Sweden became obvious and was taken for granted by the population in general, by authorities as well as media. Throughout the media the Church of Sweden was presented as an institution that serves all people in the hour of need, similar to the role of the medical service, the police or the social services: "The magnetism of the church appeals even to people not personally acquainted with any of the casualties, but who after a tragedy which affected us all try to relieve their anxiety and anguish in the fellowship of the church."[13] The population survey as well as the media analysis shows that many people who do not usually attend church services changed their behaviour in the disaster situation. Photos in newspapers gave a different image of church visitors than the usual one. Young and middle aged people appear frequently in pictures as well as in text, and it is evident that many of them do not belong to the group of regular church-goers. One of the papers published a large colour photograph of a church interior in which a teenager is lighting a candle. The caption reads: "16-year old Marta Sörling with her niece Emilia in her arms, lit the candle of hope for the eight from the village who never came back." In the article: "I just felt that I had to come here. I can't say any more, Marta says."[14] Many people who are not otherwise regular church-goers seemed to use the church as a resource in the crisis situation. Here an example from an article about a mourning service in Lindesberg's church: "A tough young man in a black bomber jacket sings hymn 217 – Heal my eye that I may see how You are present in that which happens – his eyes filled with tears."[15] This public and common role of institutional religion in the shape of the majority church is not thought of as plausible in everyday Swedish life, but was unquestioned and even expected in the face of this major disaster. Not least were expectations projected on to the church as a provider of means to handle the mental disorder.

The church was expected to have the proper tools for coping with feelings of grief and mourning in the crisis situation. All three studies show the role of the Church of Sweden as a provider of resources to handle such needs on individual as well as collective level. In the media material it is frequently emphasised that the church has the language, qualities, buildings and experience needed to fulfil the handling of mourning and grief: "…the fact that the church manages a language for the tragic

[13] *Uppsala Nya Tidning* 3.10.94.
[14] *Expressen* 3.10.94.
[15] *Expressen* 2.10.94.

dimension in our lives. [...] The church with its insight is taken out of the closet when it is needed..."[16] Media also stress the need for symbolic acts in the collective grief. Here is one example of this: "Grief needs symbolic gestures. [...] A rock of remembrance in Väckelsång in Småland, roses in the river in Norrköping, individual remembrance services in Borläng. [...] We humans are creatures of rites, we need symbolic gestures. This is said by the bishop of Linköping, Martin Lönnebo."[17]

Church buildings serve as sacred places

A number of recent studies have pointed at the significant symbolic function of church buildings in Swedish society.[18] A vast majority of the population have links with church buildings that have been established in ritualised liturgical forms in the context of birth (baptism) and death (burial). Thus church buildings can be regarded as buildings loaded with holiness linked to individually and personally important occasions for almost all people. In the disaster situation the church buildings became the natural places for collective as well as individual mourning and symbolic acts. The parish study shows that 456 churches around the country were kept open for longer from the very day of the disaster. In the population survey 9% of the whole population said that they made use of the opportunity to visit a church building in connection to the disaster. All three studies show that church buildings had the function of being important places for tranquillity, nearness, togetherness and concentrated experience. A journalist's reflections in Hedvig's church: "God meets us in the silence, beyond words". "Can life be so tangible when death has come so near?" The article ends with a statement that after the service the grief is still present. "Mute, but shared."[19] Church sanctuaries have a prominent place in both text and photo-material in the newspapers. Quite a lot of photos show people in churches, often in worship or lighting a candle. Indirectly and in different ways the press material expresses a feeling of 'the sacred' which is strongly associated with the

---

[16] *Svenska Dagbladet* 4.10.94.

[17] *Dagens Nyheter* 1.10.94.

[18] BÄCKSTRÖM & BROMANDER: *Kyrkobyggnaden och det offentliga rummet* (1995); BÄCKSTRÖM: *Livsåskådning och kyrkobyggnad* (1997); BROMANDER: 'Rör inte vår kyrka' (1998); PETTERSSON: *Kvalitet i livslånga tjänsterelationer* (2000).

[19] *Dagens Nyheter* 30.9.94.

church buildings and worship situations. A large picture of people weeping in a church has the caption: "The sorrow". The journalist writes: "Care and comfort. They are seen in here, and felt."[20]

Priests as symbolic representatives and ritual actors

In a surprising way priests frequently appeared as central symbolic officials in almost all settings of the Estonia disaster, as reported in newspapers, television and radio. Media actively appealed to clergymen and women as representatives of the local communities' crisis groups. In newspaper photographs and on television priests appeared as distinct symbolic representatives. They were stressed as important even when they just appeared without saying a word. Radio Sweden drew attention to the presence of clergy in its own evaluation of broadcasts: "The number of priests, and other representatives of religious organisations who have participated in broadcasts is strikingly large."[21] In a similar way as the church buildings, the priests of the Church of Sweden have central functions in the context of life rites, especially in the context of children's baptism and burial ceremonies. Thus priests are in a way 'loaded' with a 'holiness' character linked to birth and death, in a similar way to church buildings. Since priests are important ritual actors in certain occasions on an individual level, this can be an explanation of the broad acceptance of priests having a public role on collective level in the context of major death and crisis.

The media material contained many and often long quotations from priests' speeches and sermons. Bishop Martin Lönnebo is quoted in one article as follows: "Many peoples faith in God sank to the bottom with M/S Estonia. […] God is also at 86 meters' depth in Estonia. God is the great mystery of life. He is life, he is death. God is with us although it is incomprehensible."[22] Journalists have chosen sections of the sermons which clearly give an existential interpretation of the disaster situation. The media emphasised that the church representatives have the language and qualities needed to fulfil the role of being a spokesperson with regard to the difficult questions. One journalist asks himself: "….This inconceivably ruthless catastrophe, can we actually learn anything from it…?"

[20] *Aftonbladet* 3.10.94.
[21] LUNDIN & JONASSON: *Estonia – en kartläggning av Sveriges Radios* (1994).
[22] *Expressen* 3.10.94.

He then answers by quoting a sermon: "It can teach us that life is not to be taken for granted, said Dean Caroline Krook, it can teach us to take better care of life and of each other." The journalist then adds: "And that may be true."[23] This role as existential interpreter is seen as representing everyone, even those who are not regular church-goers or do not see themselves as religious. This is illustrated in a chronicle by an author and journalist: "In the great mourning after the ferry disaster the god-words are in use again, even for the secularised."[24]

The lighting of candles as a ritual symbolic action

According to the population survey 21% of the Swedish people lit a candle at home or in a church building in the context of the disaster. This ritual was especially observed by the media. When describing people visiting church buildings or liturgical services, media frequently mention that candles are lit, for example like this: "More people than usual found their way to the stillness of St. Jacob's church. Candles were lit for the victims and the grieving."[25] Most newspaper photos of worship and sanctuaries showed the lighting of candles or included a candle holder, often in the foreground. One large colour photograph showed candle-lighting and hundreds of lighted candles in Hedvig's church in Norrköping. The text says: "A flame for each of the missing. Every individual candle [...] is a missing mother, father..."[26]

The ritual symbolic function of church-bells

One of the categories found in the media material is the symbolic and ritualised function of the tolling of church-bells. Through the ringing of many bells at the same time, bell-ringing gains a ritually unifying function for the whole nation and at the same time expresses kinship with the disaster victims, with all grieving people, close relatives as well as affected people in general: "The bells in Sweden's 3300 churches will be ringing on Sunday in memory of the Estonia victims."[27]

---

[23] *Expressen* 3.10.94.
[24] *Dagens Nyheter* 5.10.94.
[25] *Svenska Dagbladet* 29.9.94.
[26] *Dagens Nyheter* 3.10.94.
[27] *Svenska Dagbladet* 1.10.94.

The significance of prayers

Another category that frequently appeared in the media analysis is prayer. It is described as a natural way to deal with grief and questions concerning the disaster. The media often connected the lighting of candles with the concept of prayer. The newspapers showed special interest in officially formulated prayers that were used in the special mourning and memorial services. Quotations from these prayers occur in several newspapers. A special prayer which the archbishop sent to the parishes was reproduced in its entirety in a couple of newspapers. Here is one example of a published prayer: "Lord we pray for the dead. Take them to your bosom. We also pray for the survivors, that they may rejoice in life without feeling guilt."[28]

Conclusion

The reactions in Sweden in the context of the shipwreck of M/S Estonia show the need for ritualised patterns to handle individual as well as collective anguish, grief and mourning. Previously established individual relationships with the church as provider of ritual buildings, ritual actors and ritual behavioural patterns were re-established occasionally and made public on a collective and national level. The resources of the ritual experts and the church were used as a public service function that was taken for granted. There are obvious links between the way people's ritual needs are expressed in the collective crisis of the disaster on the one hand and the way ritual needs are handled in the private life of each individual. The general practise of children's baptism and burial of the dead within the framework of the Church of Sweden, forms a ritual framework that is seen as part of the general Swedish culture. Thus the Christian majority church with its Christian ritual tools can appear as a resource for the whole society. In the discourse of everyday life Sweden is normally described as multicultural and secularised, neglecting the fact that 80% of the population belong to one and the same church and ritual provider.

In the context of the Estonia disaster the need for collectively common ritual places, actors, symbols and symbolic acts became obvious. People, public authorities and the media asked for these functions to be provided by the Church of Sweden. Church buildings turned out to be the natural places for collective gathering and ritual activities. The priests were

---

[28] *Expressen* 3.10.94.

asked to perform in all types of media, in official mourning activities and in dealing with questions concerning the handling of human and ethical aspects of the shipwreck. When it comes to rituals the most practised visible ritual behaviour was the lighting of candles in Church buildings. Since the setting for the massive death was far out in the Baltic Sea it was not possible to do something ritual or symbolic right at the place. This can explain the focus on the lighting of candles in churches all around the country. Only a number of close relatives had the possibility to join a special ferry tour for a ritual act at the place where the ship sank. The Archbishop of Sweden held a blessing service right there and the relatives put flowers on the water. This was done at the time when the state authorities had decided not to raise the boat up from the sea, but instead let the dead rest in peace and regard the place in the sea as a proper burial place.

Emerging new practises in the context of major disasters

In earlier Swedish agricultural society, church and society were integrated in a total unity. Church, society and culture were just different aspects of the same entity. In today's structurally differentiated service society the church has developed an ongoing specialisation as a professional actor in certain societal functions. Since the church inherits the means for handling collective rites this is one of the areas in which the specialisation focuses. In the context of disasters there is an interesting interplay between on the one hand the church developing towards professionalism and on the other hand people moving towards a still more service orientated behaviour. People ask for relevant tools to handle the feelings of grief and mourning and to interpret and express existential thoughts and questions. In this interplay between church and people there is a continuous development of existing ritual forms as well as new forms of expression. This is obvious when looking at the continuous change from the murder of Olof Palme in 1986 to the major discotheque fire in Göteborg 1998. In the wake of the murder of Olof Palme a lot of people came to the place of the murder to put red roses and candles on the actual spot. The use of red roses is explained by the fact that Olof Palme was strongly associated with the social democratic party that had a red rose as its party symbol.[29] This was the starting point for the development of a general practise of laying flowers and lighting candles at the

---

[29] KÄLLSTAD: 'Mordet på Olof Palme – religionspsykologiska synpunkter' (1986).

place where acute and tragic death has taken place Since 1986 this practise has grown continuously and, for example at the site for a traffic accident or a murder. is nowadays common all around the country. It was
not so before 1986.

The next tragic death with national effects was a bus accident 1988.
A group of school children from Kista in Stockholm were on their way to
the Shetland Islands. The bus's brakes failed in a tunnel in Norway and it
crashed into the tunnel wall. Twelve children and four adults died. The vicar
in the local parish of the Church of Sweden immediately took on a leading
role in organising support for the relatives. The local church building and
the parish facilities became the centre for counselling and supporting
relatives and other affected people. The church staff, priests, deacons and
others, appeared as important actors and the church got a central and broad
role in the local crisis therapy work. Authorities and journalists observed the
function of the local church and a lot was written about it in public media
and official reports. During the following years it became a more or less
regular pattern among state and municipal authorities to involve the church
as an important actor in the formation of local and regional 'crisis groups'.

A different national and even world wide crisis was caused by the perceived threat and fear of a third world war during the Gulf crisis. There
was a general worry among people that this might be the starting point
of a third world war. Many church buildings all around the country were
kept open for individual prayer the night just before the Gulf war started
on the 16th of January 1991. This was part of the development of an
expanding function for church buildings in collective crisis situations in
contemporary Sweden.

When the Estonia disaster occurred, the practise of visiting a special
place in a crisis situation to light a candle or to lay flowers was an established and common ritual. The integrated role of the church in local and
regional crisis groups was already organised as part of the pattern from
Kista parish. In local disaster planning church buildings and localities
were identified as important parts of the public resources in taking care
of peoples needs to gather and for counselling. But the persisting function of the church for the whole of modern Swedish society was not
broadly recognised until the aftermath of the Estonia disaster. In a way
one can say that a pattern and ritual tool kit for the existential handling
of a major national disaster situation was developed in the context of the
shipwreck of M/S Estonia. This pattern and ritual toolkit was used almost
in the same way four years later, 1998, when there was a fire in a

discotheque in Göteborg. The church with its personnel, church buildings and parish facilities was used as an important expert on mourning and as a ritual actor for the whole nation. Flowers and candles were put on the street outside the discotheque building but also in a local church that served as a crisis centre. People around the country lit candles in their local churches.

As a summarising comment one can say that old ritual behaviours transform and new ritual forms emerge in relation to major disasters. These processes develop in interaction between specialised religious actors and people in a service orientated societal environment.

4.2. RITUALIZING SEPTEMBER 11: A PERSONAL ACCOUNT (R.L. GRIMES)

I hold two passports, one American, one Canadian. Who I am on a given day depends on who is bombing whom and for what reason, good or ill.

On the morning of September 11, my 11-year old son got up, put on his stars-and-stripes shirt (a hand-me-down from a Texas cousin), and went off to Empire School, a monument to a political realm once so far flung that the sun could never quite escape sight of its flag. My wife and I had not turned on the news yet, and our son had not worn the ragged shirt for months.

Then came the news.

Later, in the afternoon, unsure how a stars-and-stripes shirt would play out on the school ground, I met my son after school to walk him home. He knew already. The kids and teachers had observed a minute of silence. Ritually speaking, they were ahead of me. No, he wasn't upset. He wanted to skateboard. So my parental worry was not how to play down the collapse of the towers so he would be less afraid. Rather, it was how to play the event up so it might become real rather than fictional for him and his sister. So we parents sat with the children. We watched and talked and lit candles and invited people over. We put out some special objects, hoping to bridge the gap between a televised September 11 and disastrous reality. We ritualized in order to render the event real.

After September 11, 2001, reporters surmised that disasters remind people of fundamentals, bringing out the best in people. The roles assigned to ritual were that of wrapping victims in a blanket of comfort and of replacing factionalism with solidarity. In the wake of 9/11, friends and relatives of victims found comfort in encountering other bereaved people at the site of the demolished World Trade Center and in joining

mourners at memorials, both on and off the Worldwide Web. Even the
French were reported as saying publicly, "We are Americans too."
The Democrats, who, the day before 9/11, doubted whether Bush was
really the president at all, stopped bemoaning their sorry fate and joined
the Republicans in "getting behind the President."

But there is more to disaster ritual than comfort and solidarity. For one
thing, ritualizing continues long after rites end. September 11th has become
a sacred time, a ritual date. If you don't think so, listen to the incessant
incantation: 9/11, 9/11. Everyone repeats it, gets the allusion, feels its
weight. The date, utterly symbolic in force, binds 'us' together and, in so
doing, defines 'them.' The date symbolizes who 'we' are and who 'they' are.
It created, and continues to create, a shared memory, a holiday. 9/11 was
born at breakfast time without the gods or ancestors having revealed this
awe-ful holy day, without the holy books having prescribed it. Not quite
a divine given, it is nevertheless difficult to speak of this sacred day as a
social 'construction,' even though the event was planned to a T.

The terrorist attack was ritualized. In the newspaper we read translated
excerpts from the preparation manual. It was a liturgical text prescribing
the men's activities: Shave closely. Polish your shoes. Wear tight-fitting
clothes. Chant verses. Visualize your goal. Anticipate your reward.

'They' ritualized the attack. 'We' ritualized the counterattack – flew
flags and lit candles. A moment of silence here, a moment of silence
there – several days running. Again. Then again and again. Suddenly,
the higher powers were everywhere invoked: "God bless America" (even
in Canada, where 'his' grace is more thinly scattered).

Flags, flags, flags. Here a flag, there a flag, everywhere a flag. Prayer flags
– not Tibetan, not Zuni, but pure American flags. Wave them and you'll
be a better one. Wave it and you'll know who you are. And aren't. Wave it
and you'll know who's for you. And against you. There are only two choices.
Those who are not our friends are our enemies. God is on our side.
Through our homeland runs the axis mundi; through theirs, the axis of evil.

'They' wage holy war, jihad. A new word has gate-crashed the English language, likely other languages too. It has entered with such force
and pervasiveness that we don't bother to italicize it. (Usually, foreign
words have to pay homage, serve time in italics before being let out of
jail to run freely off the tip of the tongue.)

'They' wage a particularly fanatical kind of war: holy war. When we
utter the phrase, we put the 'holy' in quotation marks. We don't really
believe jihad is holy, no matter what 'they' think or say. (The quotation

marks are everywhere. Like the date, the quotes and the authorities are thick in the air. You can pluck and then fling or chant them.)

But think about it, have we North Americans ever fought a war that was *not* holy? God 'gave' this land to 'us.' If our 'boys' die over there, they are not on sacred ground. Here is sacred ground. So bring them home in bags and flags, so they may rest in peace.

Our wars are no less holy than theirs – just holy in a different way. Holy war: war for which no price is too high. Holy war – the kind that is waged when God is on our side.

In Canada, television fed viewers three national ways of post-9/11 mourning: American, English, and Canadian. Viewers wondered aloud why they did not see other ceremonies – Japanese, German, or Dutch. The American ceremony, like the British rite, was held captive; it was indoors, in a church. It was 'interfaith' American style, which is to say, the liturgical idiom was that of Christianized civil religion. Buddhists, Sikhs, Jews, and Hindus in attendance were required to pay homage to the one particular American God. Buddhists, Sikhs, Jews, and Hindus were dragooned into singing the 'Battle Hymn of the Republic.' The prayers, like the hymns, were generic civil-Christian ones.

In Britain, they sang more and talked less. Instead of a naval choir, there was a boys' choir. Their prepubescent innocence was as clear as a crystal goblet struck with a golden spoon. (In due time they will change; no longer choir material, they will be eligible to fight against evil, the way real men do.) The British rite, like the American one, was sacralized by the use of ecclesiastical space and clerical garb. The British, like the Americans, know evil when they see it, so they too sang they 'Battle Hymn of the Republic.' Its stridency echoed across the Atlantic. The British sang the 'Star Spangled Banner,' even though it was the war cry of their rebellious offspring.

In stark contrast to the American and British rites, the Canadian rite, hardly seen or mentioned in U.S. media, was held outdoors in front of Parliament. 65,000 people participated directly in the ceremony, a proportion of the population surprising in comparison with the American or British liturgies. In Canada no privileged indoor crowd displaced a liturgically disenfranchised outdoor crowd. There were no hymns and no prayers. After all, whose god stands so clearly above the others that all of us should pray to 'him?' The crowd stood for three full minutes of silence. For three minutes CBC television sat silent, its cameras nervously cutting here and there. Silence, though ritually venerable, does not air well; it worries directors who fret over attention spans.

At the university where I teach, a town hall meeting was called. In preparing for it, I queried my colleagues in religious studies about what perspectives our discipline might contribute. There was a testy internal debate. Some thought it obscene even to consider a public discussion replete with perspectives and technical terms. Such a meeting would become a pool of empty words; we should wait a year. Now was not the time.

With my departmental colleagues' warnings in my ears, I proposed to the university's organizing committee that we ritualize the event, frame the words with elemental acts capable of grounding the talk, reminding participants of the gravity and complexity of the situation. The proposal was rejected: We don't do that kind of thing here. Here, we have no ritual tradition, no ceremonial vocabulary, on which to draw. We are a university, a place of 'higher' learning.

Ignoring the outlay of time and money spent on orientation and commencement ceremonies, the committee's chair declared that constructing and enacting ceremonies should be left to religious communities. So instead of responding ritually, a music group was invited to perform and professors invited to speak.

That, of course, was not ritual.

I seem constantly to rediscover what I already know about my community, workplace, and the culture: Ritually speaking, we are profoundly disabled. Our gestural, postural, and symbolic vocabulary is pinched, poverty stricken. We reach for candles or flowers and then deadend; that's it. We've exhausted our ritual resources. So we turn over the problem to professionals – to clergy and undertakers. But they were no better prepared for September 11 than us ordinary lay folk. They reached for what was nearby: American flags, the national anthem, military garb, and military cadences.

Unable to construct a community rite, and unwilling to join the nationalistic one, my only choice was to ritualize the talk I was to deliver at the town hall meeting. I am a ritual studies scholar. What should a ritual studies scholar say on the occasion of a disaster? Longing for a richer, more layered, more critical vocabulary, one that is not only political but also incantatory, I uttered these words:

Eleven words for September: an incantatory glossary

Symbol:
an object fraught, pregnant, laden,

and capable of acting
Symbol: a thing, action, or word
bearing many,
often contradictory, meanings.
Symbol: a multivocal device
speaking in many voices.
Symbol:
> Tower of World Trade,
> Tower of Babel.
> They all fall down.
> Tower of too much talk,
> Towers of too much money,
> Tower of arrogance.

The tower is always *over there*.
It could not possibly be *here*.
> Could it?

Myth:
a symbol dressed up in an image or a narrative
Myth: 'Wanted, Dead or Alive.'
Myth: 'Axis of Evil'
> We are cowboys, grade B; they are Indians, grade F.
> We are Christians; they are Moors...

Myth: the stories we tell ourselves during the dark nights of the global soul
Myth: the values and images and tales we are unable, or unwilling, to
question
Myth: the set of assumptions that underwrite us,
> on which we stand, like the ground:
> We, the free world, stand on guard for thee.

Sacred text:
> a myth in a book,
> a myth of a book:

the Koran says, the Gita says, the Bible says...
The king says, the pope says, the scholar says, CNN says...
Sacred text: A document that does not welcome editors.
Sacred text:
> A text that does not go out of print.

An utterance to live for,
a document to die for,
die with,
     die from.

Ritual:
a symbol embodied and enacted.
Ritual: a red, white, and blue ribbon on a custodian's lapel
Ritual: the Stars and Stripes torn between the teeth and set aflame
Ritual: the color guard, guarding the president standing by the priest
Ritual: the turbaned gathering of the Taliban to debate the fate of the nation
Ritual: the un-turbaned gathering of scholars in ivory towers
     to debate and bemoan the fate of the world.

Performative utterance:
     using words to do things.
Performative utterance:
     words that not only describe
     but also effect,
     words that transform
Performative utterance: "I pronounce you husband and wife."
Performative utterance: "This is war."

Good & Evil:
the fate of the world
held in the balance
of two hands alone;
Good & Evil:
the ultimate divide
inscribed into the ideologies and ethics
of the several religions
and the multitude of nations.
Good & Evil:
The most gaping fundamental abyss
into which all the others fall,
chasm cascading into chasm:
us and them,
East and West,

Muslim and Christian,
men and women,
terrorists and
      nice people like us.

Religion:
      that which underwrites
      deep or elemental concerns.
Religion:
      All that is implied in the phrase,
"No price is too great"
Religion:
      All that is drives people to war.
Religion:
      All that binds up people's wounds after war.
(Religions are not only that to which they aspire,
but also that which they evoke.)
Religion:
      What would we do without it?
Religion:
      How can we survive it?
Civil religion:
      that peculiar variant
      of public piety
not confined to religious institutions.
Civil religion:
Let the Americans stand and sing the *Battle Hymn of the Republic.*
      "He is trampling out the vintage where the grapes of *wrath* are
      stored.
      He hath loosed the fateful lightning of his *terrible* swift sword."
Let the British stand and join the Americans in singing the *Battle Hymn
of the Republic.*
"He has sounded forth the trumpet that shall *never* call retreat."
Civil religion:
that form of public piety discreetly closeted in Canada.
Let us mourn,
out in the open air,
without hymn,
without prayer.

Three minutes of silence,
standing,
Please.

Passage:
A moment,
a transition slicing time in half,
creating a divide,
a distinct BEFORE and AFTER.
Passage:
Life before
and life after
the fall of the great towers.
Passage:
The moment
of the loss of innocence
and entry into experience.
Passage:
the moment
after which there is no return
except in symbol, myth, and ritual.

Scapegoat:
The kid offered up.
The scapegoat is a kid,
the bleating one
sent out to starvation
or slaughter
on our behalf.
Scapegoating:
He hit me first!
No, no, he did it!
He deserves it;
he's not one of us!
Scapegoat:
Thank god for that kid.
Thank god, I am not that kid.
The scapegoat will not escape;

it carries out complicity
into the wilderness.

Peace:
The state of being reconciled,
connected with all that pulses and breathes.
Peace: What used to be.
Peace: How things were yesterday
and might be tomorrow
but are not today.
Peace:
the time when
each of us says yes
to whatever and whoever is Other.
Peace:
Even those who do not pray,
pray for it.

The house divided over these words. Some left the university's town hall meeting wishing that I had spoken more plainly and accessibly. Others left saying they should be published. To my mind both responses missed the point.

Elemental gestures

The next evening I baited the students in my Rites of Passage course. We were just starting the death section of the course, so I asked, "The time since September 11 – has that been like an extended funeral rite for you? For the nation?" They weren't sure.

I continued to probe: "Did you 'do' Diana? Or 'get into' other televised funeral rites – Mother Teresa? Pierre Trudeau? They were far too young for me to ask about Martin Luther King or John F. Kennedy.

Some confessed they had been taken by the funerals of Diana and Trudeau, so I teased them out further: "Won't you be a peculiar generation, if your most formative ritual experiences are televised funerals and memorials? Compared with funerals that you attend bodily, are televised death rites less real? Or more real?"

At the end of the discussion I posed what turned out to be the most evocative question: When there is a great imponderable (an event so profoundly questioning that anything remotely resembling an 'answer' sounds false), what is your impulse?

A young man's hand shot up instantly. "To go home," he said. "I landed in San Francisco on September 11, and all I could think about was getting back home to Canada."

A woman replied, "I just wanted to drive to New York City. I felt removed and wanted to go there, to participate."

Another added, "I become quiet, very solitary."

Then another confessed, "I flipped. After September 11, I almost lost my faith. My family worried that I'd quit school. But then we talked. We just talked and talked and talked until I came back to normal. Talk, that's what I need when there is a disaster."

The actions reported by the students were not formal ceremonies like the ones we had been discussing in class or seeing on television, but they were ritualized responses. Or, if that way of putting it seems like stretching it, then let's say that these are the impulses (go home, go to the center, pull away, go nuts, get together) on the basis of which rites of dying and healing are often constructed.

9/11 was a teaching moment if there ever was one. The surrounding weeks were fraught with pedagogical possibilities. People on the street were telling the media: "Everything is different. After September the 11th, everything is different; the world has forever changed." These words sounded like a formal definition for a rite of passage: a deep transformation, a moment with a before and after so distinct that one can never return to the previous state.

So, even though the class was designed as a lecture and discussion course, we ritualized. I prepared a few volunteers and they performed.

The script for elemental gestures

Setting: On a draped or matted table in the centre of the room:

- a mound of sand, earth, or stones; a bowl or small sandbox to contain them
- a pitcher of water; a bowl to pour it in
- a candle or lamp and matches

- a piece of fruit or a flower; a knife
- incense and matches or a wind instrument

Participant # 1 introduces the actions with words calling attention to the purpose of the gathering or to one or more of the following themes: the emptiness as well as the importance of human speech and social gatherings; the preciousness of the moment and the importance of small things; the pervasiveness of trouble.

The choice of words should fit the occasion and reflect the constituency of those gathered. The words below are only examples.

[Alternatively, no words are said and no introduction is given, especially if the rite is enacted repeatedly by the same group, in which case the actions are sometimes preceded and accompanied by words; sometimes not.]

"Buddhists say that all suffering, and all release from suffering, is now – in this very moment and in this very place."

"The Gospels say that not even a sparrow can fall without divine notice and divine compassion."

[etc.]

Participant #2 approaches the table, scoops up a handful of earth in both hands, speaks the words, then sprinkles it slowly (e.g., into the bowl, on the floor around the table, onto a flat stone or board. This and each subsequent gesture is slowly paced, enacted simply and without pomp.

[Alternatively, each participant, repeating the words, pours sand into the hands of another participant until all hands are soiled.]

"This is earth.
May it ground our words and actions
and continue sustaining the multitude of life forms
around the world."

Participant #3 approaches the table, lifts the pitcher and, speaking the words, pours the water into a bowl, slowly, so the splashing can be heard.

[Alternatively, each participant, repeating the words, pours water into the hands of another participant until all hands are washed. This alternative requires a large towel.]

"This is water.
May it cleanse us
and refresh flagging spirits everywhere."

Participant #4 approaches the table, strikes a match, lights the candle, and speaks the words.

[Alternatively, each participant, repeating the words, lights a candle from the preceding candle. This alternative requires enough candles for everyone.]

"This is light.
May it clarify decisions in high places
and enlighten choices everywhere."

Participant #5 approaches the table, picks up the flower or fruit [or other living thing] and says,

"This is living…
but not for long.
[The fruit or flower is cut.]
May its short life
and ours
fructify the planet."

[If fruit is used, it and the knife are passed so the fruit can be cut and eaten. If a flower is used, it is merely passed along with the knife.]

Participant #6 approaches the table, takes the wind instrument, speaks the words, and begins to play:

[Alternatively, incense is lit from the candle and blown into the air.]

"This is air, human breath.
May it suffuse all that throbs,
    permeate all who suffer,
        surround all who breathe,
            and all who have ceased to breathe."

Participant #1 says, "The rite is finished. We are ready to _____
[talk, work, eat, etc., what ever the main activity is.]

The actions of this tiny rite are elemental, not the property of a particular religious or ethnic group, not the product of an explicit tradition. The words do not mention 9/11, even though 9/11 was their occasion.

Of course, the actions were not perfectly generic, which is to say, universal. Nothing ever is. The aim was to create a pause in which attentiveness could deepen and a sense of connectedness could occur before discussion, debate, and other divisive moves happened. The rite was constructed as a frame inside of which different kinds of things could transpire.

After we enacted the brief gestures, I invited response and critique – in effect, transforming the meditative pause into a ritual demonstration. I explained that people need spaces in which it is possible to reflect on rituals; otherwise, we can abuse them or be abused by them.

After several minutes of appreciative but polite discussion, a mature student from Six Nations Reserve raised his hand, "Professor, I don't mean to insult you or anything, but could, maybe, that have been a little hokey?"

Other students gasped or held their breath, but I laughed, "Sure. Of course, it could. But why? Say more."

"Well," he said, "you made it up, right?"

"Right."

"Well, there was no tradition or anything. And you are not a medicine man or a priest. The whole thing was artificial."

I agreed. Rites whose constructedness is known or visible can be awkward or unconvincing. Hokey.

"How do traditions start? I asked him.

"I don't know; you're the professor," he said. More laughter.

I responded with a story. "When the Montreal Massacre occurred on December 6, 1989, at l'École Polytechnique de Montréal and fourteen women lay dead at the hands of anti-feminist murderer, people at universities had a similar debate about ritually marking the occasion. Some said, We don't have any ritual resources with which to handle traumatic public events. Others said, We should keep our mouths shut; words at such times are obscene or embarrassing. But in the end, many students and faculty ritualized their awkwardness and embarrassing silence. We did so because we felt we had to. After December 6 we invented a commemorative ceremonial tradition, and it continues to this day. The commemoration lives largely at universities, not in civil or ecclesiastical institutions, and we continue to reinvent it. Universities do have rites.

"Ritual inventiveness around September 11 has been forced upon us. Your people too have been forced to invent ceremonies. I am thinking of repatriation legislation, which returned Native burial remains to First Nations people, most of whom had no rites for re-burying bones long held in museums. Ritual creativity became a necessity.

"So, yes, when we first construct rites, invent a tradition, if you will, it seems silly, and we all become self-conscious. But rites start somewhere. And right now ceremonial innovations, borrowing from the past, are transpiring as Americans and British and Canadians and students and faculty around the world struggle to transpose their emotions and politics into gestures, postures, and ritual texts. If you don't want to be drafted into someone else's politics and religiosity, then your only option is either to ensconce yourself in a tradition you trust or to use your imagination to choreograph what you are driven to enact."

Later in the year the student who raised the question and dared to say what others were afraid to say presented his own account of a constructed rope-climbing rite used by Mohawks and other Six Nations people. He had grasped the point that even among the most traditional people, new situations require ritual invention.

9/11 began with a ritually driven attack. The event was followed up by a ritualized declaration of war on terrorism. Meanwhile, searching for bodies and sifting rubble at site of the World Trade Center was ritually conducted and ritually concluded on May 31, 2002. It became virtually impossible *not* to approach the site in a ritualizing manner – not so much in response to what *was* there but to what was *not* there. In the face of a looming, animated absence, ritualizing necessarily becomes liturgical, a way of negotiating ultimate things.

Elemental Gestures, a rite that could not be enacted in public university space, but which hatched anyway in the more protected sanctity of the classroom, is now circulating in peace centers. It is being rewritten, adapted, dismantled and reassembled. It's a small, paltry thing, but it is an alternative to waving flags. 9/11, North Americans said, drove them back to the basics, by which they meant country, family, security, the Stars and Stripes, the American way of life. *Elemental Gestures* suggests that other things – air, water, soil – are even more basic, because they are more widely shared and more profoundly endangered by both terrorism and the war on terrorism.

Neither *Eleven Words for September* nor *Elemental Gestures* is representative of the ways Americans and Canadians responded to 9/11. Both pieces were performed acts of ritual criticism, and they precipitated as many questions as answers: In the face of terrorist disaster, who are 'we,' and who are 'they?' In the face of a disaster, with whom is it most urgent to express solidarity – 'fellow countrymen' or the planet? In the face of disaster, what subtexts seep from beneath pious declarations uttered in public?

There is not only acute danger in disasters (towers falling, planes dropping, floods rising, wars breaking out) but also the chronic danger of ritually sanctioned self-righteousness. The danger in disaster rituals is that they can underwrite a desperate obsession with declaratives and imperatives: The truth is... The truth shall be... The danger is that disaster rituals can buttress an impatience with questions and an unwillingness to abide with ambiguity or uncertainty.

No one can deny that ritualizing the disaster of September 11 provided consolation and created solidarity, but it also suppressed dissent, stoked the fires of nationalism, and consolidated a move to the political and religious right.

Unless they wish to embrace their own cooption, ritual studies scholars must become as adept at analyzing disastrous rituals as they are at analyzing disaster rituals. Assuming such a posture is risky, but so is severing ritual theory and analysis from ritual criticism. It is easy to engage in retrospective ritual criticism of the 1934 Nuremburg rallies or the 1936 Olympics in Berlin. The real challenge is to think critically and analytically in the midst of politicized ritualizing rather than after it.

ILLUSTRATIONS

Op zondagavond 4 oktober 1992 om
zes minuten over half zeven stortte een
El Al Boeing 747 vrachtvliegtuig neer
op de flats Groeneveen en Kruitberg -
ter gedachtenis dit monument rondom
'de boom die alles zag'.

1. Amsterdam (The Netherlands, Bijlmer): front of memorial wall (Bijlmer
disaster, 1992), showing a part of the tile mosaic, with the tree visible behind
the wall (photograph: A. Nugteren, 2001)

2. Laren: ceramic butterfly vase in the Roman Catholic basilica at Laren
(The Netherlands, North Holland), with the names of the dead in the
aeroplane accident at Faro, Portugal (1992) (photograph: A. Nugteren, 2001)

3. Bovenkarspel: granite book in Bovenkarspel (The Netherlands, North Holland) as a memorial to the victims of the Flora disaster (1999), with a memorial text and poem by Ida Gerhardt (photograph: A. Nugteren, 2001)

4. Eindhoven: temporary monument near the site of the aeroplane crash,
Hercules disaster, The Netherlands, Eindhoven, 1996 (photograph: Hercules
Disaster Foundation, 1996)

5. Eindhoven: memorial monument, Hercules aeroplane diaster, The Netherlands, Eindhoven, 1996 (photograph: Hercules Disaster Foundation, 1996)

6. Eindhoven: memorial monument, Hercules aeroplane diaster, The Netherlands, Eindhoven, 1996, after the commemoration of July 15, 2001 (photograph: A. Nugteren)

7. Enschede: floral tribute after the fireworks disaster, Hengelosestraat fire station, The Netherlands, Enschede, May, 2000 (photograph: I. Albers)

8. Enschede: floral tribute after the fireworks disaster, The Netherlands, Enschede, May, 2000 (photograph: I. Albers)

9. Enschede: floral tribute after the fireworks disaster, The Netherlands,
Enschede, May, 2000 (photograph: I. Albers)

10. Enschede: 'Draag een steentje bij' (Do your bit) action after the firework disaster, The Netherlands, Enschede, June, 2000 (photograph: I. Albers)

11. Enschede: fencing around disaster area, fireworks disaster,
The Netherlands, Enschede, May, 2000 (photograph: I. Albers)

12. Enschede: hoarding around disaster area, fireworks disaster,
The Netherlands, Enschede, May, 2000 (photograph: I. Albers)

13. Volendam (The Netherlands): painting by Nico Jungmann,
'Kevelaer Procession in Volendam', circa 1900
(photograph: Zuiderzee Museum, Enkhuizen)

14. Volendam: Silent procession after the cafe fire, The Netherlands,
Volendam, Friday evening, January 12, 2001 (photograph: PVW Foto)

15. Volendam (The Netherlands): cemetery behind St. Vincent's Church, with the grave stones for the young people who died in the New Year's fire, 2001 (photograph: A. Nugteren, 2001)

5. CONTEMPORARY RITUAL DYNAMICS: AN EXPLORATION[1]

5.1. SIGNS OF RITUAL DYNAMICS

As we have seen in the preceding exploration, any disaster is surrounded by rituals that mark and commemorate it. In that colourful tangle of rituals – large or small, collective, public or on a smaller scale within the family – one is confronted with the dynamics of what can aptly be termed the ritual market.[2] In our analysis of the phenomenon of the silent procession, which is perhaps the most striking element in this repertoire, we have seen how it has been connected with all sorts of reflections about rituality, spirituality and even religiosity in our culture, using terms such as secularised, late-modern, postmodern or non-traditional ritual.[3]

It is obvious from the most cursory examination that the ritual market is varied, complex and dynamic. There are new rites and symbols next to familiar old rituals. There are rites which are being marginalised, or which have disappeared. There are rites which come and go, and rites which persist. Through a disaster one often also has a chance to see the ritual of a geographic or faith community, as was the case in Enschede and Volendam. A traditional repertoire appeared to be preserved (the traditional mourning ritual of hanging sheets in the windows in Volendam) or on the contrary, renewed and adapted. In this connection, responses to the first of the funerals of victims of the disaster in Enschede (May,

---

[1] This exploration is closely connected with an programme of research which has for some time been the focus of attention, in which contemporary ritual dynamics are being explored. This project focuses on the general 'milieu' in which Christian rituality must be situated. Parts of previous publications which report on this project will be drawn upon again here, somewhat in the manner of roofing slates (that is to say, always with a certain degree of overlap). In particular, in addition to the monograph POST: *Het wonder van Dokkum* (2000) see three recent articles: IDEM: 'Overvloed of deritualisering' (2001); IDEM: 'Rituell-liturgische Bewegungen' (2002) and IDEM: 'Life cycle rituals' (2002).

[2] See, in general, POST & SPEELMAN: *De Madonna* (1997); cf. POST: 'Zeven notities' (1995); IDEM: 'Liturgische bewegingen' (1996); IDEM: 'Liturgische Bewegungen' (1998); IDEM: *Het wonder van Dokkum* (2000); IDEM: 'Overvloed of deritualisering' (2001); IDEM: 'Rituell-liturgische Bewegungen' (2002); IDEM: 'Life cycle rituals' (2002).

[3] See 3.5.

2000), those of the two firemen, are interesting. The church services drew considerable media attention, and let contemporary Dutch Roman Catholic funeral liturgy be seen. For many that appeared to be a surprise, just as in 1992 the memorial service after the Bijlmer disaster also surprised through the confrontation with ritual expressions from other cultures.[4] The funeral service in Glanerbrug, near Enschede, was far from traditional, classic or old-fashioned (words that journalists and commentators readily employed), but in many respects creative and modern. The music, which was partially borrowed from contemporary popular musical culture, was particularly remarked upon. This surprise – that Catholic funeral liturgy could contain contemporary elements – is an important signal, as is also the fact that it was chiefly the selection of music and songs that provoked this response. It reveals a certain prevailing mental image when it comes to ritual. Rituals – in this case Christian, ecclesiastical rituals – are not unchanging and 'traditional', archaic or old-fashioned, but are constantly changing and undergoing inculturation.

There are a plethora of signs of movement and dynamism in the ritual market. Esoteric rites appear to be on the way out; the colourful repertoire of recent times, from Feng Shui to New Age, seems to be withdrawing into the hermetic world of alternate therapies. 'Traditional' repertoires are flourishing; the age-old pilgrims' route to the northern Spanish city of Santiago de Compostela is as busy as it was in the Middle Ages, with walking and bicycling modern pilgrims. Those being termed neo-Catholics feel themselves attracted first of all by the sacred, mysterious spell of liturgy, and monks and nuns hit the top of the pop charts with their divine office. There are also 'wild devotions'. Although by no means as widespread as has been suggested, there are small ritual agencies that produce tailor-made liturgies for rites of passage; in Flanders, for instance, one can hire a priest to conduct these from the specialised Rent-a-priest ritual agency.

Under the title *Ritual 2001*, in that year a grandly conceived series of programmes on the Dutch interdenominational television station examined this ritual landscape. From the structure it seems that they tried to cover the whole spectrum of contemporary rituality, from traditional to modern and exotic, from religious to ordinary and secular. In the end ten subjects or sub-repertoires were selected: commemoration, initiation,

---

[4] See 3.1.

healing, eating, mourning, tripping, purification, marriage, dancing and averting evil. It is interesting that in the programme the modern ritual dynamic was seen as a sign of incurable human religiosity.

Surveying the signs, one can summarise by proposing that ritual acts after a disaster are in many respects a window on the current, often remarkable dynamic of cult and culture. In this chapter we will place disaster ritual, which we have already explored both in general perspectives and through case histories, in this wider context of ritual dynamics. We are chiefly interested in an inductive appraisal of the current ritual milieu: how can we characterise and appraise the ritual climate? Are there trends? After we have discussed possible diagnoses through a comparison of two prominent authorities, we will attempt to characterise and evaluate the contemporary ritual milieu. This characterisation will have the nature of an impressionistic investigation. It is impossible to claim this is a well-considered synthesis. Yet it will be more than a purely subjective, intuitive exploration. The characterisation will be based on the general studies of the current ritual milieu that are already on the table, and various empirical case studies of ritual sub-repertoires such as rites surrounding death, marriage rites, pilgrimage, modern devotions, etc.[5]

Although the basis for this exploration will be chiefly formed by studies of religious ritual, we are nevertheless of the opinion that our sketch and characterisation will afford a first general image of contemporary rituality. In this, we are primarily thinking of rituals as symbolic acts in the contexts of sacrality and assigning meaning, such as the rites marking points in the course of the year and in life.[6] Moreover, this chapter connects with the previous broader contextual discussion of the phenomenon of the silent procession.

This chapter will also introduce a certain critical/normative perspective. It involves a diagnosis. This critical/normative dimension is in part motivated by the perspective of ritual criticism, previously introduced in the discussion of Grimes, through which characteristics, developments and tendencies with regard to rituality are approached critically and evaluated.

Further, we will employ a broad, open and international perspective in this exploration of ritual dynamics, for which in the first instance Western Europe and North America will jointly function as context. But

---

[5] For a summary, see POST: 'Religious popular culture' (1998); LUKKEN: *Rituelen in overvloed* (1999).

[6] See the broad theoretical presentation of the concept of ritual in 1.2.2.

precisely in the confrontation of the two authors chosen, Lukken and Grimes, distinctions between Europe and the United States will also become clear, so that it will once again be plain how national settings always introduce entirely peculiar dimensions into disaster ritual, as has already been seen in the sketches of Dutch, Scandinavian and North American cases in the previous two chapters.

5.2. REMARKABLE DYNAMIC IN THE DIAGNOSIS OF THE RITUAL MILIEU

For the Western situation – for convenience sake we will take the European and North American contexts together – from about 1960 to 2000 diagnoses of the general ritual milieu show a striking dynamic. In the 1960s a 'crisis in rites' was diagnosed. Ritual repertoires that had been deeply rooted in the culture were being dismantled with unprecedented speed by secularisation, with in its wake such familiar 'turbo terms' as pluriformity, individualisation, demystification and modernisation. Attention focused particularly on religious, ecclesiastical ritual. Churches emptied out and people searched and groped around in a ritual vacuum. Experts in that Christian, ecclesiastical repertoire however saw a paradox in this diagnosis: this was after all precisely the period of unprecedented creativity, experimentation and innovation, and exactly then Christian ritual lost its anchor in society, participation in it rapidly fell off, and a deficiency or void arose.

In the 1970s one could detect a reaction or compensation. That had a lot to do with the liturgical reforms that had begun in the 1960s. All sorts of movements, such as the blossoming of devotions and other rites on the very edges of or outside the Church were seen as a compensatory reaction to that new repertoire. According to observers, esoteric rites, rites of healing from gurus to Marian sites, sprang up in the void that the churches had left behind. Often the tone was critical, as in the case of leading experts like Mary Douglas and the convert Victor Turner, but Alfred Lorenzer can also be cited here.[7] The 1981 book *Das Konzil der Buchhalter*, by the last of these authorities, provoked considerable discussion.[8]

---

[7] MITCHELL: 'Emerging ritual' (1995) and MALLOY: 'The re-emergence' (1998) offer a good picture of this reaction, with examples; see also POST: 'Popular religious culture' (1998).

[8] LORENZER: *Das Konzil* (1981); see also now TOREVELL: *Losing the sacred* (2000).

In the 1980s the tone changed once again; now there was a more neutral discussion of the paradox in the crisis in rites. People had now come to see the striking dynamism in the ritual market, how on the one side repertoires went into decline, while others blossomed. There was also interest now for small rites, *The invisible religion* of Luckmann,[9] and people discovered religious popular culture and flourishing pilgrimages, without feeling a need to speak in terms of counter-movements or compensation theory.

In the 1990s this line of diagnosis was followed further, and the discussion became still more neutral and unbiased, now speaking of movement and dynamics, of the fanning out of and disappearance of borders between previously fixed repertoires, of changes in context and varying appropriations. This dynamic was certainly linked with a general religious 'background noise' in society.[10] In a general but indefinable sense the culture was rustling and crackling with religion and sacrality, with rites and symbols. Without passing any judgement on the fact, but also without much nuance, late modern or postmodern man was declared both an incurably religious and an incurably ritual being. This was readily illustrated with reference to the variegated repertoire of exotic and esoteric rituals that were collected under the heading 'New Age', which since then seems to have evaporated or moved to the margins.

By the eve of the year 2000, the reversal appeared complete: rather than 'crisis' and 'vacuum', words like 'abundance' and 'flourishing' now dominated discussion. That Gerard Lukken entitled his book on the position of Christian ritual *Rituals in abundance* is telling.[11] Where the author previously operated from the diagnosis of crisis and vacuum, he now wrote of amplitude. In the second chapter, with the title 'From crisis in ritual to rituals in abundance', Lukken explicitly articulates this reversal.[12] He is distinctly not alone in doing so. The tide has rather generally changed in the diagnosis, although for the most part the focus is on religiosity and spirituality in general, and less on rituality. Representatives of various fields that are occupied with rites in our culture have recently begun to speak of repletion and blooming, of resacralisation, the growth

---

[9] LUCKMANN: *The invisible religion* (1967); for everyday rituality and sacrality see also SEXSON: *Ordinarily sacred* (1997) and DE HAARDT: *Kom, eet mijn brood...* (1999).

[10] VAN HARSKAMP: *De religieuze ruis* (1998).

[11] LUKKEN: *Rituelen in overvloed* (1999); an English edition of this book is in preparation: IDEM: *Rituals in abundance. A critical reflection on the place and shape of Christian ritual in our culture* (to appear in the series Liturgia condenda, Leuven etc. 2003).

[12] *Ibidem*: 165-174.

of a religious sense; they also rather explicitly critique the often sombre
key of quantitative surveys and argue for qualitative research, with a different focus.[13] The secularisation and crisis thesis of the 1960s and 1970s
is increasingly on the defensive. Question marks are being placed with
respect to the demystification of our society and culture, although there
is discussion about the question whether this can still be seen in Weber-
ian terms.

But there are also other noises to be heard. There is once again more
critical diagnosis with regard to the ritual milieu. With this we have also
gone full circle in forty years. The current, somewhat double diagnosis of
rituals in abundance on the one side and tendencies toward deritualisation
on the other deserves further elaboration. We will provide that through a
comparison of two recent, important survey works by prominent experts
in ritual: the book on Christian ritual by Gerard Lukken already mentioned, which to a large extent is a general survey work on ritual, and
Deeply into the bone, a study on contemporary rites of passage by Grimes.[14]

5.3. ABUNDANCE OR CRISIS: COMPARING LUKKEN AND GRIMES[15]

Before carrying out this comparison of the two perspectives, several qual-
ifying remarks must be made. First, we must realise that the two works
differ both in context and structure. That is what makes the choice of
these two authors for our project, with both its an examination of European and North American case studies, and its direct ritual and indirect
liturgical perspective, so exciting and productive of insight. Lukken ultimately deals with the position of Christian ritual in an overwhelmingly
European context. Grimes surveys the rites connected with the course of
life in a chiefly North American context. When we then detect a much
more negative view of the ritual milieu in Grimes than in Lukken, we
may not in any sense place this in the longer tradition, mentioned immediately above, that from the 1960s has spoken in alarm about a society

---

[13] Cf. quantitative surveys with regard to classic ecclesiastical ritual in The Netherlands:
BECKER & VINK: *Secularisatie* (1994); BECKER, DE HART & MENS: *Secularisatie* (1997);
PETERS, DEKKER & DE HART: *God in Nederland* (1997); VERWEIJ: *Secularisering* (1998);
SCHEPENS: 'Een statistische documentatie' (1999); BURGGRAEVE, CLOET, DOBBELAERE &
LEIJSSEN: *Het huwelijk* (2000); KNULST: *Werk* (1999).
[14] GRIMES: *Deeply into the bone* (2000).
[15] This comparison is developed at greater length in POST: 'Overvloed of deritualis-
ering' (2001) and 'Life cycle rituals' (2002).

supposedly 'without rituals'.[16] Precisely over against this supposed absence of ritual Grimes places all sorts of new, rising rituals, which he prefers to term 'emerging ritual'. In an address to the annual meeting of the North American Academy of Liturgy in St. Louis, Missouri, in 1990 he launched the term 'emerging ritual', and argued for abandoning a narrow, rigid conception of ritual linked to fixed paradigms, and a widening of the perspective to include all sorts of forms of ritualisation (thus also including new rituals).[17] When Grimes engages in a critical diagnosis in respect to the current ritual milieu, it does not involve the absence of rituals, but the process of ritual dynamics and ritualisation itself. The issues are the anchoring of rites in our culture, and the time, place and energy that we have for them, and our capacity for ritual acts.

The comparison between Lukken and Grimes will be carried out on the basis of six themes. Almost all of these points will be taken up again in the closing section of this chapter. They are successively the designation of the current ritual dynamic, new rites, distance and involvement, the peculiar character of the ritual domain, the media and the ritual expert or leader.

(a) Both Lukken and Grimes are attentive to the fluidity, dynamism and development in the ritual market. Both see radical shifts taking place. Grimes interprets tendencies and developments regarding rituality critically and often negatively; for instance, through the whole study he suggests a process of deritualisation. He sometimes phrases this in very strong terms: in our present Western culture there is less and less time and energy (and, it could also be added, space, both figuratively and literally) for ritual actions.[18] This is not an absence of demand and need: there is need aplenty for language, form and space for ritual, but things generally do not get beyond the expression of this need. In his critical diagnosis Grimes continually focuses on ritual practice. The anchorage (or the renewal of the anchorage) of rituality in the lives of people would often appear to be an extremely difficult question. For Grimes rites of passage – and in particular initiation rites and the present hiatus between marriage and death rites – provide striking proof of this. The character of the

---

[16] For a summary: MITCHELL: 'Emerging ritual' (1995).

[17] GRIMES: 'Emerging ritual' (1990).

[18] See, for instance, GRIMES: *Deeply into the bone* (2000) 111: (in the context of initiation rites) "Comparatively speaking, Western industrial societies spend less time and energy on rites than do people living in more traditional, small-scale societies and less than Asian, Middle Eastern, and African peoples."

life cycle is by now so fundamentally altered that nearly all ritual repertoires are left standing in a vacuum.[19] In reality, only wedding ritual is still
present as a public rite of passage. Much more than Lukken, Grimes thus
sees the main problem in the design of rituality. People are empty-handed,
they search assiduously but find little: "Sir, do you have any satisfying
rituals today?"

Communication with the sacred, expression of emotions, marking the
successive steps in life or important, radical events: these all demand
suitable language, space, expression. But people have arrived in a cul de
sac of eclectic experiments, bizarre collages or especially what Grimes
terms 'ritual substitutes': ritual fantasies and impressions from the media
rather than ritual experience now define the ritual act. It all becomes a
matter of projections.[20]

(b) In that connection, both Lukken and Grimes bestow ample attention on the dynamic of the new, creative and experimental in ritual design,
but their tone differs. Lukken warms to the experimental. It breaks through
the exclusivity and uniformity of traditional repertoires, it is a sign of attention for pluriformity and the search for forms of adequate and inductive rites
and symbols, rites that fit for this or that situation. For Grimes creativity
and innovation, the process of 'reinventing' ritual, is often a dream, an ideal
that takes on real form only with difficulty, a utopia that gets stuck at the
level of clumsy searching, in talking *about*, rather than successful, physical
ritual performance. He then links this with physicality and the sensory, the
role of the professional or ritual expert, and the media (see below).[21]

(c) The question of distance and involvement is an important theme
that recurs in both.[22] In Lukken it is, for instance, elaborated in connection with the theme of musealisation, a cultural process that Grimes
never develops (does the difference in social-cultural contexts between
Europe and North America also play a role in this?).[23] Grimes always

---

[19] *Ibidem*, particularly Chapt. 5, 286ff.

[20] He is here referring primarily to the world of advertising and media, the supply
of virtual ritual, but also to academics: cf. *ibidem*, 111, 273-275; see further under (e),
below. Grimes elaborates this 'fantasy perspective' into what he terms the 'initiatory
dilemma'; see GRIMES: 'The initiatory dilemma' (1998).

[21] Grimes further develops this for initiation ritual, for example: GRIMES: *Deeply into
the bone* (2000) 111ff.

[22] It indeed forms a separate theme for Lukken: LUKKEN: *Rituelen in overvloed* (1999),
Chapt. 5, 197-212.

[23] *Ibidem*, 198ff.

connects the distance with the direct sensory performance of the ritual. He sees ritual inculturation failing in many places because we do not succeed in being engaged (that is to say, in acting physically and in sensory terms) in our rites. The indispensable physical dimension of rituality has become problematic, and is in part the reason for a deep crisis in rites[24] – in part, because numerous other factors also play a role, such as, for instance, a long tradition of aversion in Western culture with regard to ritual.

(d) Closely connected with this for Grimes is the deep chasm between gratuitous ritualistic acts on the one side and non-ritualistic, utilitarian, functional acts on the other.[25] Elsewhere he speaks of a distinction between an orientation to *meaning* and one to *doing* and efficacy.[26] The latter category of action is dominant in our culture, and has undermined the credibility and legitimacy of ritual acts. In a context where economic and technological discourse predominates there is hardly any space for ritual and symbol. Again, particularly our rites of passage and rituals at turning points in life are signals of this. For example, at birth and death, as Grimes illustrates extensively, the room for ritual is at a minimum, also quite literally. Even in therapeutic settings the instrumentality and function of ritual is dominant. Lukken also comments on the dominance of rites by technological and economic orders, but prefers to speak of an ambiguous situation for ritual in our culture, and sets it off against renewed interest in the symbolic order.[27]

(e) A further, more focused theme where the difference between the two authors comes to light is that of media, old and new. Both bestow relatively large amounts of attention on this theme. Lukken is open and accepting of new perspectives. That can be seen particularly when he discusses the internet and World Wide Web.[28] He points to new forms of participation that come with these (participation at a distance) and the new mythic dimensions that are introduced. Grimes in contrast is critical of new media.[29] At the level of description both are quite in agreement. It is impossible to conceive of our society now without these

---

[24] Grimes here introduces the term 'disembodying': see GRIMES: *Deeply into the bone* (2000) 275.

[25] *Ibidem*, 28.

[26] *Ibidem*, 34 (in the context of birth rituals).

[27] LUKKEN: *Rituelen in overvloed* (1999) Chapt. 3, section 2, 176-179.

[28] *Ibidem*, 188-189; 197-198.

[29] GRIMES: *Deeply into the bone* (2000) 273-275.

media. These media make the transmission of a tremendous amount of information possible, and we are confronted with an enormous variety of ritual repertoires. But, suggests Grimes, the media 'mediate' this in a very specific way: they compose, there is always a degree of selection, of processing, of shots. The media themselves are also mythic; the scripts of television soaps supply their own 'fantastic' mythic directions. Media offer a virtual world free of sensory ritual performance. All of this has far-reaching effects for authentic ritual acts. Grimes points especially to what he terms 'ritual idealism'. The rites people have seen through media cause them to develop high expectations for rituals, while everyday ritual reality is generally grey and mediocre. Not every marriage is a fairy-tale royal marriage and not every funeral draws media attention. Aside from, and sometimes in addition to literature and cultural transmission, it is chiefly the ever-present visual culture (television, video and film) that is not only the provider of substitutionary fantasy ritual,[30] but also of a substitute rituality, resulting in disappointment and a lack of quality.[31]

(f) As a last point in this comparative exercise we can point to the classic ritual theme of the ritual expert or leader. Although neither of the two authors deal with this subject separately, it is nevertheless discussed indirectly. In the case of Lukken this comes, for instance, when he speaks of the role of experts in the creation and evaluation of ritual.[32] Naturally, as an anthropologist Grimes shows interest in the role of the priest as a ritual expert, but further develops the contrast between the ritual expert and the ritual authority, between the expert in ritual drama and the professional student of rites. He then brings this distinction into relationship with his critical diagnosis of the current ritual situation and the above-mentioned issues of distance and involvement, and fantasy and idealism.[33] He observes how leaders of ritual acts in our culture (to reiterate: for Grimes that is chiefly North American culture) have become authorities on ritual. They are the professionals, no longer specialised in performance, in ritual language and ritual acts, but in the setting, the background. These authorities focus in the meta-procedural level, concentrate on preparation and evaluation. This posture of distance, of theory and procedure, has by now permeated through the structure to the participants and those who

---

[30] *Ibidem*, 111.

[31] See, for instance, in the context of initiation rites, *ibidem*, 98ff.

[32] LUKKEN: *Rituelen in overvloed* (1999) 186-188.

[33] See for instance GRIMES: *Deeply into the bone* (2000) 98ff.

attend ritual celebrations. Today they too are amply conversant with the phases of processing grief and degrees of liminality, and grade their ritual acts on the scale of ideal phasing and experience.[34]

5.4. Dynamics of Ritual Repertoires:
Types, Trends, Qualities and Deficiencies

In the comparison of the models represented by Lukken and Grimes just presented, in addition to sampling the general diagnosis of the ritual milieu, specific trends and qualities in contemporary rituality have been mentioned. We will now continue in this line through a series of characterisations on the basis of research, both ongoing and already reported. We will first offer a pluralistic typology of contemporary rituality, which will be drawn with broad strokes. Thereafter some obvious trends and characteristics of modern ritual will be sketched out.

Expansion, pluriformity

First of all, we see how since about the 1960s an until then rather homogenous and fixed ritual repertoire has uninterruptedly fanned out along four lines. There is first the Christian line, sometimes ecclesiastical and sometimes a more general Christian variant. Second, there is the line that could be termed more generally religious, which sometimes is inspired by the Christian ritual tradition, but sometimes simultaneously includes non-Christian elements. The third is the secular/profane line; and finally, here and there, much less than is often suggested, and often precisely on such peculiar occasions as disasters and commemorations, there is intercultural or interreligious ritual. These distinctions are theoretical, and primarily of service as a guide.

One tendency which is immediately clear is that present-day rituality is characterised by an increasing interaction among these lines. The walls between them have become porous, and one can speak of a falling away of borders. Particularly in the context of rituals surrounding death, burial and remembrance we see fluid boundaries among the various repertoires.

A good illustration, and one much cited (including in this book) is the funeral of Princess Diana. In her memorial service the Christian repertoire was represented by High-Church elements such as the liturgical

---

[34] See, for instance, through rituals involving death, *ibidem*, 221ff.

space, clerical dignitaries, chasubles, hymns and prayers, but the general religious line was also present in the reading on love from I Cor. 13 by Tony Blair (although it is a passage from Christian scriptures, with authentic Christian community life and discussion of the gifts of the Spirit, prophecy and speaking in tongues as its context, the praise of love was lifted out of that context and placed in a general setting), as was also the profane, in the saccharine popular song 'Candle in the Wind' by Elton John (which was originally intended for Marilyn Monroe).[35] One can also look to the explorations of the various case studies in the preceding chapter for other illustrations.

Further, it is important to see this expansion and falling away or boundaries in relation to the previously mentioned shifts in diagnoses in the latter half of the 20th century. The first diagnosis mentioned, of a crisis in rites, involves chiefly the non-ecclesiastical lines. There has indisputably been a great movement making up lost ground; since the 1980s creativity has focused more and more on the great need for secular, general religious and general Christian rites, particularly in the area of life-cycle rituals. Apparently many experienced ecclesiastical rites as too much of a straitjacket. Rites surrounding death provide a good example. This development has repeatedly been described and evaluated. The dead person was no longer laid out at home, the neighbourhood and parish community were less involved in the rites, there was no longer any real close-knit repertoire of rites, piety and support. The funeral industry blossomed, filling the hole in the market in a businesslike, efficient and uniform manner. Church funerals in this context became 'super-valued' rituals that were nonetheless appropriated by increasing numbers of people as a framework or surrogate for general Christian, general religious or even profane/secular ritual. Only since the 1980s has the situation changed; there is now a more pluriform selection, more personal and creative. This development is now having more and more influence on church funerals.[36]

[35] For a somewhat different interpretation of this ritual, see SPEELMAN: 'The 'feast' of Diana's death' (2001).

[36] See LUKKEN: *Rituelen in overvloed* (1999) 272ff; GRIMES: *Deeply into the bone* (2000) Chapt. 4, 217-284; for a recent ritual-litugical discussion: GERHARDS & KRANE-MANN (eds.): *Liturgie im Umfeld von Sterben und Tod* (2002).

Contextual changes

With this we touch on another important tendency, which for brevity's sake we will term contextual change.[37] Often connected with the disappearance of the boundaries between previously fixed tracks in rituality, the contemporary ritual dynamic is characterised by contextual changes. Churches become museums, their liturgical repertoire a museal exhibit. Gregorian chant is popular with harried managers seeking rest and repose; old pilgrimage routes are unprecedentedly popular with long distance hikers. The concept of appropriation discussed previously plays an important role in this.[38] Although this general point of contextual change has everything to do with tendencies in sacrality (see below), and particularly with the previously cited point of distance and involvement, we will not develop this tendency further here because it has a less direct relationship with our subject of disasters and rituals. It will be sufficient to make a general reference to processes such as musealisation, folklorisation, developments in the concept of tourism, commercialisation, etc.[39] Reference can also be made to several signs such as the phenomenon of disaster tourism, the tensions that always exist between documentary and museal dimensions on the one side and ritual on the other in the design of memorial sites or ritual landscapes (the preferred term here is 'memorial centres'), and increasing criticism in The Netherlands of the commemoration of the Second World War, with its accusations of bad taste and commercialisation. The Peace Education Foundation has observed a trend in the field of war commemorations: memorials and education are being transformed into "entertainment with Disney-like effects. […] All kinds of things are invented to make the history of World War II more attractive or commercially viable."[40]

Feast and remembrance

A third general typological characteristic of the ritual milieu is the dominance of the dimensions (or categories) of feast and remembrance in

---

[37] For a summary see POST: *Het wonder van Dokkum* (2000) 33-36 and IDEM: 'De moderne heilige' (2000).

[38] See 1.1.

[39] For a summary of these cultural processes, see POST: *Het wonder van Dokkum* (2000) 33-36; IDEM: 'Het verleden in het spel' (1991); IDEM: 'Traditie gebruiken' (1991); NISSEN: *De folklorisering* (1994) and STURM: 'Museifizierung' (1990).

[40] See *Trouw*, April 28, 2001, 3.

our ritual repertoires. We will here confine ourselves to noting that our rituals often take on the character of a feast.[41] That is true for general profane/secular ritual in our modern culture, but the figures are also telling for the Christian-liturgical repertoire: many note that Christians have again become 'feast Christians', whose relation to the church is only for rituals in the course of the year (witness facetious remarks about 'C&E' ((Christmas and Easter)) or sometimes 'A&P' ((Ashes and Palms)) Christians) or in the course of life (baptism, marriage, burial or cremation).

As well as feast, another dominant dimension is that of remembrance, mentioned so often in this book.[42] The traditional national war memorial repertoire is the model here, but there are also all sorts of new commemorative repertoires, as discussed in the previous chapter in our examination of the phenomenon of the silent procession.

The two dimensions, feast and remembrance, have all sorts of interfaces. For instance, the collective, the communal, and the contrast with everyday life play important, if not decisive, roles.

Emerging ritual

Alongside the genres of feast and remembrance there is a varied repertoire of new, rising rituals, which in ritual studies is now being termed 'emerging ritual'. We have already indicated how Grimes launched the concept of emerging ritual in 1990.[43] The term applies to the new rites springing up in contemporary culture. Initially this generic term was used primarily in the context of debates about the purported absence of rituals in modern Western culture, to refer to the ritual dynamic. What is involved here is seeing things from another perspective. In that context Nathan Mitchell pointed to a number of factors and characteristics.[44] For instance, the new rites were often connected with the domestic and family sphere, and with the public domain. To an important degree this was also marginal ritual, in the sense of being linked to marginal groups such as homosexuals, Alcoholics Anonymous, AIDS victims, the women's

---

[41] For feast and feast culture, see BIERITZ: 'Nächstes Jahr' (1994/5); SCHILSON: 'Fest und Feier' (1994), and with extensive bibliography, POST et al.: *Christian feast and festival* (2001).

[42] PERRY: *Wij herdenken* (1999).

[43] GRIMES: 'Emerging ritual' (1990); MITCHELL: 'Emerging ritual' (1995).

[44] MITCHELL: 'Emerging ritual' (1995).

movement, etc. It is 'fresh' ritual, still wet behind the ears, newly 'discovered', still bearing the traces of experiment and creativity.

Qualities and deficiencies

Next, for a general characterisation of the current ritual milieu, there are the more specific qualities and deficiencies of our rites. In the footsteps of researchers such as Schilson, Bieritz, Grimes, Englert, Lukken, Voyé and many others, by tracing demonstrable ritual tendencies or characteristics an effort was made to describe our modern rituality through certain 'qualities', which subsequently in a more normative, critical perspective could be evaluated in terms of quality or deficiencies.[45] This double nature of the concept of 'quality' has been elaborated elsewhere;[46] what is important here is to focus attention on the otherwise always closely mutually connected characteristics or qualities and deficiencies, which then come in view:

(a) Contemporary rituality is, for instance, characterised by a strong emphasis on experience. Unmediated experience of emotion is central. It is about being touched directly. It is on this basis that rites are evaluated, as judgements such as "it left me cold" and "it really did something for me" testify. Other ritual dimensions such as creativity, content and analysis appear to play a subordinate role, if any. The era of rites of protest in which there was room for critical analysis seem to be definitively over. That does not say, however, that protest can no longer be expressed through ritual. For this, see the discussion of the phenomenon of the silent procession, in section 3.5 above.

(b) This tendency is coupled with more of a consumer attitude in regard to the rite. One consumes the ritual, and therefore one cannot speak of real participation or engagement. This is expressed, for example, in the nonchalant combination of the lines of ecclesiastical/Christian, general religious and secular rituality identified above, which could be thought of as 'shops' in the ritual market. This aspect further touches

---

[45] SCHILSON: 'Das neue Religiöse' (1996); IDEM: 'Den Gottesdienst fernsehgerecht inszenieren?' (1996); IDEM: 'Musicals' (1998); BIERITZ: 'Nächstes Jahr' (1994/5); GRIMES: *Deeply into the bone* (2000); ENGLERT: 'Les valeurs sacrées' (1999); LUKKEN: *Rituelen in overvloed* (1999); VOYÉ: 'Effacement' (1998).

[46] See the Introduction to Part II of POST: *Christian feast and festival* (2001) 47-78, particularly 57ff.

on the general tendency toward increasing distance which we have already discussed. People zap, choose, quote, borrow, combine and associate, cut and paste brazenly. Much ritual is quoted ritual, at second or even third hand. In the humanities this tendency is of course further connected with postmodern thought.

(c) This has a good deal to do with the homogenisation and globalisation of rites observed by many. Everything is beginning to look like everything else. Ritual is often very general. People in turn react to that by making ritual very local, and linking it with the search of identity on the part of local communities. Likewise, another generally recognisable response is to make ritual unique, specific and new, often resulting in a bizarre show in which script and symbols are at the same time surprising, disorientating and unrepeatable, and which defy active participation. This tendency to homogenisation and globalising, and the reaction to it, was already discussed in the exploration of the phenomenon of the silent procession (cf. the later tendency toward specificity in the titles given to the processions).[47]

(d) Next, and again connected with the tendencies we have just noted, there is the emphasis on spectacle and event: above all else, ritual must be feast and festival, must be striking and spectacular. That is also to say, it must be large-scale, exceptional, new and different, but at the same time, short-lived. Our rites seem to be primarily focused on entrancement in the here and now.

(e) It is striking how the collective and the individual both receive a place in our rites. Speaking only of individualisation and personalisation seems inadequate. There is unmistakeably a tendency to make a feast, a memorial, a rite of passage into a personal expression, but at the same time people appear to be seeking *communitas*, the familiar 'we-feeling'.

For the rest, we must be aware here that we are introducing an extremely complex and multi-layered concept with the term individualisation. Particularly in sociology this has been worked out in very diverse ways, letting us see that very diverse and sometimes contradictory processes can lie behind this general term, as the distinction between utilitarian and expressive individualisation illustrates.[48] This always involves differing visions of the relation between the individual and

---

[47] See 3.5.

[48] L. Laeyendecker insisted on this in his contribution to the 'Rituals after Disasters' symposium at Tilburg, May 14, 2002.

community. In our closing chapter we will return briefly to this, from the ritual-liturgical perspective.

(f) Finally, our rites are concrete, functional and instrumental. Rites are – and here we pick up again Grimes's argument from our comparison between Lukken and Grimes – judged heavily on their effectiveness. This quality provokes thought, because to an important degree it seems to be at odds with one of the fundamental 'qualities' of ritual, namely gratuity and uselessness. While in essence ritual is uninhibited and pointless play, present-day rituality is readily judged on, and legitimated by, purpose and function. Funerary ritual is praised therapeutically as grief processing (or even replayed at the urging of the therapist, with the costs being picked up by health insurance), and in Protestant circles on hears the plea with increasing frequency for the Roman confessional as a ritually functional manner for expressing guilt, dealing with shame and failure, and reconciliation with fate and life.[49]

One can surmise that this operative or instrumental dimension coheres closely with the fact that many rituals are related (or again related) with evil, or, more generally formulated, the contingency in life. One could also advance the thesis that our rituals have become (or again become) apotropaic in nature. This hypothesis is particularly important for disaster ritual. The powers of evil and woe appear not to be banished. The mutability of society appears to be an illusion, the power of government and science to protect us or solve problems limited, the perfectibility of life a dream. Calamity threatens from all sides. The streets are ruled by violence that is neither to be predicted nor restrained; despite the fact that traffic always seems to be gridlocked, road accidents claim the lives of three persons a day in The Netherlands; new illnesses are not instantly followed by new cures; disasters and explosions suddenly strike close at hand; experience and statistics indicate that calm and harmonious family life is a fragile blessing. Against this background people search for safety and well-being; they seek healing and conciliating rites and symbols, and thus our rites are increasingly taking on an apotropaic and prophylactic character. We see this as linked with the tendency to instrumentalise rituals. How can they be employed strategically and effectively for protection and healing? Is this also perhaps why, in contrast to the receding tide in the rest of the liturgical repertoire, the Christian rites of passage such

---

[49] See for instance NAUTA: 'Rituelen als decor' (1997) 92.

as baptism, marriage, First Communion and funerals continue to be so valued? Modest empirical studies now available seem to confirm this; for instance, the desire for God's blessing and protection is given as the motivation for the celebration of marriage in church.[50]

---

[50] See POST: *Het wonder van Dokkum* (2000) 154; PIEPER: *God gezocht* (1988).

6. SYNTHESIS AND PERSPECTIVE

This final chapter is intended as a bird's-eye survey of our theme. Just as structures, trends and tendencies which were not visible, or only barely visible in the separate disasters are perceptible in an overview, so this survey will enable us to see those broader lines that might especially be of importance for future studies. We will thus enumerate a number of points again, and single out for discussion several salient aspects with regard to rituals and disasters. We will do this in three steps. First we will draw up a balance, then formulate perspectives – first some more general research perspectives, and then several additional ritual-liturgical perspectives. We have already introduced the term 'ritual-liturgical' in our first chapter. We also refer to the series of perspectives previously listed in the introduction, which in our view are valid for the recommended subsequent research.

6.1. SYNTHESIS

Rituals after disasters: an overlooked theme for research

A first general observation is that the subject of rituals after disasters is thoroughly underexamined, both from the perspective of disasters and from that of ritual. By now there are academics, often in separate centres devoted to the subject, who produce large-scale studies on responses to disasters; governmental policy, medical, legal, psychosocial and psychotraumatic aspects all receive attention; centres of expertise are set up, and manuals written. But ritual rarely enters the picture in all this. The same is true from the perspective of ritual. Surveying the full breadth of ritual studies, there too the subject of rituals after disasters is absent. This is remarkable. Does the 'hard' quantitative medical and psychotraumatic perspective so dominate the field that people ignore the more elusive area of symbolic acts? But how can this be squared with the increasing interest in rituals in therapeutic contexts? Indeed, in ritual studies scholars in disciplines ranging from liturgical studies to European ethnology and cultural anthropology turn their attention to the most diverse and marginal rituals, certainly now that anthropologists have massively discovered their own homelands as research fields. And is disaster ritual not a locus par excellence for the popular theme of supposedly multicultural and multireligious ritual?

This lacuna is remarkable. It should be all the more a stimulus to research. After each disaster the ritual repertoire, such as the silent procession, is characterised, placed and evaluated in journalistic essays or short cultural-sociological explorations. But these judgements are seldom if ever based on or followed by research or more thorough observation of the separate facts. Although several studies dealing with parts of the topic are available, this exploration is one of the first studies of ritual after disasters to examine the phenomenon in its relationships and contexts. Accordingly, it fills a conspicuous gap.

A settled, coherent and orderly repertoire

The ritual repertoire after a disaster in The Netherlands in the period we have defined is strikingly coherent and orderly. Although in a formal sense it is an example of what we in ritual studies term emerging ritual, the collective and public Dutch disaster ritual in the 1990s reveals itself as new, rising ritual, but without the features of emerging ritual that indicate it has not yet been licked into shape. From our bird's-eye perspective it is striking that the 'classic' repertoire of rituals after disasters apparently just sprang up spontaneously when a fitting form was sought for collective mourning and remembrance after the crash of the El Al freighter in the Bijlmer in 1992.[1] When we look further back to the years which preceded that, we may surmise that in our first case study a number of separate factors came together, which were experienced as right and fitting to such a degree that this entity, albeit with some variations each time, was more or less ready for use, and was repeated at later disasters.

The four fixed pillars of it are the silent procession, the collective service of remembrance, a monument, and annual commemoration. We can therefore speak of a ritual scenario. Around these four basic elements we see variable factors that are adjusted according to the situation. How these variable factors are introduced and organised in each case also seems to be related to the centre of power: who exercises the direction in the

---

[1] We have already noted the influence of the mourning rituals after the 1989 aeroplane disaster in Paramaribo, Surinam, on the mourning rituals after the Bijlmer disaster; this chiefly involved the collective memorial service.

week or weeks after the disaster. Is this the next of kin, the burgomaster, clergy, local authorities, the 'guilty' institutions, the media?

The following can be listed among the separate, variable factors:

(a) the demarcation of the disaster zone;
(b) the creation of a spontaneous memorial site with in particular rites involving light and flowers, as well as a varied corpus of 'grave gifts': notes, cards and drawings appear along with some stuffed animals or personal attributes;
(c) the composition of the ranks of the silent procession, the members of which comprise those immediately involved (families, survivors, neighbours), the larger circle of fellow residents of the town or city expressing their sympathy, the local authorities (burgomaster, aldermen), provincial and national political figures (Royal Commissioner, Prime Minister, government ministers), at least one representative of the royal family, and representatives of religious institutions;
(d) the reading of the names of the victims during the collective service of remembrance, and the listing of the names on the monument; particularly the phenomenon that the names are given a place in the ritual (read off or projected) is an important new, emerging element, one which was emphatically present in the rites connected with Belgium's 'Dutroux affair' (with, as its culmination, the White March in Brussels, 1996), the observance after the Hercules disaster (1996) and the memorial in Enschede (2000);
(e) the alternate and deliberate use of poetic and more mundane language, as well as of musical forms of expression;
(f) the involvement of much larger circles of people, as appears in the number of participants who come long distances for silent processions, the minutes of silence observed simultaneously elsewhere, prayers in churches and tolling of bells elsewhere;
(g) the monument and the rituals surrounding the site of the disaster itself; these differ from those at an individual grave, indicating a double set of separation rituals.

It is clear that we are here dealing with a coherent, orderly repertoire that is also clearly recognisable in the international perspective. We want to once again emphasize that we are conscious of the many forms of anger and protest that also seek expression after a disaster. These however seldom are expressed in their raw forms in the rituals we have studied, either in the ritual conduct shortly after the disaster, or in the annual commemorations. We would, though, also want to point out that investigations into the causes of the disaster, and the designation of the guilty, takes on an almost ritual character. Both acknowledgement and compensation appear to be of great importance in coping with loss, but it seems precisely the peculiar characteristic of collective mourning rituals that people are somewhat restrained in them, deferring the anger for the time being in order to be able to grieve sincerely and allow others to grieve.

While in our study we have devoted ample attention to the first two of the settled components, namely the silent procession and the collective memorial service, it would appear that an entirely separate investigation into the process by which both the monuments and the annual commemorations arise and develop would be worthwhile. Our research on both topics did not go beyond the level of general description, but it has become clear that the monuments discussed often came to be only after a great deal of consultation, wrangling and conflicting opinions. It is striking that the choice often fell on an artist from the local region. A following question concerns the function that such a monument or place of remembrance could fulfil, apart from the annual commemoration. In the Bijlmer we have already seen initiatives toward this. At the same time, important questions could be asked about the design of the commemorative services as they will be further developing over the course of time: what elements from the very first memorial services will be retained, which altered, what added or what perhaps will gradually disappear?

The silent procession: typically Dutch and general

In the Dutch situation the silent procession has been allocated a dominant place in the ritual repertoire after disasters. The rise of the silent procession and its rapid development into the standard ritual for a disaster can be connected primarily with a series of memorial rites around 1996/1997, as well as with the previously mentioned Bijlmer disaster. Although a number of international references could be cited, nevertheless this in many respects can be termed a typically Dutch ritual. The silent procession is an extremely popular ritual with an ambiguous nature. It is a very general and basic ritual. Both its strength and its weakness as a form of ritual expression lie in that. It is generally applicable and recognisable, but at the same time is increasingly experienced as too general and homogenous. Although disaster ritual is readily seized upon as an illustration of the contemporary dynamism or flowering of ritual – in the same way internationally the reference to the 'explosion of rituals' after the death of Princess Diana scores highly – we are more restrained in our judgement. In particular, the dominance of the silent procession perhaps points instead to an incapacity to find collective forms of ritual expression which are both generally recognisable and have a character all of their own that fits with the unique circumstances of their situation.

In addition to the apparently inevitable flood of words in addresses and speeches (in which, in the ritual opening, it is observed that in these situations we are struck dumb, are at a loss for words, or that words fall short), people join one another in a silent march. The procession can thus be seen as an important place to catch sight of the current development of rituals after disasters. For us, it is a sort of key ritual. Therefore we devoted ample attention to it.

We sketched the various backgrounds against which the rise of this form of ritual in the 1990s must be placed. We saw how both Dutch references (the 'silent rounds' and Dutch processional culture) and international references played a role. We called attention to the ambivalence which we have just mentioned again. It is both an extremely powerful and generally applicable ritual, as well as a ritual that precisely through its general character is increasingly experienced as faceless. The recent attempts to find a more focused name for each individual procession (procession of compassion, of solidarity, of reconciliation) speak for themselves. That here and there, in the face of the proliferation of the phenomenon, voices are raised in protest against the illegitimate use of such processions points toward a process of setting standards and canonisation.

In addition to being crisis ritual and a rite of passage, the silent procession is also a ritual linked with a specific location. It is in one way or another directly connected to a particular place. That is generally the site of the disaster. This can be included in the route taken, but it can also be the terminus of the procession. This linkage to a place appears to have been decisive for the fact that, as far as is known, nowhere in The Netherlands (or elsewhere for that matter) was there any serious consideration after September 11, 2001, of organising a silent procession for the victims of the terrorist attacks in New York and Washington, D.C., while there certainly were numerous memorial services.[2]

---

[2] The marches that ultimately did take place in The Netherlands, and in other lands including the United States itself, had more the nature of protest marches, focused on the military intervention in Afghanistan.

The silence can also be designated as an important dimension. Disaster ritual such as the silent procession is closely connected with the symbolic-ritual role of silence in our culture. Further investigation of the regimes or repertoires of silence would be productive here: where are they located, how do they interrelate, why is the quality of silence so valued (and at the same time feared)? Is silence perhaps an important ritual component that links various religions and cultures? Is silence in this ritual one of the most basic forms of expression, or (once again) is it instead a sign of the present impotence when it comes to ritual acts? In the latter case, is this perhaps the explanation for the fact that memorial ritual is often such an amazing combination of reticence, silence, deferment and simplicity on the one side, and a deluge of words on the other?

Disaster ritual as arena

A more general perspective can be derived from the key position of the silent procession which we have sketched, namely that rituals after disasters are an arena in which all sorts of trends and tendencies in Western culture encounter, and sometimes collide, with one another. This can involve very practical dimensions, or more general cultural developments.

In our explorations we referred to the important point of ritual performance. Disaster ritual reflects our ritual clumsiness, often magnified by the media and its collective, massive nature. Not only does this include the search for adequate forms of ritual expression, but also, and chiefly, the conduct of the ritual play. Real physical acts seem difficult; distance and commentary often are dominant. Here the important role of ritual space and time must also be mentioned. This is not the place to translate these general perspectives of ritual criticism into a series of concrete recommendations. We will content ourselves with a reference to the necessity of training and evaluation with regard to the *ars celebrandi*.

In conducting the ritual play, the key role is reserved for the leaders and ritual experts. Here we once again encounter the location-specific character of the ritual. The ritual experts and leaders are seldom 'hired in' from outside. The concern for rites and symbols is in that respect separated from the other concerns. While expertise in the fields of management, trauma processing and specific victim support (such as the links and exchange of expertise and experience between the disco fire in Göteborg and the cafe fire in Volendam) gained from other disasters is often called upon after a new disaster, there is little or no continuity in the role of ritual experts, developed in a previous disaster, when in a following disaster elsewhere in the country rituals once again need to be 'invented', adapted or performed. Apparently disaster ritual, unlike the other professional expertise mentioned above, is something 'among ourselves', something that is perhaps influenced by what people have seen on television from previous disasters, but which should be shaped in their own circles. The churches, with their ritual experts and worship leaders, often seem to fulfil a prominent role, as we have seen in the cases discussed. Yet this role is also specific to the place: it is not the official representatives, such as bishops or synod presidents, who are on the podium, but intimately involved local clergy.

The image of the arena also applies when we more generally consider the current situation with regard to ritual and public domain and the relation of disaster ritual with the traditional ecclesiastical repertoire. Ecclesiastical ritual, i.e. Christian liturgy, has almost vanished from the public domain, withdrawing into the church, or if it does remain outside its walls, it does so as museal, theatrical or decorative expression. It is, we suspect, characteristic of the Dutch situation that, in contrast to many European countries, the ritual landscape has not yet been definitively reallocated. Sometimes the church seeks to reenter the public domain through old and new forms of ritual presentation (for instance, through meditation centres), or people mark the key moments in the course of the year or life more or less publicly.

When it comes to memorial services, the church buildings in The Netherlands are not public stages or settings. From the whole of the rites in England after the death of Princess Diana, those in Scandinavia (especially Sweden and Finland) after the sinking of the ferry boat 'Estonia' (1994), and after the terror attacks in America in September, 2001, it appears that in the countries involved the churches occupy a different place in the public domain than they do in The Netherlands. In The Netherlands too, as in America, churches were opened after the terrorist attacks, but here they drew few people apart from their own members. After the Estonia disaster, the church (nota bene, the state church) was the central ritual mediator.[3] The church provided the place, the buildings, the repertoire and the leaders. The two international case studies in

---

[3] Another notable difference is that white crosses were prominently present in the commemorations for the Estonia disaster, while crosses rarely appeared in the public domain in The Netherlands. Cf. further section 4.1.

Chapter 4 offer important material here. This point touches on the perspective or context of 'civil religion', which will shortly be developed.

The supposed multicultural and multireligious dimension

The contemporary ritual situation is readily characterised as dynamic and
pluriform. Alongside ecclesiastical, Christian, generally religious and
secular or profane ritual, multicultural and multireligious ritual is also
differentiated. Disaster ritual is often called upon as an example of this.
Our exploration of rites after disasters rather considerably relativises this,
as intercultural and/or interreligious encounters through emerging ritual
in a general sense also form only a very modest dimension. Although
today other cultures certainly are a source of inspiration in the process of
seeking and feeling one's way toward fitting personal expressions, in the
public domain of collective rituals after disasters which we have studied
there is no real process of multicultural or multireligious appropriation.

The general positive regard for the multicultural mourning rituals after
the Bijlmer disaster (Amsterdam, 1992) did not lead to a real change or
supplement to the ritual scenario which was ready for use in subsequent
disasters in The Netherlands. In the same way that in the planning of the
collective memorial service an effort was made to have a balanced or at
least reasonable representation on the platform from the population
groups involved, so each time in the rituals after subsequent disasters we
saw an attempt to allow many voices to be heard, proportionally represented both in presence and presentation. It is rather this multiplicity
of voices which was copied in the following disaster rituals, and not,
as is sometimes suggested, multiculturality that is being held up as an
example.

One critical observation must yet be added here. In the atmosphere
of Western cultural uneasiness after the 1960s, here and there the obligation was felt to seek out the distant and different, which was treated as
a sort of neo-colonialist territory. In the period we have studied we do
not see much of this, but the praise expressed after the massively watched
Bijlmer rituals sometimes betrayed an undeserved depreciation of Western (or Dutch) ritual capacities. In the case of the fireworks disaster in
Enschede (2000), in the context of which several private funerals were
shown by the media, it further appeared that many were likewise pleasantly surprised by the fact that apparently so much new and flowing from
our own culture was possible within the walls of a traditional church.

For the rest, much also remained unseen. That was literally the case for the Moroccan and Turkish victims, whose bodies were immediately flown out to their country of origin. A complex and unfamiliar ritual repertoire that belongs to group and religious tradition also remained invisible. Multicultural and/or multireligious ritual is here by definition marginal and reserved for very specific situations, because ritual is pre-eminently linked to groups and traditions. All sorts of multireligious risk areas also remain out of the picture, such as the difference in the duration of mourning, the culturally defined aversion on the part of some to a silent procession that was held in the dark, and the presumably culturally shaped use of silence, or on the other hand vehemence to express deep mourning.

With the attacks of September 11, 2001, the multicultural and multireligious aspect was emphatically present, but in a very different way. After all, for the perpetrators and their accomplices it was the background and cause for the attack. Although the case study of September 11 included in this book does not take this dimension explicitly into consideration, in a general sense it can be said that the specific multicultural and interreligious aspects of anti-Western Moslem fundamentalism have strongly influenced disaster ritual, and were a sharp stimulus for its nationalistic dimensions.

6.2. RESEARCH PERSPECTIVES

International comparisons

The importance of the comparative international perspective has already been stressed several times. With the Estonia disaster and September 11 we presented two international case studies. In our introduction we pointed to the complicating factor that disaster ritual is both extremely local and specific to its place, because it is ritual that to an important degree is attached to the site of the catastrophic events, while at the same time having international dimensions through the nature of the disaster (in the case of aeroplane disasters, for instance, the connection with international air traffic), through their impact spreading internationally in the media, and through international ritual references. Disaster ritual thus always has important international references, without there however being anything of the nature of a general international ritual repertoire. On the contrary: let us again emphasize that disaster ritual is always deeply bound up with its place and situation, and the silent procession, for example,

despite its many international references, is to be considered as a typical
Dutch ritual, even as the striking role of the church in Sweden in the case
of the Estonia disaster, and the nature of the September 11 rites are likewise related to the particular nations.

Particularly through the influence of the media (see below) there are
constantly direct and indirect interferences across national borders. We
saw how these often involve specific appropriations. For instance, The
Netherlands formed its own image of the White March in Brussels. The
funeral of Princess Diana has become a standard reference in discussions
of ritual dynamics in public mourning ritual.

This national/local ambivalence and the international references could
well be the subject of interesting comparative research. On the one hand
we have ritual that is connected to both place and situation, intertwined
with national, regional and local contexts; on the other such ritual,
because of its public character and the universal or supranational nature
of a disaster, is immediately connected with forms of ritual expression
taken from or to other countries. Through international comparisons
that which is specific to The Netherlands (or any other country) would
more clearly be seen. There is much in these comparisons that indicates
that the phenomenon of the silent procession, as it developed in the
1990s in The Netherlands, is in many respects a very Dutch ritual that
has no real counterpart in any other land. We have previously discussed
the important theme of rituality and the public domain, and the altered
position of Christian ecclesiastical ritual.

As far as we can determine, almost no comparative investigation into
disaster ritual has been done. There are constant references to the 'Diana
rituals', but this hardly qualifies as a thorough international comparison
– with the exception of the research by the social scientist A. Bäckström,
from Uppsala, who placed the rituals after the Estonia disaster into a wider
international perspective.[4]

In an adjacent field, that of collective rituals after the death of celebrities, we find particularly in the cases of the violent deaths of the Swedish
statesman Olof Palme (1986) and Israeli Prime Minister Yitzhak Rabin
(1995) a series of studies taking the role of the media and international

---

[4] Unpublished lecture at Soesterberg, June 7, 2000; see also Chapt. 1, note 42. This
lecture also plays a role in the recently issued collection of articles by MENKEN-BEKIUS,
BAL & VAN DIJK-GROENEBOER: 'De kerk en stille tochten' (2001); see further
section 4.1.

comparisons as their subject. Such research could be the model for a wider comparison of disaster ritual.[5]

A yet underestimated and insufficiently understood factor in the international dimension of disaster ritual is the role of the new electronic media, such as the internet.

The role of the media

Another important field for further research involves the role of the media. Disaster ritual is to a great extent media ritual. In this exploratory study we could only mention the role of the media briefly in each case.[6] Because, to our mind, this is an extremely important topic, and also because the more general subject of ritual and media is too little discussed, in this section of synthesis and perspectives we will enter somewhat more extensively into the issues at stake here. It is important that we not only address the role of television, but also that of the new electronic network media.

Rituals after a disaster are directly 'mediated' by media, and the information is distributed both nationally and internationally, sometimes on a grand scale. Media themselves have become an integral part of the ritual. In the case of media and disaster ritual, it is primarily the role of television that is important. Internet appears to play a lesser role, although the death of Princess Diana and the disasters in Enschede and Volendam reveal how in each case an entirely peculiar assembly of rituals arose which has hardly been documented. In addition to the familiar electronic condolence registers there were all sorts of indications of national and international involvement to be found, in the form of poems, first-hand narratives, prayers, and virtual symbolic acts with flowers, candles, photographs, etc.

An important issue in this regard is the territory between virtuality and reality. Modern network media are constantly being connected with the ambiguity of 'real' and 'non-real'. The nature of the media communication is contrasted with existing mediation in which particularly physical presence and encounter are the parameters. Terms such as 'simulation' are

---

[5] SCHARFE: 'Totengedenken' (1989); PERI (ed.): *The assassination of Yitzhak Rabin* (2000).

[6] See, for example, JACOBS: 'Folklore in Cyberië' (2001); POST: 'De kus door het glas' (2002).

employed, and dichotomies such as 'real' and 'unreal', or 'real' and 'virtual' assumed. The key question in the case of television and internet rituality is whether the conception of ritual is actually at stake. On this matter, as we saw in the preceding chapter, Grimes for instance is critical and reserved.[7]

The question of how 'real' virtual ritual is proceeds too much from the assumption of discontinuity if participants are not physically present. However, the real issue is how 'virtual' media ritual actually is. After all, virtual ritual indeed has thoroughly physical dimensions: someone is typing on the keyboard, and looking at the monitor. It is notable that the image is primary, while word and act are secondary. The connection to the local also comes to the fore in virtual ritual: through virtual cemetery rites a virtual cemetery simulates the function of a 'real' cemetery as the place to mourn, commemorate and encounter.

Grimes, as we saw too in the chapter on ritual dynamics, also connects the subjects of media (old and new) and rituality with the tension between ideal and reality.[8] The media makes a tremendous interchange of information possible, and almost all familiar ritual repertoires are in principle accessible. But, Grimes suggests, the media do not act purely as a conduit, but compose; there is always selection, editing, shots. The media provide a virtual world that is separated from physical ritual performance. This all has far-reaching consequences for authentic ritual action; ritual becomes idealised. Expectations constructed from rites seen in the media become too high, while everyday ritual reality is generally rather thin and average. Seen from this perspective, disaster ritual, which to such a large degree is also media ritual, probably has a great influence on our ritual actions, or at least on our vision of them. Here too a perspective for research beckons. As a parallel, it is rather generally supposed that the broadcast of church services on radio – and especially on television – has an influence on the liturgical practice in parishes and congregations.

The theme of the ambivalence of distance and engagement, also developed in ritual studies, is also to be encountered in questions about the role of media. The media also force us to reevaluate our ideas here. At great distance, in their own living rooms, people feel deeply involved; they cry and are really emotionally affected. There is, however, a clear

---

[7] GRIMES: *Deeply into the bone* (2000) 273-275.
[8] For a summary, see POST: 'Overvloed of deritualisering' (2001).

difference between the visual medium of television and cyberspace. With televised rituals, the camera often functions as a magnifying glass that reduces distance, sharply visualising a facial expression or the nature of an act. In cyberspace the most extremely personal of emotions can be anonymous, concealed, or manipulated.

The tension between the individual and community is closely connected with this. Media create new forms of community. Especially the developments in the new network media demand a fundamental reevaluation of the relation between ritual and community. Is it possible to maintain the primacy of sensory, physical presence? Are not forums, and incidental, situational sub-communities more important? This issue of new forms of community will later be the subject of further discussion, as a ritual-liturgical perspective par excellence.

At the same time there is mingling of the public and private domains taking place. A personal, emotional expression is made publicly, or at least becomes accessible to the general public. This sometimes leads to irritation, which is related to the ambiguity, the ambivalence of distance and involvement. It is precisely this point to which reference is often made in the journalistic evaluations of ritual after disasters we have discussed. The private and the public become fused, and a lack of discretion and distance is the result. For that matter, ritual does not always accommodate that tension, even apart from media intervention. Ritual lives by the grace of a delicate balance between involvement with this unique situation or person on the one side, and transcending this situation or person on the other. Ritual always incorporates a certain objectivity and general order. In this manner the private and intimate is transcended and the personal emotion is channelled.

Ritual narrative: a privileged source

As potential sources, research into rituals after disasters has available to it all of the possible sources that ritual studies has at its disposal, from empirical, quantitative surveys to qualitative case studies based on participant observations. We wish to spotlight one potential source. We will indeed recommend it as a privileged source, especially because the previously discussed issue of appropriation and conferring significance is directly accessible through it. This source is what is termed ritual narrative, the account of the experience of those involved. This source could only be employed here and there in this exploratory project.

The investigative relevance of the ritual narrative is connected with the broader field of oral history and ego documents, through to the narrative interview in the social sciences and humanities. Since the 1970s the personal narrative has been explored in its theoretical aspects and employed in the discipline of ethnology, particularly in Germany, Scandinavia and the United States. In the wider interest in stories and narrative culture which was present there, more and more attention was paid to the personal narrative. Specifically, this source has been fruitfully employed in pilgrimage research.[9] For an extensive theoretical and methodological positioning of the personal narrative as a source for ritual investigations, the reader is referred to research based on these pilgrim accounts.[10] Here only a subdivision of the personal narrative is relevant, namely the ritual narrative, the personal account that provides insight into the effect of ritual on the personal handling of suffering and loss.

In his recent study of rites of passage, Grimes makes this his central source.[11] He employs this source not purely for illustration or characterising a trend or theme, but also as an expression of how rituals are interpreted and evaluated. Through the ritual narrative he combines the level of the local and particular with the more universal and general. The aspect of experience is at the heart of this. He is surprised that this source is so little used, and conjectures that this has to do with the assumption that stories would be irrelevant in the case of rituals. After all, rituals by definition involve transcending the personal dimension. Grimes disputes that they primarily concern something objective and universal. On the contrary, the autobiographical ritual narrative is a unique source in which the involved person themselves 'opens up' the ritual, decodes it ('makes sense of a rite'). The stories can give the rites much more meaning in hindsight than they had at the actual moment of performance, but they can also flatten a rite, talk the meaning out of it.

By employing ritual narratives researchers can come upon the traces of important themes, and can support interpretations and evaluations, or

---

[9] For a general overview, see POST: 'Pelgrimsverslagen' (1992) particularly 297-304; further BREDNICH: *Lebenslauf* (1982); RÖHRICH: 'Erzählforschung' (1994); DEKKER, ROODENBURG & ROOIJAKKERS: *Volkscultuur* (2000) Chapt. 6 on narrative culture.

[10] POST, PIEPER & VAN UDEN: *The modern pilgrim* (1998) 221-242; see also FREY: *Pilgrim stories* (1998).

[11] GRIMES: *Deeply into the bone* (2000) 9ff.; IDEM: *Marrying & burying* (1995). This is actually one composite personal/ritual narrative.

even put them into words. The range of ritual narratives is great: they can include diary fragments, interviews, fragments from books based on personal experience, documentaries, newspaper articles, etc.

Memorial culture

We further consider the general context of the flourishing general memorial culture in The Netherlands and other countries as an indispensable perspective for follow-up research. Developments in this repertoire are directly connected with rituals after disasters. We have already drawn attention to several important developments. For instance, all sorts of subgroups, such as the next of kin of cancer patients, road traffic victims and other groups of victims, regularly create memorials with their own rites, symbols and myths. These new forms of memorial culture, a real example of emerging ritual, in part define the context in which disaster ritual should be studied. Through this contextual approach one catches sight of trends and developments which are already beginning to reveal themselves in the field of disaster rituals.

As was already mentioned, we have devoted but little attention to the creation of the monuments or developments in the annual memorial services. Historiography in this field would throw an interesting light on trends and tendencies in memorial culture in general and that surrounding disasters in particular.

Many have pointed out that developments in the field of memorial culture cohere closely with the ritual dynamic sketched here and the changes in the relationship between the individual and the community. Beginning in the second half of the 1990s all sorts of groups or communities of fellow-sufferers, for example next of kin of disaster victims, road traffic victims or particularly victims of certain illnesses such as cancer, have coalesced. These groups of fellow-sufferers are typical examples of communities of interest, or interest groups, people who come together around a theme, who have an interest in common. To an increasing degree these groups want to act, to do something. A rather general form of action is an annual memorial ritual at a particular place. The annual commemoration of a disaster at a memorial monument has thus by now a broad context in a sought-after memorial repertoire. That repertoire can even develop long after a disaster, as can be seen in the case of the great aeroplane disaster on the island of Tenerife, where a Dutch KLM passenger liner crashed into an American Pan Am jet liner on the runway (1977, over 570 fatalities). Only in 2002, undoubtedly prompted by recent disasters, did the next of kin come together into a group which, among other activities, is organising annual services of remembrance. There had already been a monument placed in an Amsterdam cemetery, and at the time a large memorial service was held in a hanger at Schiphol Airport.

Civil religion

When it comes to finally characterising and evaluating the repertoire, we wish to be more reticent than most of the journalistic essays that set out with this purpose (see Chapter 1.1. and 3.5.). It is our conviction that the phase of characterisation, interpreting and evaluating can only follow after a phase of descriptive, analytical and contextual research. Only now and then have we made pronouncements on ritual capacity and incapacity, on the role of the community, on interference with the ecclesiastical repertoire, and on play of ritual, and its players, in the public domain.

The concept of civil religion can perhaps offer direction in this context. The concept of civil religion is generally related to the public conferring and deriving of meaning in ritualised aspects of the state, politics and citizenship. In the context of disaster ritual, this conferring of meaning takes place on the street, in the most literal sense. The disaster rituals we have studied shows not only how mourning is expressed collectively, but also how comfort is given collectively. The 'positive mass' which arises thereby however also involves a collective expression of helplessness and vulnerability, in which resignation and protest each appear to have their own course.

The manner in which the term 'civil religion' developed, from Rousseau to Bellah, via Durkheim, allocates space for collectivity as an ideal in itself: most participants in disaster ritual, as participants or observers, did not know the victims personally, but feel involved; they show their sympathy and take part in something that is larger than themselves.[12] They draw comfort from each other's company, the words, music, flowers and silence. In view of the popularity of the theme of social cohesion, interesting illustrations could be found here. A more general characterisation and evaluation could be linked with the functions and dimensions of rituals, which we previously designated as relief, orientation, channelling, mediation of community, prophylaxis and contrast between the ordinary and supramundane.

---

[12] NUGTEREN: 'Collective/public ritual behaviour' (2001).

Looking back over our descriptions of disaster ritual once again, it is striking that they contain no heavy religious propositions; what is shared does not consist of scripturally prescribed certainties, but lays bare human powerlessness. The critical question which must be asked about this is for whom this discourse on mourning was intended, and if it is perhaps the case that this is perhaps a self-justifying exercise on the part of those who have had a lucky escape. The acknowledgement that "this could have happened to me" should not be underestimated as a motivation for entering the public domain.

Disaster rituals appear to mobilise large numbers. Study of collective mourning rituals after disasters could shed light on vital trends in the community as a whole. The place where disaster strikes turns into a ritual laboratory. The large convention centre where a service of mourning is held affords a cross section of a dynamic society. In a silent procession one of the foundations of contemporary efforts to find meaning is literally exposed on the street. These could well be the places where to an increasing degree civil religion can be found.

6.3. RITUAL-LITURGICAL PERSPECTIVES

A tendency to sacrality

As we now in closing sketch several more ritual-liturgical perspectives, first general connections can be made with the presently very vital demand for a diagnosis of the current ritual milieu. Such a diagnosis touches directly the fundamental liturgical project of liturgical inculturation. Ultimately it involves the position of Christian ritual in that milieu and possible connections with that milieu. These can take the form of radical analogy, or of discrepancy, of continuity or discontinuity. Ultimately we here encounter the question of the identity of Christian rituality.[13] We do not deal with that question here; that fits more into a liturgical-theological context. With this diagnosis of the milieu from disaster ritual in mind, however, it is certainly important to mention here the concept of sacrality tendencies, which is rising in liturgical studies.[14] In addition to,

---

[13] For this programme of ritual studies research, see: POST: 'Interference and intuition' (2000); IDEM: 'Programm und Profil' (2002).

[14] For a summary, see: ENGLERT: 'Les valeurs sacrées' (1999). Further: POST: *Het wonder van Dokkum* (2000) 115ff. and IDEM: 'De moderne heilige' (2000); IDEM: 'Life cycle rituals' (2002).

and increasingly often in opposition to a process of desacralisation, researchers now also observe a general anthropological, cultural *persistance du sacré*; increasingly in our supposedly demystified culture there are references to forces and powers, perspectives and dimensions which transcend us: reference to sacred transcendence through which one goes beyond the banality of the ordinary. Particularly at the key moments in life ritual comes to the fore – but also at moments of crisis. It has been argued that precisely for modernity these tendencies surrounding sacrality are extremely complex and dynamic. It is interesting to see how disaster ritual is often cited as an illustration for supposedly ineradicable fundamental sacrality and rituality. In the recent, strongly programmatic book by David Torevell, *Losing the sacred*, postmodern disaster ritual is directly linked with a general indelible need for rituals as acts which order and give meaning to life.[15] A longer quote will not be out of place here:

> Within more secular contexts, too, ritual often finds expression, particularly at times of intense doubt or fragility after tragic events. Davie's account (1995) of the highly ritualised behaviour at the Anfield football ground after the Hillsborough disaster and the numerous ritual layings of flowers at the spots where people have been killed or murdered suggests that rituals have far from disappeared in modern consciousness and still hold existentialist meaning and importance. The national response to the death of Diana, Princess of Wales, tells a similar story. Such rituals might be far removed from those ecclesiastically managed during the medieval period, but they do point to the need for many people to mark important stages in life with ritualised actions which help secure order and meaning.[16]

Beyond repetition

The dimension of repetition has an important place in the theory of rites. Ritual lives by grace of repetition, and repeatability. But recently that concept too has been relativised.[17] After all, sought-for ritual, when found, is usually experimental, inductive, and wholly tailored to a particular and unique situation (see below), and as such is not repeatable. We see that in much disaster ritual, which is one-off. Only a few silent

---

[15] TOREVELL: *Losing the sacred* (2000).
[16] *Ibidem*, 203.
[17] See ROUWHORST: 'Rituelen in overvloed' (2001).

processions are later repeated or grow into a real ritual tradition, as happened with the Bijlmer disaster. Without here becoming involved in the theoretical debate about to what extent the aspect of repeatability is part of the core domain of ritual (for instance, Lukken defends this aspect strongly while Bell argues that repetition is not per se related to ritual[18]), modern ritual still reveals a detached attitude toward the element of repetition. It is precisely disaster ritual which illustrates that. As we have said, there is one-off, unique ritual, and alongside it new 'traditional' ritual that can be employed and repeated for other situations which arise. The silent procession is, once again, a salient and popular example of this.

This ritual-theoretical, and at the same time extremely practical point of repetition as a basic category or quality of ritual touches directly on two other important points, the aspect of new, emerging rituals, and that of inductive or deductive ritual. The latter point we will soon discuss in another section; here we will briefly touch again on emerging rituals.

When we look at the paper in which Grimes introduced the term emerging ritual, it is notable that he actually chiefly deals there with the aspect of the creative malleability of ritual.[19] In that connection he formulates eight 'principles of ritualizing', with regard to which it is striking that they sound more like principles which have to do with inductivity, creativity and practice rather than 'classic' principles such as tradition and collectivity.[20] He lists successively the dialectic of body and culture, of individual and society (not beginning with rituals as massive or collective), the principle of temporary community (certainly in our segmented society), the principle that ritual is always dependent on performance, of the actual acts, and finally of 'ritual inventability': you can learn and create rites, invent them through trial and error and experimentation.

Inductive and adequate ritual

We find that regard for creativity and experiment as a characteristic of contemporary ritual dynamics not only in the academic study of ritual, but also among liturgists. It is often discussed in liturgical studies in the broader context of liturgical inculturation, and in arguments for inductive

---

[18] LUKKEN: *Rituelen in overvloed* (1999) 47-55; cf. ROUWHORST: 'Rituelen in overvloed' (2001).

[19] GRIMES: 'Emerging ritual' (1990).

[20] *Ibidem*, 25ff.

and adequate ritual. Particularly Lukken has developed this theme many times, in particular for modern ritual relating to death.[21] A brief examination of this important perspective of inductive and adequate ritual will not be out of place in our context of disaster ritual.

Lukken opposes inductive ritual with deductive ritual. Deductive ritual is uniform, ahistorical ritual, which in the case of funeral rites is always performed in the same way, irrespective of the ever changing new situation. It is the general applied to the specific. Inductive ritual works the other way around: it begins with the specific and goes from there to the general. The situation is given a place in the ritual, which is 'opened up' (a favourite key concept for Lukken) for it; the tradition is reappropriated, and what was done before is done again from this unique situation. This repetition is free and creative; the new, unique performance is central. Inductive ritual is open, and in the doing the perspective jumps. The one-dimensionality is broken through by language and symbolic act. Now, a swing to this more inductive ritual, in which personal wishes and creativity rather than ceremony and protocol are the desired qualities, is a general tendency in our culture. We have already referred to the dangers in this movement: extravagance, dominance of emotionalism, consumption and commercialism.

Lukken connects inductive ritual with adequate ritual. With this strongly normative quality he points to the necessity of seeking accommodation with the pluriformity of convictions and spirituality in the contemporary context. Today's context demands multiple models and types in the rituals available. In essence this is about the acknowledgement of the lines of rituality (Christian ecclesiastical, general religious and secular) elaborated in Chapter 5.

Disaster ritual as death ritual and rite de passage[22]

Disaster ritual can be seen as a particular form of transition ritual and – more specifically – as a death rite. This perspective touches also on the point of coping with trauma and processing grief, which will shortly be discussed. Here we will briefly deal with some aspects of death ritual

---

[21] LUKKEN: *Rituelen in overvloed* (1999) 216-231 and IDEM: 'De liturgie rond een overledene' (2000).

[22] In addition to consulting the abundance of literature on rites surrounding death (including especially recent work by Lukken and Grimes), the ideas in this section were gathered particularly from a conference on contemporary funeral ritual in Schmochtitz, Germany, in September, 2000; see GERHARDS & KRANEMANN (eds.): *Christliche Begräbnisliturgie* (2002).

which in our opinion are relevant and of current interest. In doing so we will keep disaster ritual in mind.[23]

Taking death ritual as a structure of acts in which three sorts of orientations play a role offers a perspective for ritual and liturgy. First, there is the orientation to values. In culture there are always preconceived ideas about ritual acts. 'Values' are at work here. Some things must be, others not. '"We can't do that to the deceased" is a popular reflection of that attitude. Those values which in a general sense determine our ritual acts in their design and performance are always in flux. Previously Christian values were dominant. In his study of contemporary rites of passage Grimes indicates how modern rites of death are becoming less emotional and personal and more professional, and how this exposes other patterns of values.[24] For ritual acts that produces all kinds of confusion. Is death ritual a ritual for the deceased, or for the survivors? Do we look to the dead, or does the dead person speak to us? With increasing frequency in the ritual it is indeed the deceased who is presented as speaking to the survivors. The second orientation is to purpose. This involves the direct functions of the ritual: leave-taking, the marking of the last phase of life, and ultimately (and literally) assigning a place to the dead body. Especially today, marking the withdrawal from active life is no longer exclusively linked with rituals surrounding death, but expands over a series of moments of transition and leave-taking. This has relativised the function of death rituals in our culture as rites of passage. There are now, as people become older, a whole series of moments of leave-taking and transition, which are often also being marked by ritual. People retire, turn 65, move into senior citizen centres, etc. A sudden death, as in the case of a disaster, breaks this step-by-step process of disengagement radically. For this reason the aspects of transition and leave-taking, and the suddenness and arbitrariness of death – elsewhere often less accentuated – are found in strength in disaster ritual. In this way disaster ritual distinguishes itself fundamentally from other death ritual. This brings us emphatically to the third orientation, namely that of emotion. Precisely in the case of

---

[23] Here we will take up again some perspectives which were discussed in the international conference mentioned in note 22, *Liturgie im Umfeld von Sterben und Tod im Kontext der säkularen Gesellschaft*, September, 2000, in Schmochtitz, Germany. Particularly the lecture on contemporary funerary and cemetery culture by R. Sörries, director of the Museum für Sepulkralkultur in Kassel, deserves notice here. See the conference report: SÖRRIES: 'Bestattungs- und Friedhofskultur der Gegenwart' (2002).

[24] GRIMES: *Deeply into the bone* (2000) Chapt. 4.

'atypical death' (often termed sudden or undeserved) is there a great need for a ritual oriented to feelings. Prescriptions and frameworks, efficient procedures are experienced as very exasperating. Much of the ritual available is too thin, or completely unsuitable. Crisis ritual is primarily emotionally oriented, and challenges those dealing with it to inductive and creative responses.

A next aspect of rituals surrounding death is that a development in their 'economic cycle' has been observed. Very schematically, and therefore undoubtedly without the necessary nuances, the following picture emerges. After the Second World War rituals surrounding death were hardly considered; people focused on living worthily, and on reconstruction. Until the 1980s growing old with dignity, and dying with dignity, were central. Now we have reached the point of dealing with the dead and death itself in a dignified way. What is still to come is worthy remembrance. Slowly that is growing as a concern, although the fact that in our society memorial rites and maintenance of cemeteries are given little thought should itself stimulate reflection.[25] In our view, the increasing search for new and suitable memorial repertoires to which we have repeatedly drawn attention in this study, would confirm this cycle.

Closely related to this is the issue, also often raised here, of the relation between individuality and collectivity. Our culture has few collective rites of death. There are national war commemorations; churches have annual memorials for the dead (for instance, All Saints' Day, and in Germany there is a *Totensonntag*). After disasters one sees the search for an adequate form of collective memorial ritual. We saw already how particularly a place can play a role in this. The rites of remembrance come in addition to those at the individual grave (which at the same time in the case of Volendam is part of a collective plot), and are generally connected with a place, usually the site of the disaster. While presently the link between death and dying and any particular place is relaxing – where a person dies and is buried is to a great extent dependent on the accidents of mobility – with a disaster a place again enters the picture. Despite sometimes great practical problems, a specific spot is cherished and turned into a ritual landscape. That is illustrated by the many roadside shrines along our roads, by the way that the site of Princess Diana's crash in Paris continues to be ritually marked, and the

---

[25] This is an important observation from the lecture by Sörries (see note 23, above). He noted that within Europe The Netherlands was nevertheless leading the way.

fact that, after many objections and much opposition, a memorial monument for the Hercules disaster in Eindhoven was constructed on the military base close beside the runway.

A final aspect that we want to mention is the role of mourning attributes. With rituals in general, and with rites surrounding death in particular, rites are linked with objects. That can be seen, for example, in the metaphors that dominate the texts and images: bridges, stair, ship, labyrinth, door, cradle, etc. These are concrete things. But it can also be seen in the fact that things are employed in the ritual: torches, candles, balloons, flowers, wreathes, photographs. A trend that has been observed by many but which can be explicated by few is the placement of toys, stuffed animals and teddy bears. What is happening here? Is this a new variant in grave gifts? A spontaneous attempt at post-death communication? Or is the stuffed animal a bearer of transcendent concepts, as grave lights were in the past (and still are in many regions in Europe where they remain a general practice)? Or are they, more generally and vaguely, a material representation of emotions such as love, comfort, security and solidarity? People could be expressing these feelings in soft toys rather than in words or acts.[26]

By viewing disaster ritual as a rite of passage and death ritual, it can further be seen as a part of a complex whole of related rituals, and thus as part of a process. As collective death ritual, disaster ritual is part of a series of processes which often have unsuspected connections and links. Thus caution and sensitivity are recommended here. As a ritual process, death ritual channels, carries those involved from lock to lock, as it were. This course comprises private and public, religious and profane components. But the sub-repertoire of collective, public disaster rites also forms a process with successive, more or less fixed, prescribed phases. For instance, the memorial service, possible silent procession, construction and dedication of a monument and annual gatherings at that monument together form one whole.

In most cases there appears to be a dichotomy: individual burial and collective mourning. Sometimes this yields a painful dilemma, for instance when the timing of the memorial service and silent procession must be established while other victims are still fighting for their lives. If both ritual components are seen as parts of a phased death ritual, the

---

[26] Many have observed the role of stuffed toys, but little research has been done into it. Recently there has been a fine article on the material culture of hospitals, where stuffed toys likewise surface: see HOLMBERG: ""Anders hätte ich es gar nicht überlebt"" (2001).

later fatalities fall outside it. In fact, no real transition can be made as long
as the number of dead is not definitively established. Thus here the individual domains are at cross-purposes with the collective domain and the
time line for the fixed steps collides with the uncertainties regarding individual victims.

Coping with disaster

Often disaster ritual is primarily seen as, and employed as a functional
ritual. Rituals can play a role in coping with traumas. The familiar designation for this is the coping dimension. In Chapter 3.3., with regard
to the case of the Volendam cafe fire of 2001, coping was characterised
as psychosocial adaptation after a serious occurrence. One can here note
a lacuna in professional psychological literature. The role of rituals in
processing trauma is rather widely acknowledged, but seldom does one
find follow-up research into the effectiveness of individual or collective
rituals after a disaster. Here at the same time perhaps lies the problem.
Rituals can make a meaningful contribution to coping with suffering and
loss after a disaster, but it must not be expected that rituals are a panacea.
In addition, there is the question of whether the instrumental perspective should be permitted to be decisive. One can conceive of other perspectives that might be more decisive – for instance, honour to the dead.

Moreover, the effect of a rite is not amenable to control. Processing
of suffering – in this case after a disaster – seems to coincide to an important extent with becoming reconciled to the blindness of existence and
to chance. This demands surrender. The purely instrumental employment of rites negates this fundamental attitude of submission and grace
that is a condition for the effectiveness of the ritual.

Powerlessness is one of the essential points about a trauma. When a
ritual is performed deliberately, a certain degree of control is regained, but
when the model of control becomes too dominant with regard to the
model of reconciliation, the nature of coping as a process is short-cir-
cuited. A certain restraint here with regard to the instrumental employment of rituals after a disaster would therefore seem to be recommended.

If more exhaustive use were made of ritual narratives (see above) in
order to assay the personal experience of the effect of mourning rituals,
the voice of individual experience could be better heard. At the same
time there is here a question about the psychohygienic operation of anger
and protest: there is the search for acknowledgement, the desire to see

the guilty named and shamed, and a commitment to preventing the recurrence of the event. To what degree the aftermath of the disaster, in the form of investigations and public pillorying is developing into a ritual of its own which effectively contributes to the coping process, is a question that requires separate further study.

Through the dimension of coping we now directly encounter the question of functionality and instrumentality in ritual.

Functionality and instrumentality versus gratuity

In focusing on the coping dimension the central question of the suggested gulf between dominant instrumental, functional and effective acts on the one hand and the gratuitous domain of rite and symbol on the other once again comes into the picture. With regard to this issue, which plays a role in ritual studies (and particularly liturgical studies) in numerous ways and at many points, we will briefly formulate two remarks.

First, it is good to keep in mind the theoretical framework for the discussion. The discussion about the functionality of ritual has for a long time been related to two currents in anthropology. One can there see the distinction between functionalist and symbolist approaches to ritual.[27] The one current sees the significance of ritual as linked with its function, particularly in social contexts; the other sees the rite as having significance in itself. Lukken, following Spiro, correctly emphasizes that these are do not exclude each other, but complement one another (although he subsequently wishes to avoid any appearance of functionalism and exchanges the term 'function' with regard to ritual for the word 'dimension'). It is thus of great importance to always see how 'functional' and instrumental the approach to ritual functions is.

A second remark involves the perspective that sociology can offer. There a distinction is made between functionality and intentionality. The critical attitude toward instrumentalisation of rituality involves intentionality – that is to say, the conscious, deliberate employment of ritual for certain instrumental processes.

For the rest, we refer the reader to that which was said in the previous chapter, by way of the discussion of Grimes, about the characteristic ritualistic discourse that in our society is becoming ever less accepted, as everything is coming to be measured on use, effect and function.

---

[27] Cf. LUKKEN: *Rituelen in overvloed* (1999) 47. See above in 1.2.2.

*Two basic liturgical concepts reconsidered: active participation
and community*

Surveying the development of disaster ritual within the broader context
of tendencies in the ritual market, one is struck by how certain basic
concepts come to stand in a different perspective, and perhaps must be
reevaluated. At a number of points that touches Christian ritual in particular. This would appear to be the case, for instance, for the pair of
active participation and community which, as is well known, were and
are the key concepts of what is termed the Liturgical Movement. This
rethinking has much to do with an entirely new relation between distance
and involvement in and through ritual in the modern context. A strong
incentive here could be the important (though in ritual studies far too
little recognised) issue of new media in our culture. The cultic explosion
accompanying the death of Princess Diana in 1997 is a good and often
cited example.[28] As well as the distance of the medium (following a
funeral in another country from your own sofa) there was also extreme
involvement. Many considered Diana as their best friend, while none of
them had ever really met the Princess in their lives! Distance was transformed into the most intimate involvement by the media. In the face of
this, can one maintain the primacy of spatial, physical presence for
participation and community? The same complex situation applies for
individual and community: the most individual emotion and expression
is paired with the search for – and for many, the finding and experience
of – *communitas*. Here we are confronted with the important point of the
perhaps lamentably specific interpretation of the concept of 'community'
(and closely, or perhaps even inseparably connected to that, of 'active
participation'). In the modern communications sciences, in cyberan-
thropology and cyberethnology there is much reflection ongoing about
this point of community, which traditionally was supported by such elements as time and space, broad sensory communication, being together,
coming together, knowing one another, sharing with one another in all
facets of life, certain organisational structures, and a certain tradition, a
sense of 'from generation to generation'.[29] In our modernity there is also

---

[28] See, among others, LUKKEN: *Rituelen in overvloed* (1999) 228 and 273; POST:
Het wonder van Dokkum (2000) 124-126 and 152; GRIMES: *Deeply into the bone* (2000)
275-280; SPEELMAN: 'The 'feast' of Diana's death' (2001).

[29] A good *status quaestionis* with literature is provided by JACOBS: 'Folkore in Cyberië'
(2001); cf. further: GABRIEL: *Kulturwissenschaften* (1997); SCHWIBBE & SPIEKER: 'Virtuelle
Friedhöfe' (1999) and O'LEARY: 'Cyberspace' (1996); POST: 'De kus door het glas' (2002).

now another interpretation of community coming into being. It involves a plural and complex community, more random, temporary and incidental encounters, with more emphasis on the individual, and especially less fixed. The World Wide Web indicates the nature of this shift: communities there chiefly take on the nature of interactive forums and platforms.[30] An important factor with more or less virtual communities of this sort is that active participation is often built in beforehand via interaction – indeed, it is perhaps the core of such forum communities.

For some time now those in ritual and liturgical studies have been relativising the massive emphasis on conscious and active participation. For some time they have seen the deritualising dimensions of strongly expository, explanatory, word-oriented ritual. They are now also aware of growth and dynamics in time, of silence, of the small *geste* as participatory ritual act, and of individual devotional ritual in which involvement in *communitas* is not excluded.

Studies of emerging and newly established ritual repertoires such as disaster ritual and its adjacent rites can thus provide important perspectives for current reflection on and reevaluation of those key concepts for liturgy and liturgical studies, active participation and community. This stimulus from outside fits in well with the discussion on these issues that is being set in motion from inside.[31]

[30] Just as was the case at the time television was a rising medium, there is hardly any research being performed into the ritual implications of the new media. See: LUKKEN: *Rituelen in overvloed* (1999) 155ff. and critical about rituality and the internet: GRIMES: *Deeply into the bone* (2000), for instance 273-275. See further the literature listed in the previous footnote.

[31] Cf. the discussion on *participatio actuosa* in the various phases of the Liturgical Movement through and into the effects and application of the Vatican II documents and the rewritten liturgical books. For this debate see for instance: RATZINGER: *Der Geist der Liturgie* (2000) and: GY: 'Ist 'Der Geist der Liturgie' Kardinal Ratzingers dem Konzil treu?' (2002) and RATZINGER: ''Der Geist der Liturgie'' oder: Die Treue zum Konzil' (2002).

BIBLIOGRAPHY

ABRAHAMS, M.J. et al.: 'The Brisbane floods, January 1974: their impact on health', *The Medical Journal of Australia* 2 (1976) 936-939.

ALBERS, I.: 'Stille tochten, heilige plaatsen' (series: Liturgie in geseculariseerde context), in *Eredienstvaardig. Tijdschrift voor liturgie en kerkmuziek* 16 (2000) 6, 204-207.

ALEXANDER, B.C.: *Victor Turner revisited. Ritual as social change* (Oxford 1991).

AL-KRENAWI, A.: 'An overview of rituals in Western therapies and intervention. Argument for their use in cross-cultural therapy', in *International Journal for the Advancement of Counselling* 21 (1999) 3-17.

ALWART, I., U. MACNACK, C. PENGEL-FORST & M. SARUCCO: 'Rouw en rituelen na de vliegramp. Ervaringen van allochtone hulpverleners', in *Maandblad voor de Geestelijke Volksgezondheid* 48 (1993) 10, 1056-1066.

AMERICAN PSYCHIATRIC ASSOCIATION: *Diagnostic and statistical manual of mental disorders*, second edition (DSM-II) (Washington 1968).

ANGEL, H-F.: *Der religiöse Mensch in Katastrophenzeiten. Perspektiven kollektiver Elendsphänomene* (Frankfurt 1996).

ANNUAL BOOK OF THE YEAR: yearly supplement *Encyclopaedia Britannica*, 15th ed.

ANSEMS, H.: 'Weet u misschien een leuk ritueel?', in *Psychologie* 15 (1996) 4, 49ff.

APOSTEL, L.: 'Rationaliteit in ritueel en mystiek', in *Ons Erfdeel* 37 (1994) 3, 393-404.

ARIÈS, PH.: *Western attitudes toward death: from the Middle Ages to the present* (Baltimore 1977).

ARIÈS, PH.: *L'Homme devant la mort* (Paris 1987).

AUNE, M.B. & V.M. DeMARINIS (eds.): *Religious and social ritual. Interdisciplinary explorations* (Albany, New York 1996).

AVESAATH, M. VAN & P. DE BRUIN: *De psychosociale gevolgen van rampen en de begeleiding van de slachtoffers: een literatuuronderzoek* (= thesis) (Leiden 1994).

BÄCKSTRÖM, A.: 'Från institution till rörelse' (From institution to movement), in *Religion och samhälle* 12 (1989) Religionssociologiska institutet (Stockholm 1989).

BÄCKSTRÖM, A.: 'Believing in belonging. The Swedish way of being religious', in R. RYÖKÄS & E. RYÖKÄS: *Urban faith 2000. Publications of Church sociology, Helsinki University A8/1993* (Helsinki 1993).

BÄCKSTRÖM, A.: *Livsåskådning och kyrkobyggnad* (= Tro och tanke 4 (1997) Svenska kyrkans forskningsråd) (Uppsala 1997).

BÄCKSTRÖM, A. & J. BROMANDER: *Kyrkobyggnaden och det offentliga rummet* (The church building and the public place) (= Svenska kyrkans utredningar 1995:5, Svenska Kyrkans Information) (Uppsala 1995).

BAEYENS, E.F.: *Herald of Free Enterprise: het verslag van de ramp* (= Kroniek van de Noordzeekust 1) (Hulst 1992).

BAL, L.: *De stille tocht in Gorinchem. Een pastoraal-psychologische verkenning van een eigentijds collectief ritueel* (= Master's thesis Faculty of Theology, UU4-12.00) (Utrecht 2000).

BALDOVIN, J.: *The urban character of Christian worship. The origins, development and meaning of stational liturgy* (= Orientalia Christiana Analecta 228) (Rome 1987).

BARNARD, M. & P. POST (eds.): *Ritueel bestek. Antropologische kernwoorden van de liturgie* (Zoetermeer 2001).

BARNARD, M.: 'De nationale herdenking en nationale viering bevrijding op 4 en 5 mei', in M. BARNARD & P. POST (eds.): *Ritueel bestek. Antropologische kernwoorden van de liturgie* (Zoetermeer 2001) 187-193.

BARTON, A.H.: *Communities in disaster: a sociological analysis of collective stress situations* (New York 1969).

BAUMEISTER, R.F.: *Meanings of life* (New York 1991).

BECK, R. & S.B. METRICK: *The art of ritual. A guide to creating and performing your own rituals for growth and change* (Berkeley 1990).

BECKER, J.W. & W.R. VINK: *Secularisatie in Nederland 1966-1999* (= Sociale en culturele studies 19) (Den Haag 1994).

BECKER, J.W., J. DE HART & J. MENS: *Secularisatie en alternatieve zingeving in Nederland* (Den Haag 1997).

BELL, C.: *Ritual theory, ritual practice* (New York/Oxford 1992).

BELL, C.: *Ritual. Perspectives and dimensions* (New York/Oxford 1997).

BELLAH, R.N.: *Varieties of civil religion* (San Francisco 1980).

BERNET KEMPERS, A.J.: 'Volkskunde en 'bijzondere vormgeving'', in *Bijdragen en mededelingen van het Rijksmuseum voor volkskunde 'Het Nederlands Openluchtmuseum'* 33 (1970) 2, 25-52 (= inaugural lecture University of Amsterdam 1969).

BERREN, M.R., A. BEIGEL & S. GHERTNER: 'A typology for the classification of disasters', in *Community of Mental Health Journal* 16,2 (1980) 103-111.

BEUNDERS, H.: 'Nationale rouw loopt uit op 'media-event'', in: *NRC Handelsblad* 01.10.1996.

BEYER, P.: *Religion and globalization* (London 1994).

BHOLA, R.: *Rouwrituelen onder Hindoestanen* (Den Haag 1997).

BIERITZ, K.-H.: 'Nächstes Jahr in Jerusalem. Von Schicksal der Feste', in *Jahrbuch für Liturgik und Hymnologie* 35 (1994/5) 37-57.

BLAIKIE, P., T. CANNON, I. DAVIS & B. WISNER: *At risk. Natural hazards, people's vulnerability and disasters* (London/New York 1994).

BORG, M. TER: 'Vanwaar die gewijde sfeer', in *Trouw* 23.01.1999.

BORG, M. TER: *Het geloof der goddelozen: essays* (Baarn 1996).

BOT, M.: *Een laatste groet. Uitvaart- en rouwrituelen in multicultureel Nederland* (Rotterdam 1998).

BOUDEWIJNSE, B.: 'The conceptualisation of ritual. A history of its problematic aspects', in *Jaarboek voor liturgie-onderzoek* 11 (1995) 31-56.

BOURRIAU, J.: *Understanding catastrophe* (Cambridge 1992).

BOWLBY, J.: 'Processes of mourning', in *International Journal of Psycho-Analysis* 42 (1961) 317-340.

BOWLBY, J.: *Attachment and loss. (Volume III): Loss, sadness and depression* (London 1980).

BOXTEL, H. VAN: 'Het monument is van iedereen. Balanceren tussen respect en uitbundigheid', in *Landelijke Allochtonenkrant* 6 (1999) 3.

BRÅKENHIELM, C.R.: 'Den demokratiska staten och medborgarnas religioner' (The democratic state and the religions of the citizens), in *Tro och tanke* 3 (1992) 83-94 Svenska kyrkans forskningsråd (Uppsala 1992).

BREDNICH, R.W. et al. (eds.): *Lebenslauf und Lebenszusammenhang. Autobiographische Materialien in der volkskundlichen Forschung* (Freiburg 1982).

BRENDEL, C.: 'De kerk als reddingsboei bij rampen', in *Algemeen Dagblad* 10.10.1994.

BRESLAU, N.: 'Epidemiology of trauma and post-traumatic stress disorder', in R. YEHUDA (ed.): *Psychological trauma* (Washington 1998) 1-30.

BREUKEL, TH.: *Stilte Atlas van Nederland. Meer dan 100 plaatsen om tot rust te komen* (Amsterdam 2000).

BROEKSMA, A.: 'Huilen om Diana', in *de Humanist* 52 (1997) 12, 28-29.

BROER, TH. et al.: 'Blind geweld – selectieve verontwaardiging', in *Vrij Nederland* 23.01.1999, 6-10.

BROMANDER, J.: 'Rör inte vår kyrka. Några kyrkliga traditionsbärares berättelser om kyrkorummet", in *Tro och tanke* 7 (1998). Svenska kyrkans forskningsråd (Uppsala 1998).

BROMANDER, J. (ed.): 'Då, nu och sedan. Perspektiv på Svenska kyrkans statistik 2000', in *Tro och tanke* 4 (2001), Svenska kyrkans forskningsråd (Uppsala 2001).

BURGGRAEVE, R., M. CLOET, K. DOBBELAERE & L. LEIJSSEN (eds.): *Het huwelijk* (= KADOC-Studies 24) (Leuven 2000).

CALICHER, E.: 'Publieke rouwverwerking vervangt ritueel in kerk', in *de Gooi en Eemlander* 30.12.1998, 2.

CAPLAN, G.: *Principles of preventive psychiatry* (New York 1964).

CAPUZZI, D. & D.R. GROSS: *Counseling and psychotherapy: theories and interventions* (Upper Saddle River 1999).

COHEN, G.B.: 'De militaire parade', in *Te elfder ure* 13 (1996) 257-260.

COREY, G.: *Theory and practice of counseling and psychotherapy* (Pacific Grove 1996).

COUWENBERGH, M.: *Servicemap stervensbegeleiding; rouwrituelen en rouwverwerking in de multiculturele samenleving* (Rotterdam 2000).

CUISINIER, M.: 'Rituelen; rouwen om een miskraam', in *Psychologie* 17,7/8 (1998) 66-69.

D'AQUILI, E. & CH.D. LAUGHLIN JR.: 'The neurobiology of myth and ritual', in E. D'AQUILI, CH.D. LAUGHLIN JR., J. MCMANUS & T.R. BURNS (eds.): *The spectrum of ritual. A biogenetic structural analysis* (New York 1979) 152-182.

D'AQUILI, E. & A.B. NEWBERG: *The mystical mind. Probing the biology of religious experience* (Minneapolis 1999).

D'HONDT, E. (ed.): *Zinloos geweld herdacht* (Hilversum 2000).

DAVIE, G.: 'You'll never walk alone: the Anfield pilgrimage', in I. READER & T. WALKER (eds.): *Pilgrimage in popular culture* (Houndmills etc. 1993) 201-219.

DAVIE, G.: *Religion in modern Europe. A memory mutates* (Oxford 2000).

DAVIES, D. et al.: *Church and religion in rural England* (Edinburgh 1991).

DAVIS, L.A.: *Manmade catastrophes: from the burning of Rome to the Lockerbie crash* (New York 1992).

DEKKER, T., H. ROODENBURG & G. ROOIJAKKERS (eds.): *Volkscultuur. Een inleiding in de Nederlandse etnologie* (Nijmegen 2000).

DEPONDT, P.: 'Monumenten voor de gehavende ziel', in *de Volkskrant* 17.10.1997, 11.

DOBBELAERE, K., L. LEIJSSEN & M. CLOET (eds.): *Het vormsel* (= KADOC-Studies 12) (Leuven 1991).

DOORN, J.A.A. VAN & C.J. LAMMERS: *Moderne sociologie* (Utrecht 1984).

DRIVER, T.F.: *Liberating rites. Understanding the transformative power of ritual* (Boulder 1988).

DUIN, M. VAN: 'Een beschouwing van het 'rampjaar' 1992, in *Alert, tijdschrift voor civiele verdediging, hulpverlening en rampenbestrijding* jan. (1993).

DUIN, M.J. VAN & U. ROSENTHAL, M.M.V. H.W. VAN BEELEN-BERGSMA: *De Herculesramp 15 juli 1996: individuen, organisaties en systemen* (Den Haag 1996).

DURKHEIM, E.: *Les formes ÈlÈmentaires de la vie religieuse: le système totémique en Australie* (Paris 1960).

DYNES, R.R.: *Organized behavior in disaster* (Disaster Research Center, Ohio State University 1969).

DYNES, R.R., B. DE MARCHI & C. PELANDA (eds.): *Sociology of disasters: contribution of sociology to disaster research* (= Collana dell'istituto di sociologia internazionale, Gorizia) (Milaan 1987).

ELIADE, M.: *Das Heilige und das Profane: vom Wesen des Religiösen* (Hamburg 1957).

ELLEMERS, J.E.: *De februari-ramp: sociologie van een samenleving in nood* (= Bouwstenen voor de kennis der maatschappij 30) (Assen 1956).

ELLEMERS, J.: 'Rampen in Nederland', in *Sociologische Gids* 48,3 (2001) 231-252.

ENARSON, E. & B. HEARN MORROW (eds.): *The gendered terrain of disaster* (Westport, Conn. 1998).

ENGLERT, R.: 'Les valeurs sacrées des hommes et les signes sacrés de L'Église', in *Lumen vitae. Revue internationale de catéchèse et de pastorale* 54,4 (1999) 404-422.

ENKLAAR, M.: *Onder de groene zoden. De persoonlijke uitvaart. Nieuwe rituelen in rouwen, begraven en cremeren* (Zutphen 1995).

FELBECKER, S.: *Die Prozession: historische und systematische Untersuchungen zu einer liturgischen Ausdruckshandlung* (= Münsteraner theologische Abhandlungen 39) (Altenberge 1995).

FLANNERY, R.B.: 'Social support and psychological trauma', in *Journal of Traumatic Stress* 3 (1990) 593-613.

FOOTE, K.E.: *Shadowed ground. America's landscapes of violence and tragedy* (Austin 1997).

FORTUIN, J., J. VAN KILSDONK et al.: *Afscheid nemen van onze doden. Rouw en rouwgebruiken in Nederland* (Kampen 1988).

FRANCES, A.: *Diagnostic and statistical manual of mental disorders, DSM-IV-TR* (Washington 2000).

FRANKE, A., U. FRIEDRICHS & H. MEHL: 'Unfallskreuze an Schleswig-Holsteins Autostraßen', in *Kieler Blätter zur Volkskunde* 26 (1994) 189-212.

FRANKE, H.: *De dood in het leven van alledag* ('s Gravenhage 1985).

FREDERICK, C.J.: 'Effects of natural versus human-induced violence upon victims', in *Evaluation and Change* (special issue) (1980) 71-75.

FRERKS, G.E.: *Omgaan met rampen* (n.p. 1998).

FREY, N.L.: *Pilgrim stories: on and off the road to Santiago* (Berkeley/Los Angeles/London 1998).

FRIJHOFF, W.: 'Traditie en verleden. Kritische reflecties over het gebruik van verwijzingen naar vroeger', in *Jaarboek voor liturgie-onderzoek* 7 (1991) 125-136.

FRIJHOFF, W.: 'Toe-eigening van bezitsdrang naar betekenisgeving', in *Trajecta* 6,2 (1997) 99-118.

FRIJHOFF, W.: *Heiligen, idolen, iconen* (= inaugural lecture Vrije Universiteit Amsterdam) (Nijmegen 1998).

FRITZ, C.E.: 'Disasters', in R.K. MERTON & R.E. NISBET (eds.): *Contemporary social problems* (New York 1961) 651-694.

GABRIEL, N.: *Kulturwissenschaften und neue Medien. Wissensvermittlung im digitalen Zeitlater* (Darmstadt 1997).

GENNEP, A. VAN: *The rites of passage* (Chicago 1960).

GERGEN, K. & M. GERGEN: 'Narratives of the self', in TH. SARBIN & K. SCHEIBE (eds.): *Studies in social identity* (New York 1983) 254-273.

GERGEN, K. & M. GERGEN: 'Narrative form and the construction of psychological science', in TH. SARBIN (ed.): *Narrative psychology. The storied nature of human conduct* (New York 1986) 22-44.

GERGEN, K. & M. GERGEN: 'Narrative and the self as relationship', in *Advances in Experimental Social Psychology* 21 (1988) 17-56.

GERHARDS, A. & B. KRANEMANN (eds.): *Christliche Begräbnisliturgie und säkulare Gesellschaft* (= Erfurter Theologische Schriften 30) (Leipzig 2002).

GERSONS, B.P.R.: 'Adaptive defense mechanism in post-traumatic stress disorders and leave-taking rituals', in O. VAN DER HART: *Coping with loss. The therapeutic use of leave-taking rituals* (New York 1988) 135-149.

GIEBEN, S.: 'Rook, klei, kaarsen en dansen om een dood paard', in *Elsevier* 04.07.1998, 104ff.

GIJSWIJT-HOFSTRA, M.: *Vragen bij een onttoverde wereld* (= inaugural lecture University of Amsterdam) (= Amsterdamse Historische Reeks, kleine serie 37) (Amsterdam 1997).

GIJSWIJT-HOFSTRA, M. & F. EGMOND (eds.): *Of bidden helpt? Tegenslag en cultuur in West-Europa, circa 1500-2000* (Amsterdam 1997).

GILS, T. VAN: *Verlies en rouw* (Baarn 1998).

GOVAART, A.: 'Spreken en horen', in M. BARNARD & P. POST (eds.): *Ritueel bestek. Antropologische kernwoorden van de liturgie* (Zoetermeer 2001) 131-144.

GRAY, D.: 'Bridging the gap' (= Presidential address), in *Studia Liturgica* 20 (1990) 1-7 (= 'Jeter un pont', in *La Maison-Dieu* 179 (1989) 7-14).

GRIMES, R.L.: *Beginnings in ritual studies* (Washington DC 1982).

GRIMES, R.L.: *Ritual criticism* (Columbia SC 1990).

GRIMES, R.L.: *Reading, writing and ritualizing. Ritual in fictive, liturgical, and public places* (Washington DC 1993).

GRIMES, R.L.: 'Emerging ritual', in: IDEM: *Reading, writing, and ritualizing: rituals in fictive, liturgical and public places* (Washington DC 1993) Ch. 2, 23-38; original article in *Proceedings of the North American Academy of Liturgy* (1990) 15-34.

GRIMES, R.L.: *Marrying & burying: rites of passage in a man's life* (Boulder 1995).

GRIMES, R.L.: 'The initiatory dilemma: cinematic fantasy and ecclesiastical rarification', in *Bulletin ET* 9 (1998) 161-170.

GRIMES, R.L.: *Deeply into the bone. Re-inventing rites of passage* (= serie Life passages 1) (Berkeley/Los Angeles/London 2000).

GRIMES, R.L.: 'Ritual', in W. BRAUN & R.T MCCUTCHEON (eds.): *Guide to the study of religion* (London/New York 2000) Ch. 18, 259-270.

GUSTAFSSON, B.: *Svenska folkets religion* (The religion of the Swedish people) (Falköping 1969).

GUSTAFSSON, G. & L. AHLIN: *Två undersökningar om Estonia och religionen* (Two surveys concerning Estonia and religion) (= Religionssociologiska studier nr 1, Teologiska institutionen, Lunds universitet) (Lund 1995).

GUSTAFSSON, G. & T. PETTERSSON (eds.): *Folkkyrkor och religiös pluralism den nordiska religiösa modellen* (Stockholm 2000).

GY, P.: 'Ist 'der Geist der Liturgie' Kardinal Ratizngers dem Konzil treu?', in *Liturgisches Jahrbuch* 32 (2002) 59-65.

HAAN, N.: 'Coping and defense mechanisms related to personality inventories', in *Journal of Consulting Psychology* 29 (1965) 373-378.

HAAN, N.: 'Assessment of coping, defense and stress', in L. GOLDBERGER & S. BREZNITZ (eds.): *Handbook of stress: theoretical and clinical aspects* (New York 1992) 258-273.

HAARDT, M. DE: *Kom, eet mijn brood... Exemplarische verkenningen naar het goddelijke in het alledaagse* (= inaugural lecture) (Nijmegen 1999).

HAASTRECHT, R. VAN, G. MARLET et al.: *Enschede, de ramp* (= *Trouw* dossier NL 9) (Amsterdam 2001).

HAMBERG, E.: 'Kristen på mitt eget sätt' (Christian in my own way), in *Religion och samhälle* no. 48-49 (1989) 10-11, Religionssociologiska institutet (Stockholm 1989).

HAMBURG, D.A. & J.E. ADAMS: *Coping and adaptation* (New York 1974).

HAMERSMA, H.: 'Naamloze vermisten in de Bijlmer', in *Streven* 59,14 (1992) 1251-1254.

HANEGRAAFF, W.: *New Age religion and Western culture: esotorism in the mirror of secular thought* (Leiden/New York/Köln 1996; paperback: Albany 1998).

HANEGRAAFF, W.: *Het einde van de hermetische traditie* (= inaugural lecture) (Amsterdam 1999).

HARSKAMP, A. VAN et al. (eds.): *De religieuze ruis in Nederland. Thesen over de versterving en de wedergeboorte van de godsdienst* (Zoetermeer 1998).

HART, O. VAN DER: *Overgang en bestendiging: over het ontwerpen en voorschrijven van rituelen in psychotherapie* (Deventer 1978).

HART, O. VAN DER: 'Het gebruik van mythen en rituelen in psychotherapie', in O. VAN DER HART et al.: *Afscheidsrituelen in de psychotherapie* (Baarn 1981) 16-32.

HART, O. VAN DER: 'Symbolen in afscheidsrituelen', in O. VAN DER HART et al.: *Afscheidsrituelen in de psychotherapie* (Baarn 1981) 33-42.

HART, O. VAN DER: *Rituelen in psychotherapie. Overgang en bestendiging* (Deventer 1984, 2^d rev. and elab. ed.).

HART, O. VAN DER: *Coping with loss: the therapeutic use of leave-taking rituals* (New York 1988).

HART, O. VAN DER et al.: *Afscheidsrituelen in de psychotherapie* (Baarn 1981).

HARTINGER, W.: *Religion und Brauch* (Darmstadt 1992).

HEILER, F.: *Das Gebet. Eine religionsgeschichtliche und religionspsychologische Untersuchung* (München 1921).

HELLEMANS, S. (ed.): 'Wit van het volk: de zaak-Dutroux en de protestgolf in België in de herfst van 1996', = *Sociologische Gids XLV* (1998).

HOBFOLL, S.E. & M.W. DE VRIES: *Extreme stress and communities: impact and intervention* (Dordrecht 1995).

HOFSTRA, S.: *Het functiebegrip in de sociologie* (Amsterdam 1946).

HOLAHAN, C.J., R.H. MOOS & J.A. SCHAEFFER: 'Coping, stress resistance and growth: conceptualizing adaptive functioning', in M. ZEIDNER & N.S. ENDLER (eds.): *Handbook of coping: theory, research, applications* (New York 1996) 24-43.

HOLMBERG, Chr.: ' "Anders hätte ich es gar nicht überlebt" Magische Objekte im Krankenhaus', in M. SIMON & M. KANIA-SCHÜTZ (eds.): *Auf der Suche nach Heil und Heilung; religiöse Aspekte der medikalen Alltagskultur* (= Volkskunde in Sachsen 10/11) (Dresden 2001) 197-212.

HOOG, T. DE: 'De ramp, de rituelen', in *de Groene Amsterdammer* 27.05.2000.

HOOGEN, T. VAN DEN: 'Is de zonde nog te redden? Civil religion – ongeneeslijk ziek of vals sentiment?', in E. D'HONDT (ed.): *Zinloos geweld herdacht* (Hilversum 2000) 81-88.

HOOGHE, M.: 'De 'witte mobilisatie' in België als moral crusade: de vervlechting van emotie en politiek', in S HELLEMANS (ed.): *Wit van het volk* (1998) 289-309.

HOROWITZ, M.J. & N.B. KALTREIDER: 'Brief treatment of post-traumatic stress disorders', in *New directions for Mental Health Services* 6 (1980) 67-78.

HOROWITZ, M.J.: *Stress response syndromes* (New York 1976; 1986).

HOROWITZ, M.J.: 'Psychological response to serious life events', in V. HAMILTON & D.M. WARBURTON (eds.): *Human stress and cognition: an information processing approach* (Chisester 1979) 235-263.

HORST, P. VAN DER: 'Silent prayer in Antiquity', in *Numen* 41 (1994) 1-25.

HUMPHREY, C. & J. LAIDLAW: *The archetypal actions of ritual. A theory of ritual illustrated by the Jain rite of worship* (= Oxford Studies in Social and Cultural Anthropology) (Oxford 1994).

JACOBS, J.L.: Religious ritual and mental health, in J.F. SCHUMAKER: *Religion and mental health* (Oxford 1992) 291-299.

JACOBS, M.: 'Folklore in Cyberië in het jaar twee kilo', in *Volkskundig Bulletin. Tijdschrift voor Nederlandse cultuurwetenschap* 26,1 (2001) 3-41.

JANSSEN, J.: 'Stille Omgang: een zoeken naar samenleving. Plechtigheden en morele verontwaardiging rondom 'zinloos geweld'', in E. D'HONDT (ed.): *Zinloos geweld herdacht* (Hilversum 2000) 65-79.

JANSSEN, J., M. PRINS, C. BAERVELDT & J. VAN DER LANS: 'Structuur en varianten van bidden. Een onderzoek bij Nederlandse jongeren', in M. VAN UDEN & J. PIEPER (eds.): *Wat baat religie? Godsdienstpsychologen en godsdienstsociologen over het nut van religie* (Nijmegen 1998) 67-96.

JOHNSON, D.R., S.C. FELDMAN, H. LUBIN & S.M. SOUTHWICK: 'The therapeutic use of ritual and ceremony in the treatment of post-traumatic stress disorder', in *Journal of Traumatic Stress* 8,2 (1995) 283-298.

JONG, J.T. DE & M.M. VAN SCHAIK: 'Culturele en religieuze aspecten van rouw- en traumaverwerking naar aanleiding van de Bijlmerramp', in *Tijdschrift voor Psychiatrie* 36,4 (1994) 291-303.

JONGEDIJK, R.I. et al.: 'Is er plaats voor de Complexe Posttraumatische Stress Stoornis? PTSS en DES NOS nader beschouwd', in *Tijdschrift voor Psychiatrie* 37,1 (1995) 43-54.

KÄLLSTAD, T.: 'Mordet på Olof Palme – religionspsykologiska synpunkter' (The murder of Olof Palme-religion – psychological aspects), in *Religion och samhälle* 10 (1986) 1-12, Religionsssociologiska institutet (Stockholm 1986).

KERKHOF, T. VAN DE: 'Rituelen bij rampen. Je handelt waar handelen onmogelijk werd', in *de Bazuin*, 18.05.2001, 6-9.

KERSTTOESPRAAK KONINGIN BEATRIX, afgedrukt in o.a.: *de Volkskrant* 27.12.2000, 6.

KIMMERLE, H.: *De dood is (g)een einde. Over het dubbele gezicht van het einde in intercultureel perspectief* (Rotterdam 1992).

KINSTON, W. & R. ROSSER: 'Disaster: effects on mental and physical state', in *Journal of Psychometric Research* 18 (1974) 437-456.

KLASHORST, P. VAN DER: *Dodendans. Ontdekkingsreis rond de dood in verschillende culturen* (Amsterdam 1990).

KLEBER, R.J.: *Het trauma voorbij. Over de grenzen van de psychotraumatologie* (= inaugural lecture) (Tilburg 1999).

KLEBER, R.J., D. BROM & P.B. DEFARES: *Traumatische ervaringen, gevolgen en verwerking* (Amsterdam/Lisse 1986).

KLEBER, R.J., D. BROM & P.B. DEFARES: *Coping with trauma. Theory, prevention and treatment* (Amsterdam 1992).

KLEBER, R.J., C.R. FIGLEY & B.P. GERSONS: *Beyond trauma. Cultural and societal dynamics* (New York 1995).

KLEBER, R.J., C. MITTENDORFF & O. VAN DER HART: 'Posttraumatische stress', in W.T.A.M. EVERAERD, A.P. BAK & W.T.M VAN BERLO (eds.): *Handboek klinische psychologie* (Houten 1997) 1-30.

KLEBER, R.J., & C. MITTENDORFF: 'Opvang na schokkende gebeurtenissen. Stand van zaken in het wetenschappelijke onderzoek', in *Maandblad voor de Geestelijke Volksgezondheid* 55 (2000) 889-904.

KNIPSCHEER, J.W. & R.J. KLEBER: 'Migranten, psychische (on)gezondheid en hulpverlening', in *de Psycholoog* april (1998) 151-157.

KNIPSCHEER, J.W.: *Cultural convergence and divergence in mental health care: empirical studies on mental distress and help-seeking behaviour of Surinamese, Ghanaian, Turkish and Moroccan migrants in the Netherlands* (Veenendaal 2000).

KNULST, W.: *Werk, rust en sociaal leven op zondagen sinds de jaren zeventig* (= inaugural lecture) (Tilburg 1999).

KOENIG, H.G.: *Religion, health and aging: a review and theoretical integration* (Connecticut 1988).

KOENIG, H.G.: *Research on religion and aging: an annotated bibliography* (Westport 1995).

KROEBER, T.C.: 'The coping functions of the ego mechanisms', in R.W. WHITE (ed.): *The study of lives: essays on personality in honor of Henry A. Murray* (New York 1963) 178-189.

KÜBLER-ROSS, E.: *Death: the final state of growth* (Englewood Cliffs, New Jersey 1975).

KÜBLER-ROSS, E.: *On death and dying* (New York 1993).

LANG, B.: *Sacred games. A history of Christian worship* (New Haven 1997) = *Heiliges Spiel. Eine Geschichte des christlichen Gottesdienstes* (München 1998).

LANGE, H. DE: 'Het aantal stille tochten neemt toe, maar de ene is de andere niet', in *Trouw* 14.01.2000, 1.

LAZARUS, R.S.: *Psychological stress and the coping process* (New York 1966).

LAZARUS, R.S.: 'The stress and the coping paradigm', in C. EISDORFER et al. (eds.): *Models for clinical psychopathology* (New York 1981) 177-214.

LAZARUS, R.S. & A. DELONGIS: 'Psychological stress and coping in aging', in *American Psychologist* 38 (1983) 245-254.

LAZARUS, R.S. & S. FOLKMAN: *Stress, appraisal and coping* (New York 1984).

LEIJSSEN, L., M. CLOET & K. DOBBELAERE (eds.): *Geboorte en doopsel* (= KADOC-Studies 20) (Leuven 1996).

LIFTON, R.J. & E. OLSON: 'Death imprint in Buffalo Creek', in H.J. PARAD, H.L.P. RESNIK & L.G. PARAD (eds.): *Emergency and disaster management: a mental health sourcebook* (Bowie 1976) 295-309.

LORENZER, A.: *Das Konzil der Buchhalter. Die Zerstörung der Sinnlichkeit. Eine Religionskritik* (Frankfurt a.M. 1981).

LUCKMANN, TH.: *The invisible religion* (New York 1967) = orig.: *Das Problem der Religion in der modernen Gesellschaft* (Freiburg i.Br. 1963).

LUGT, F. DE: *De ramp van Enschede* (Enschede 2000).

LUKKEN, G.: *Rituelen in overvloed. Een kritische bezinning op de plaats en de gestalte van het christelijke ritueel in onze cultuur* (Kampen 1999) = *Rituals in abundance. A critical reflection on the place and shape of Christian ritual in our culture* (to appear in the series *Liturgia condenda*, Leuven etc. 2003).

LUKKEN, G.: 'De liturgie rond een overledene. Over inductieve en adequate dodenliturgie', in *Rond de Tafel* 55,1 (2000) 3-14.

LUNDIN, I. & J. JONASSON: *Estonia – en kartläggning av Sveriges Radios agerande i samband med m/s Estonia förlisning onsdagen den 28 september 1994* (Estonia – an investigation of how radio Sweden acted in connection to the Estonia disaster Wednesday 28th of September 1994), (Sveriges Radios styrelse, Stockholm 29 November 1994).

LUYTEN, M.: 'Moderne religie zit verstopt in stille tocht', in *de Volkskrant* 04.03.1999.

MALLOY, P.: 'The re-emergence of popular religion among non-Hispanic American catholics', in *Worship* 72,1 (1998) 2-15.

MARGRY, P.J.: *Amsterdam en het Mirakel van het Heilig Sacrament. Van middeleeuwse devotie tot 20e-eeuwse stille omgang* (Amsterdam 1988).

MARGRY, P.J.: 'Gebed en verbod. Processies en bedevaarten in en om Brabant', in L. VAN LIEBERGEN & G. ROOIJAKKERS (eds.): *Volksdevotie. Beelden van religieuze volkscultuur in Noord-Brabant* (Uden 1990) 41-44.

MARGRY, P.J.: 'Processie versus stille omgang. Het probleem van de openbare godsdienstuitoefening buiten gebouwen en besloten plaatsen in Holland', in *Historisch Tijdschrift Holland* 25,3-5 (= Themanummer Geloof in Holland) (1993) 174-196.

MARGRY, P.J.: 'Processie-exercities. Strategieën van overheid en kerk bij de beteugeling en de stimulering van processies in Nederland en België, 1815-1825', in M. MONTEIRO, G. ROOIJAKKERS & J. ROSENDAAL (eds.): *De dynamiek van religie en cultuur. Geschiedenis van het Nederlands katholicisme* (Kampen 1993) 60-79.

MARGRY, P.J.: 'Bedevaartrevival? Bedevaartcultuur in het Bataafs-Franse Nederland (1795-1814)', in *Trajecta* 3,3 (1994) 209-232.

MARGRY, P.J.: 'Accommodatie en innovatie met betrekking tot traditionele rituelen. Bedevaarten en processies in de moderne tijd', in M. VAN UDEN, J. PIEPER & P. POST (eds.): *Oude sporen, nieuwe wegen. Ontwikkelingen in bedevaartonderzoek* (= UTP-Katernen 17) (Baarn 1995) 169-202.

MARGRY, P.J. (ed.): *Goede en slechte tijden: het Amsterdams Mirakel van Sacrament in historisch perspectief* (Aerdenhout 1995).

MARGRY, P.J.: *Teedere quaesties: religieuze rituelen in conflict. Confrontaties tussen katholieken en protestanten rond de processiecultuur in 19e-eeuws Nederland* (Hilversum 2000).

MATTEEUWS, G.: "De stilte zingt U toe'. Over de betekenis en de mogelijkheden van rituele stilte', in *Collationes* 31,4 (2001) 371-382.

MENKEN-BEKIUS, C.: 'Een kanaal voor onze emoties. Rituelen rond de dood', in *Rondom het woord* 38,2 (1996) 30-37.

MENKEN-BEKIUS, C.: 'Oude en nieuwe rituelen: een kwestie van vraag en aanbod?' in *Praktische theologie* 24,2 (1997) 190-194.

MENKEN-BEKIUS, C.: *Rituelen in het individuele pastoraat. Een praktisch-theologisch onderzoek* (Kampen 1998).

MENKEN-BEKIUS, C.: *Werken met rituelen in het pastoraat* (Kampen 2001).

MENKEN-BEKIUS, C., L. BAL & M. VAN DIJK-GROENEBOER: 'De kerk en stille tochten tegen geweld' (= collection of articles), in *Praktische Theologie* 28,3 (2001) 272-301.

MERTON, R.K.: *Social theory and social structure* (Glencoe 1957).

MINISTERIE VAN DEFENSIE: Videoband viering Herculesdienst (1996).

MINISTERIE VAN VERKEER EN WATERSTAAT, DIRECTIE VOORLICHTING, DOCUMENTATIE EN BIBLIOTHEEK: *Ramp met El Al-toestel in de Bijlmermeer op 4 oktober 1992: media-overzicht* (= Bidoc-Publicaties 37) (Den Haag 1992).

MITCHELL, N.: 'Emerging ritual in contemporary culture', in *Concilium* 31,3 (1995) 121-129.

MITCHELL, N.: *Liturgy and the social sciences* (Collegeville 1999).

MOOS, R.: *Coping with life crises: an integrative approach* (New York 1980).

MOOS, R.H. & J.A. SCHAEFFER: 'Coping resources and processes: current concepts and measures', in L. GOLDBERGER & S. BREZNITZ (eds.): *Handbook of stress: theoretical and clinical aspects* (New York 1993) 234-257.

MULDER, A.: *Geloven in crematieliturgie. Een pastoraal-liturgisch onderzoek naar hedendaagse crematieliturgie in een rooms-katholieke context* (= UTP-Katern 23) (Baarn 2000).

NAUTA, R.: *Ik geloof het wel* (Assen 1995).

NAUTA, R.: 'De militaire parade', = in 'Rituele repertoires: actores en personages', in M. BARNARD & P. POST (eds.): *Ritueel bestek. Antropologische kernwoorden van de liturgie* (Zoetermeer 2001) 100-101.

NAUTA, R.: 'Rituelen als decor. Over het geheim van de leegte', in P. POST & W.M. SPEELMAN (ed.): *De madonna van de Bijenkorf. Bewegingen op de rituele markt* (= Liturgie in perspectief 9) (Baarn 1997) 73-94.

NEISSER, U.: *Cognition and reality: principles and implications of cognitive psychology* (San Francisco 1976).

NISSEN, P.: *De folklorisering van het onalledaagse* (Tilburg 1994).

NUGTEREN, A.: 'Collective/public ritual behaviour after disasters: an emerging manifestation of civil religion?', *Cyberproceedings of the 2001 International Conference on The Spiritual Supermarket,* www.cesnur.org/2001/london 2001/index.htm.

NURMI, L.: 'The Estonia disaster. National interventions, outcomes, and personal impact', in E.S. ZINNER & M.B. WILLIAMS (eds.): *When a community weeps. Case studies in group survivorship* (Ann Arbor 1999) 49-72.

O'LEARY, S.: 'Cyberspace as sacred space: communicating religion on computer networks', in *Journal of the American Academy of Religion* 64,4 (1996) 781-808.

OBENCHAIN, J.V. & S.M. SILVER: 'Symbolic recognition: ceremony in a treatment of post-traumatic stress disorder', in *Journal of Traumatic Stress* 5,1 (1992) 37-43.

OOMEN, M. & J. PALM: *Geloven in de Bijlmer: over de rol van religieuze groeperingen* (Amsterdam 1994).

ØRNER, R.J.: 'Intervention strategies for emergency response groups: a new conceptual framework', in S.E. HOBFOLL & M.W. DE VRIES (eds.): *Extreme stress and communities: impact and intervention* (Dordrecht 1995) 499-521.

PARGAMENT, K.I.: *The psychology of religion and coping. Theory, research and practice* (New York 1997).

PARKER, K.J., & N.S. ENDLER: 'Coping with coping assessment: a critical review', in *European Journal of Psychology* 6 (1996) 321-344.

PARKES, C.M.: *Bereavement: studies of grief in adult life* (London 1986).

PEETERS, B.: 'Stilte', in M. BARNARD & P. POST (eds.): *Ritueel bestek. Antropologische kernwoorden van de liturgie* (Zoetermeer 2001) 155-161.

PERI, Y. (ed.): *The assassination of Yitzhak Rabin* (Stanford 2000).

PERLOFF, L.S.: 'Perceptions of vulnaribility to victimization', in *Journal of Social Issues* 39,2 (1983) 41-61.

PERRY, J.: *Wij herdenken, dus wij bestaan. Over jubilea, monumenten en de collectieve herinnering* (Nijmegen 1999).

PESSIRERON, S.: *Rouwen in zeven 'Nederlandse' culturen* (Utrecht 1999).

PETERS, J., G. DEKKER & J. DE HART: *God in Nederland 1966-1996* (Amsterdam 1997).

PETERSON, C. & M.E.P. SELIGMAN: 'Learned helplessness and victimization', in *Journal of Social Issues* 39 (1983) 103-116.

PETTERSSON, P.: *Svenska kyrkans folkreligiösa funktion i anslutning till Estonia-katastrofen* (The folk religious function of the Church of Sweden in the context of the Estonia disaster) (paper in sociology of religion at The Department of Theology, University of Uppsala 1995).

PETTERSSON, P.: *Kvalitet i livslånga tjänsterelationer. Svenska kyrkan ur tjänsteteoretiskt och religionssociologiskt perspektiv* (Quality in lifelong service relationships. The Church of Sweden in service theoretical and sociology of religion perspective) (Stockholm 2000).

PIAGET, J.: *Structuralism* (London 1971).

PIEPER, J.: *God gezocht en gevonden? Een godsdienstpsychologisch onderzoek rond het kerkelijk huwelijk met pastoraal-theologische consequenties* (Nijmegen 1988).

POLAK, K. (ed.): *Een stilte die spreekt. Herdenken in diversiteit* (Amsterdam 2000).

POOT, T.: *Waar is uw God? Predikatie n.a.v. de treinramp te Harmelen* (Middelharnis 1962).

POST, P.: 'Het liturgische spel: implikaties en voorwaarden vanuit omgang met symbolen', in *Werkmap voor Liturgie* 20,3 (1986) 157-173.

POST, P.: 'Het verleden in het spel? Volksreligieuze rituelen tussen cultus en cultuur', in *Jaarboek voor liturgie-onderzoek* 7 (1991) 79-124.

POST, P.: 'Traditie gebruiken. Sint Hubertus in Muiderberg', in: M. VAN UDEN et al. (eds.): *Bij geloof. Over bedevaarten en andere uitingen van volksreligiositeit* (= UTP-katernen 11) (Hilversum 1991) 191-208.

POST, P.: 'Pelgrimsverslagen: verkenning van een genre', in *Jaarboek voor liturgie-onderzoek* 8 (1992) 285-332.

POST, P.: *Ritueel landschap: over liturgie-buiten* (= inaugural lecture) (= Liturgie in perspectief 5) (Heeswijk-Dinther/Baarn 1995).

POST, P.: 'Zeven notities over rituele veranderingen, traditie en (vergelijkende) liturgiewetenschap', in *Jaarboek voor liturgie-onderzoek* 11 (1995) 1-30.

POST, P.: 'Liturgische bewegingen en feestcultuur', in *Jaarboek voor liturgie-onderzoek* 12 (1996) 21-55.

POST, P.: 'Paysage rituel: la liturgie en plein air (II). La visite du pape, action de graces pour la moisson, rites autour d'une mort subite', in *Questions liturgiques / Studies in Liturgy* 77 (1996) 240-256.

POST, P.: 'Liturgische Bewegungen und Festkultur. Ein landesweites liturgiewis-senschaftliches Forschungsprogramm in den Niederlanden', in *Liturgisches Jahrbuch* 48 (1998) 96-113.

POST, P.: 'Religieuze volkskunde en liturgie. Geïllustreerd pleidooi voor een benadering', in J. LAMBERTS (ed.): *Volksreligie, liturgie en evangelisatie* (= Nikè-reeks 42) (Leuven/Amersfoort 1998) 19-78 = 'Religious popular culture and liturgy', in *Questions liturgiques/Studies in Liturgy* 79 (1998) 14-59.

POST, P.: 'Het rituele perspectief: zes notities over rituele bewegingen', in A. VAN HARSKAMP et al. (eds.): *De religieuze ruis in Nederland. Thesen over de ver-sterving en de wedergeboorte van de godsdienst* (Zoetermeer 1998) 47-55.

POST, P.: 'Van paasvuur tot stille tocht. Over interferentie van liturgie en volks-religieus ritueel', in *Volkskundig Bulletin. Tijdschrift voor Nederlandse cultuur-wetenschap* 25,2/3 (1999) 215-234.

POST, P.: 'Rijke oogst: literatuurbericht liturgiewetenschap', in *Praktische Theologie* 26,1 (1999) 94-117.

POST, P.: 'Rituele dynamiek in liturgisch perspectief: een verkenning van vorm, inhoud en beleving', in *Jaarboek voor liturgie-onderzoek* 15 (1999) 119-141.

POST, P.: 'Speelruimte voor heilig spel', in H. BECK, R. NAUTA & P. POST (eds.): *Over spel. Theologie als drama en illusie* (Leende 2000) 139-167.

POST, P.: 'Acht woorden bij 'Rituelen in overvloed" (= Presentation and review of: Lukken: *Rituelen in overvloed*), in *Eredienstvaardig* 16,1 (2000) 31-33.

POST, P.: 'De moderne heilige: sacrale interferenties. Een terreinverkenning', in *Jaarboek voor liturgie-onderzoek* 16 (2000) 135-160.

POST, P.: 'Interference and intuition. On the characteristic nature of research design in liturgical studies', in *Questions liturgiques/Studies in Liturgy* 81,1 (2000) 48-65.

POST, P.: *Het wonder van Dokkum. Verkenningen van populair religieus ritueel* (Nijmegen 2000).

POST, P.: 'Overvloed of deritualisering. Lukken en Grimes over het actuele rituee-liturgische milieu', in *Jaarboek voor liturgie-onderzoek* 17 (2001) 193-212.

POST, P.: 'Personen en patronen: literatuurbericht liturgiewetenschap', in *Prak-tische Theologie* 28,1 (2001) 86-110.

POST, P.: 'Ritualiteit: teken, symbool, rite, mythe', in M. BARNARD & P. POST (eds.): *Ritueel bestek. Antropologische kernwoorden van de liturgie* (Zoetermeer 2001) 33-46.

POST, P.: 'La marche silencieuse: perspectives rituelles et liturgiques sur de nouveaux rites populaires aux Pays-Bas', in *La Maison-Dieu* 228,4 (2001) 143-157.

POST, P.: 'Silent procession: ritual-liturgical perspectives of an emerging popular Dutch ritual', in *Studia Liturgica* 32 (2002) 89-97.

POST, P.: 'De kus door het glas. Moderne media als ritueel-liturgisch milieu', in C. STERKENS & J.A. VAN DER VEN (eds.): *De functie van de kerk in de hedendaagse maatschappij. Opstellen voor Ernest Henau* (Averbode 2002) 263-286.

POST, P.: 'Life cycle rituals: a ritual-liturgical perspective', in: *Questions liturgiques / Studies in Liturgy* 83,1 (2002) 10-29.

POST, P.: 'Programm und Profil der Liturgiewissenschaft. Ein niederländischer Beitrag', in W. RATZMANN (ed.): *Grenzen überschreiten. Profile und Perspektiven der Liturgiewissenschaft* (= Beiträge zu Liturgie und Spiritualität 9) (Leipzig 2002) 81-100.

POST, P.: 'Rituell-liturgische Bewegungen: Erkundungen von Trends und Perspektiven', in A. GERHARDS & B. KRANEMANN (eds.): *Christliche Begräbnisliturgie und säkulare Gesellschaft* (= Erfurter Theologische Schriften 30) (Leipzig 2002) 25-60.

POST, P., A. NUGTEREN & H. ZONDAG: *Rituelen na rampen. Verkenning van een opkomend repertoire* (= Meander 3) (Kampen 2002).

POST, P. & W.M. SPEELMAN (eds.): *De Madonna van de Bijenkorf. Bewegingen op de rituele markt* (= Liturgie in perspectief 9) (Baarn 1997).

POST, P., J. PIEPER & M.VAN UDEN: *The modern pilgrim. Multidisciplinary explorations of Christian pilgrimage* (= Liturgia condenda 8) (Leuven 1998).

POST, P. & P. SCHMID: 'Centrum van stilte', in M. BARNARD & P. POST (eds.): *Ritueel bestek. Antropologische kernwoorden van de liturgie* (Zoetermeer 2001) 162-170.

POST, P. et al. (eds.): *Christian feast and festival: the dynamics of Western liturgy and culture* (= Liturgia condenda 12) (Leuven 2001).

PRO BIBLIO (ed.): *Leesmap Begrafenisgebruiken* (Den Haag 2000).

QUARANTELLI, E.L. (ed.): *Disasters: theory and research* (London 1978).

RAMSEY, R.W. & J.A. HAPPÉE: 'The stress of bereavement: components and treatment', in C.D. SPIELBERGER & I.G. SARASON (eds.): *Stress and anxiety Vol. 4.* (Washington 1977) 53-64.

RAPPAPORT, R.A.: *Ritual and religion in the making of humanity* (= Cambridge Studies in Social and Cultural Anthropology 110) (Cambridge 1999).

RATZINGER, J.: *Der Geist der Liturgie. Eine Einführung* (Freiburg/Basel/Wien 2000).

RATZINGER, J.: '"Der Geist der Liturgie" oder: die Treue zum Konzil', in *Liturgisches Jahrbuch* 52 (2002) 111-115.

REIMERS, E.: *Dopet som kult och kultur* (Baptism as cult and culture) (Stockholm 1995).

REIJNOUDT & STERK: *Tragedie op Tenerife* (Kampen 2002).

RENSSEN, H. VAN: 'Achter de stille tocht', in *de Volkskrant* (katern Reflex) 26.02.2000, 5.

RINPOCHE, S.: *The Tibetan book of living and dying* (San Francisco 1998, 15th ed.).

RITUELEN EN RELIGIE: *Kultuurleven: tijdschrift voor cultuur en samenleving* (Leuven November 1997) .

RITUELEN IN JE LEVEN: *de Humanist* 12,1 (1997/1998).

ROEBBEN, B., 'Spiritual and moral education in/and cyberspace: preliminary reflections', in *Journal of Education and Christian Belief* 3 (1999) 85-95.

RÖHRICH, L.: 'Erzählforschung', in R.W. BREDNICH (ed.): *Grundriss der Volkskunde* (Berlin 1994 2ᵈ ed.) 285-332.

ROMIJN, P. et al.: *Herdenken en vieren in vrijheid. Praktische handreiking voor 4 en 5 mei* ('s Gravenhage 1994).

ROOIJAKKERS, G.: *Rituele repertoires. Volkscultuur in oostelijk Noord-Brabant 1559-1853* (Nijmegen 1994).

ROSENBLATT, P.C., H.P. WALSH & D.A. JACKSON: *Grief and mourning in cross-cultural perspective* (New Haven 1976).

ROSENTHAL, U.: *Rampen, rellen, gijzelingen: crisisbesluitvorming in Nederland* (Amsterdam 1984).

ROSSEELS, C.: *Rituelen vandaag* (Antwerp/Baarn 1995).

ROTHBAUM, F.M., J.R. WEISZ & S.S. SNYDER: 'Changing the world and changing the self: a two-process model of perceived control', in *Journal of Personality and Social Psychology* 42 (1982) 5-37.

ROUWHORST, G.: 'Rituelen in overvloed', in *Praktische Theologie* 28,1 (2001) 71-85.

RUYTER, J.: 'Nieuwe rituelen door aids', in *Concilium* 29,3 (1993) 28-36.

SARAFINO, E.P.: *Health psychology: biopsychosocial interactions* (New York 1994).

SAUDIA, T.L., M.R. KINNERY, K.C. BROWN & L. YOUNG-WARD: 'Health locus of control and helpfulness of prayer', in *Heart and Lung* 20 (1991) 60-65.

SAX, M. et al.: *Zand erover. Afscheid en uitvaart naar eigen inzicht* (Amsterdam 1989).

SCHARFE, M.: 'Totengedenken. Zur Historizität von Brauchtraditionen. Das Beispiel Olof Palme 1986', in *Ethnologia Scandinavica* 19 (1989) 142-153.

SCHEFF, T.J.: 'The distancing of emotion in ritual', in *Current Antropology* 18,3 (1977) 483-490.

SCHEFF, T.J.: *Catharsis in healing, ritual and drama* (Berkeley 1979).

SCHEPENS, TH.: 'Een statistische documentatie', in W. GODDIJN, J. JACOBS & G. VAN TILLO: *Tot vrijheid geroepen. Katholieken in Nederland 1945-2000* (Baarn 1999) 499-525.

SCHILLEBEECKX, E.: 'Naar een herontdekking van de sacramenten: ritualisering van religieuze momenten in het alledaagse leven', in *Tijdschrift voor Theologie* 40,2 (2000) 164-187 = 'Hin zu einer Wiederentdeckung der christlichen Sakramente. Ritualisierung religiöser Moemente im alltäglichen Leben, in A. HOLDEREGGER & J.-P. WILS (ed.): *Interdisziplinäre Ethik: Grundlagen, Methoden, Bereiche. Festgabe für Dietmar Mieth zum 60. Geburtstag* (= Studies zur theologischen Ethik 89) (Freinburg i.Br. 2001) 309-339.

SCHILSON, A.: 'Fest und Feier in anthropologischer und theologischer Sicht', in *Liturgisches Jahrbuch* 44,1 (1994) 4-32.

SCHILSON, A.: 'Das neue Religiöse und der Gottesdienst. Liturgie vor einer neuen Herausforderung?', in *Liturgisches Jahrbuch* 46,2 (1996) 94-109.

SCHILSON, A.: 'Den Gottesdienst fernsehgerecht inszenieren? Die Verantwortung der Liturgie angesichts des 'Medienreligiösen'', in *Stimmen der Zeit* 8 (1996) 534-546.

SCHILSON, A.: 'Musicals als Kult. Neue Verpackung religiöser Symbolik?', in *Liturgisches Jahrbuch* 48,3 (1998) 143-167.

SCHNABEL, P.: 'Nieuw ritueel na zinloos geweld', in *het Financieele Dagblad* 22.01.2000.

SCHOOTS-WILKE, H., I. SPEE & R. FIDDELEARS-JASPERS: *Als een ramp een school treft. Omgaan met calamiteiten in het onderwijs* ('s-Hertogenbosch 2000).

SCHUMAN, N.: 'Gedenken', in M. BARNARD & P. POST (EDS.): *Ritueel bestek. Antropologische kernwoorden van de liturgie* (Zoetermeer 2001) 181-186.

SCHUYT, K. & E. TAVERNE: *1950. Welvaart in zwart-wit* (Den Haag 2000).

SCHWIBBE, G. & I. SPIEKER: 'Virtuelle Friedhöfe', in *Zeitschrift für Volkskunde* 95,2 (1999) 220-245.

SELIGMAN, M.E.P.: *Helplessness: on depression development and death* (San Francisco 1983).

SEXSON, L.: *Ordinarily sacred* (Charlottesville 1992, orig. New York 1982).

SHEPPY, P. (ed.): *Funerals, death and liturgy* (Aldershot 2001).

SILVER, S.M.: 'Post-traumatic stress disorders and the death imprint: the search for a new mythos', in W.E. KELLY (ed.): *Post-traumatic stress disorder and the war veterans patient* (New York 1985) 43-53.

SITTERLE, K.A. & R.H. GURWITCH: 'The terrorist bombing in Oklahoma city', in E.S. ZINNER & M.B. WILLIAMS (eds.): *When a community weeps. Case studies in group survivorship* (Philadelphia, Penn. 1999) 161-190.

SLIJKERMAN, F.: 'Legionella, een 'stille ramp'', in *Alert* 5 (1999) 5-10.

SLOTERDIJK, P.: 'Huiveren bij CNN. Peter Sloterdijk over de mondiale rampencultuur', in *Filosofie Magazine* 8,4 (1999) 8-12.

SÖRRIES, R.: 'Bestattungs- und Friedhofskultur der Gegenwart. Vom angebots- zum nachfrageorientierten Markt', in A. GERHARDS & B. KRANEMANN (eds.): *Christliche Begräbnisliturgie und säkulare Gesellschaft* (= Erfurter Theologische Schriften 30) (Leipzig 2002) 204-217.

SPEE, I., D. ROOS & R. FIDDELAERS: *Veelkleurig verdriet. Afscheid nemen in verschillende culturen* (Den Bosch 2000).

SPEELMAN, W.M., 'The 'feast' of Diana's death', in P. POST et al. (eds.): *Christian feast and festival. The dynamics of Western liturgy and culture* (= Liturgia condenda 12) (Leuven 2001) 775-802.

SPRUIT, R. & B. SORGEDRAGER: *De dood onder ogen. Een cultuurgeschiedenis van sterven, begraven, cremeren en rouw* (Houten 1986).

STAAL, F.: 'The meaninglessness of ritual', in *Numen* 26,1 (1979) 2-22.

STEENBERGHE, M.: 'Witte rozen en blauwe ballonnen voor René Klijn', in *Nieuwsblad* 09.09.1993.

STOCK, A.: *Poetische Dogmatik 1: Namen* (Paderborn 1995).

STOCK, A.: 'Namen', in M. BARNARD & P. POST (eds.): *Ritueel bestek. Antropologische kernwoorden van de liturgie* (Zoetermeer 2001) 303-317.

STRINGER, M.D.: *On the perception of worship. The ethnography of worship in four Christian congregations in Manchester* (Birmingham 1999).

STURM, E.: 'Museifizierung und Realitätsverlust', in: W. ZACHARIAS (ed.): *Zeitphänomen Musealisierung: das Verschwinden der Gegenwart und die Konstruktion der Erinnerung* (Essen 1990) 99-113.

TAYLOR, S.E.: 'Adjustment to threatening events: a theory of cognitive adaptation', in *American Psychologist* 38 (1983) 1161-1173.

TAYLOR, S.E., R.R. LICHTMAN & J.V. WOOD: 'Attributions, beliefs about control and adjustment to breast cancer', in *Journal of Personality and Social Psychology* 46 (1984) 489-502.

TEESELING, I. VAN: *Het oog van de storm. Slachtoffers in actie* (Amsterdam/Antwerp 2001).

TERR, L.C.: 'Childhood trauma's: an outline and overview', in *American Journal of Psychiatry* 148 (1991) 10-20.

TIEMERSMA, D. (ed.): *De vele gezichten van de dood. Voorstellingen en rituelen in verschillende culturen* (Rotterdam 1996).

TITCHENER, J.L., F.T. KAPP & C. WINGET: 'The Buffalo Creek syndrome: symptoms and character change after a major disaster', in H.J. PARAD, H.L.P. RESNIK & L.G. PARAD (eds.): *Emergency and disaster management: a mental health sourcebook* (Bowie 1976) 283-295.

TOREVELL, D.: *Losing the sacred. Ritual, modernity and liturgical reform* (Edinburgh 2000).

TURNER, V.W.: 'Betwixt and between: the liminal period in rites de passage', in V.W. TURNER: *The forest of symbols. Aspects of Ndembu ritual* (Ithaca/London 1967) 93-112.

TURNER, V.W.: *The ritual process: structure and anti-structure* (Chicago 1969).

TURNER, V.W.: *Dramas, fields and metaphors. Symbolic action in human society* (Ithaca/London 1974).

TYHURST, J.S.: 'Individual reactions to community disaster: the natural history of psychiatric phenomena', in *American Journal of Psychiatry* 107 (1951) 23-27.

UDEN, M. VAN: *Religie in de crisis van de rouw* (Nijmegen 1985).

UDEN, M. VAN: *Rouw, religie en ritueel* (Baarn 1988).

VAILLANT, G.E.: 'Theoretical hierarchy of adaptive ego mechanisms', in *Archives of General Psychiatry* 24 (1971) 107-118.

VAILLANT, G.E.: *Adaptation to life* (Boston 1977).

VELDEN, P. VAN DER: 'Rampen op het net. Suggesties voor een website bij crises', in *Alert* 5 (1999) 30-33.

VELDEN, P.G. VAN DER, J. ELAND & R.J. KLEBER: *Handboek voor opvang na rampen en calamiteiten* (Zaltbommel 1997).

VERHOEVEN, C.: 'Wat moeten die bloemen verbloemen?', in *Trouw* 23.01.1999.

VERWEIJ, J.: *Secularisering tussen feit en fictie: een internationaal vergelijkend onderzoek naar determinanten van religieuze betrokkenheid* (Tilburg 1998).

VISSCHER, J. DE: *Een te voltooien leven. Over de rituelen van de moderne mens* (Kapellen/Kampen 1996).

VOSKUIL, B.V. et al.: *Bomen voor Oranje* ('s Gravenhage 1991).

VOSSEN, E.,: 'Religieuze zingeving', in B. VEDDER et al. (eds.): *Zin tussen vraag en aanbod* (Tilburg 1992) 301-319.

VOYÉ, L.: 'Effacement ou relégitamtion de la religion populaire?', in *Questions liturgiques/Studies in Liturgy* 79,1-2 (1998) 79-94 = 'Uitwissing of nieuwe legitimatie van de volksreligie?', in J. LAMBERTS (ed.): *Volksreligie, liturgie en evangelisatie*) (= Nikè-reeks 42) (Leuven/Amersfoort 1998) 129-152.

VRIES, M.W. DE: 'Twee minuten lang stilstaan bij de doden. De betekenis van de Overveense stille tocht in de jaren '80', in J. BOISSEVAIN (ed.): *Feestelijke vernieuwing in Nederland?* (= Cahier van het P.J. Meertens-Instituut 3) (Amsterdam 1991) 15-26.

VRIES, M.W. DE: 'Culture, community and catastrophe: issues in understanding communities under difficult conditions', in S.E. HOBFOLL & M.W. DE VRIES (eds.): *Extreme stress and communities: impact and intervention* (Dordrecht 1995) 375-393.

WAGENVOORT, J.: 'De stille tocht als verwerking', in *Inzet* 30,1 (2001) 2-8.

WALGRAVE, ST. & B. RIHOUX: *De Witte Mars: een jaar later. Van emotie tot politieke commotie* (Leuven 1997).

WALGRAVE, ST. & B. RIHOUX: 'De Belgische witte golf: voorbij de sociologische bewegingstheorie?', in HELLEMANS: *Wit van het volk* (1998) 310-339.

WALGRAVE, ST. & J. MANSSENS: 'De Witte Mars als product van de media: de pers als mobilisatie-alternatief voor bewegingsorganisaties', in HELLEMANS: *Wit van het volk* (1998) 340-375.

WALLACE, W.A., J.M. ROWLES & CHR.L. COLTON (eds.): *Management of disasters and their aftermath: with experiences from the M1 plane crash, the Manchester aircraft fire disaster, the Hillsborough football disaster, the Northern Ireland troubles and other accidents* (London 1994).

WALTER, T.: 'War grave pilgrimage', in I. READER & T. WALTER (eds.): *Pilgrimage in popular culture* (Houndmills etc. 1993) 29-62.

WILLIAMS, M.B., G.R. BAKER & T. WILLIAMS: 'The great Hanshin-Awaji earthquake. Adapted strategies for survival', in E.S. ZINNER & M.B. WILLIAMS (eds.): *When a community weeps. Case studies in group survivorship* (Philadelphia, Penn. 1999) 103-118.

WIT, J. DE: 'Maatwerk in rituelen. Tussen kerk en markt', in *de Bazuin* 83,9 (2000) 20-23.

WITHUIS, J.: 'Levensbeschouwing en doodsdreiging', in *Maandblad voor de Geestelijke Volksgezondheid* 52,5 (1997) 467-484.

WITHUIS, J.: 'Geestelijke oorlogsschade. De oorlog in het maandblad', in *Maandblad voor de Geestelijke Volksgezondheid* 56,5 (2001) 394-449.

WOOLFENDEN, G.: 'How ritual forms holiness', in *Studia Liturgica* 30 (2000) 170-188.

WOUTERS, C.: *Van minnen en sterven: informalisering van omgangsvormen rond seks en dood* (Amsterdam 1990).

WOUTERS, C.: 'Moderne rituelen rond sterven en rouwen', in *Socialisme en Democratie* 53,6 (1996) 321-328.

WOUTERS, D.N.: *Er valt een gat... Over crisiscounseling bij een grote ramp* (Kampen 1993).

YATES, J., et al.: 'Religion in patients with advanced cancer', in *Medical and Pediatric Oncology* 9 (1981) 121-128.

ZEIDNER, M. & N.S. ENDLER: *Handbook of coping: theory, research, applications* (New York 1996).

ZIJDERVELD, G.: 'Collectieve emoties', in *het Financieele Dagblad* 30.01.1999.

ZINNER, E.S.: 'Group survivorship: a model and case study application', in E.S. ZINNER (ed.): *Coping with death on campus* (San Francisco 1985) 51-68.

ZINNER, E.S.: 'The Challenger disaster. Group survivorship on a national landscape', in E.S. ZINNER & M.B. WILLIAMS (eds.): *When a community weeps. Case studies in group survivorship* (Philadelphia, Penn. 1999) 23-48.

ZINNER, E.S. & M.B. WILLIAMS (eds.): *When a community weeps. Case studies in group survivorship* (= The series in trauma and loss) (Philadelphia, Penn. 1999).

ZONDAG, H.J.: 'De herinnering aan 'Putten'. Een cultuurpsychologisch perspectief op de verwerking van leed', in *Psyche en Geloof* 3 (1999) 129-143.

ZOUTMAN, D.: 'Rituelen in overvloed, maar ze moeten wel worden geoefend', in *Inzage* September (2000) 3-6.

ON THE AUTHORS

Ronald R. Grimes is professor Religion and Culture, Wilfrid Laurier University, Waterloo, Ontario, Canada.

Albertina Nugteren is University lecturer in phenomenology and history of religion at the Tilburg Faculty of Theology.

Per Pettersson is doctor in sociology of religion at Service Research Center – CTF, Karlstad University and at Uppsala University in Sweden. He is combining sociology of religion with service research. His main interest is in the relationship between the Swedish people in general and the Church of Sweden.

Paul Post is Professor of Liturgical Studies and Director of the Liturgical Institute at the Tilburg Faculty of Theology.

Hessel Zondag is University lecturer in psychology at the Tilburg Faculty of Theology.

INDEX